VA-VA VOOM

TOM WILLIAMS

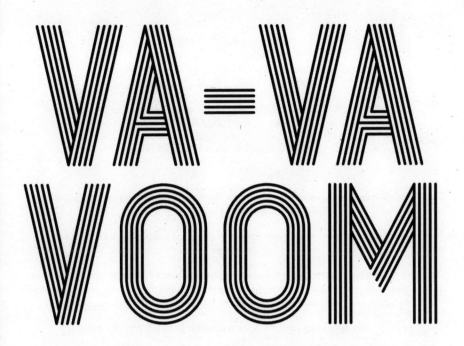

VA-VA VOOM

THE MODERN HISTORY OF FRENCH FOOTBALL

BLOOMSBURY SPORT

LONDON · OXFORD · NEW YORK · NEW DELHI · SYDNEY

BLOOMSBURY SPORT
Bloomsbury Publishing Plc
50 Bedford Square, London, WC1B 3DP, UK
29 Earlsfort Terrace, Dublin 2, Ireland

BLOOMSBURY, BLOOMSBURY SPORT and the Diana logo are trademarks of
Bloomsbury Publishing Plc

First published in Great Britain 2024

A catalogue record for this book is available from the British Library

Library of Congress Cataloguing-in-Publication data has been applied for

ISBN: HB: 978-1-3994-0395-5; eBook: 978-1-3994-0394-8

2 4 6 8 10 9 7 5 3 1

Typeset in Adobe Garamond Pro by Deanta Global Publishing Services, Chennai, India
Printed and bound in Great Britain by CPI Group (UK) Ltd., Croydon, CR0 4YY

To find out more about our authors and books visit www.bloomsbury.com
and sign up for our newsletters

For Ffion

Map of France showing principal football locations

CONTENTS

PROLOGUE

LES POTEAUX CARRÉS

'We had to put Plexiglas around the posts because people kept touching them – it was like they were touching the rock beside the Virgin Mary at Lourdes.'

Saint-Étienne museum director Philippe Gastal

In the early summer of 1987, The Farmer's Boy in Kidderminster acquired an unusual architectural feature. The pub stood on the corner of Comberton Hill and Comberton Place, to the east of the town centre, a short walk from Kidderminster Harriers' Aggborough Stadium and just around the corner from the train station. A two-storey brick building with a gable roof, it hosted live bands, staged regular disco nights and occasionally served as a meeting point for local Birmingham City fans travelling to matches at St Andrew's. Led Zeppelin frontman Robert Plant, who lived locally, sometimes popped in for a pint. On top of its flat-roofed porch, in front of two windows on the building's gabled end, a set of goalposts stood on display: posts, crossbar, goal net and all. In a previous life, they had stood at the eastern end of the pitch at Hampden Park in Glasgow. And it was there, on the evening of Wednesday 12 May, 1976, that they broke the hearts of an entire nation.

Playing Bayern Munich in the European Cup final, the great Saint-Étienne team of the mid-1970s twice hit the crossbar in front of Hampden's East Stand before going on to lose 1–0. The chief peculiarity of the Hampden goalposts was that they were square rather than cylindrical and French football fans were quick to devise a theory that if the posts had been rounded, Dominique Bathenay's long-range shot and Jacques Santini's flying header would have glanced off the bar and gone in, rather than bouncing out, and Saint-Étienne would have become France's first European club champions. The legend of the *poteaux carrés*, or square goalposts, was born.

In its ceaseless quest for uniformity, FIFA ultimately outlawed quadrilateral goalposts and prior to gracing the Hampden pitch for one last time in a Rous Cup[1] match between Scotland and Brazil in May 1987, the *poteaux carrés* were put up for auction. Amid rumours of interest from Sean Connery and Rod Stewart, an 11-strong consortium of investors paid £6,200 to buy the posts and obtain for themselves a physical piece of Scottish – and French – football history. 'They actually did the bidding on the pitch before a Scotland–England game,' says Bill Campbell, a straight-talking Scot who was the leader of the consortium. 'I hate to think what my good lady thought of it, because I made my mind up that I wasn't going to go over five grand and then you just get carried away. My dad said to me: "Have you lost your marbles?" I'd never been to an auction before and I've never been to one since.'

Campbell, now 77 and living in Worcester, was the landlord of The Farmer's Boy (which has since been turned into a veterinary practice). He had the goalposts transported to Kidderminster and mounted upon the roof of the pub, where they became a local tourist attraction. 'We borrowed some scaffolding to support them, but then the scaffolding guy started calling up and asking when he could have his scaffolding back!' he says with a chuckle. Wary of their weight and warned by the local council that he would require planning permission to keep them in situ, Campbell took down the heavy crossbar a few months later and stored it on some wooden blocks in the yard of the pub, leaving the uprights to fend for themselves against the Worcestershire elements. The goalframe returned to Hampden – via a stint at the Glasgow Museum of Transport – when Campbell loaned it to the Scottish Football Museum ahead of its opening in May 2001. But its size and flea-bitten state meant that it was never put on display; when a group of journalists from Rhône-Alpes regional newspaper *Le Progrès* visited

---

1 Running from 1985 to 1989, the Rous Cup – named after former FIFA president Sir Stanley Rous – was an international tournament contested by England, Scotland and, from 1987 onwards, a guest team from South America.

Hampden in the spring of 2012, they found the goalposts gathering dust on a pile of cinder blocks in an unvisited corner of the museum's storeroom.

Saint-Étienne were preparing to open their own museum and upon hearing of the goalposts' fate, they struck a deal with Campbell and his fellow investors to buy them for €20,000. Transported free of charge by a local haulier who regularly travelled to Scotland, the *poteaux carrés* made the 36-hour, 1,000-mile journey down to Saint-Étienne in October 2013, arriving in the early hours of a Saturday morning to be greeted by club co-president Roland Romeyer and emblematic former players Dominique Rocheteau and Georges Bereta, accompanied by a gaggle of journalists. After being touched up and repainted, they took pride of place at the Musée des Verts and have stood there ever since, looming large at one end of the main exhibition room in eternal tribute to French football's flair for the agonising near miss. 'In the first four days after the museum opened, we had 10,000 visitors,' says museum director Philippe Gastal. 'We had to put Plexiglas around the posts because people kept touching them – it was like they were touching the rock beside the Virgin Mary at Lourdes. Even people who aren't football fans have heard of *les poteaux carrés*.'

Les poteaux carrés will always be part of the furniture in Saint-Étienne, where, among other things, they have lent their name to a restaurant, a popular fan website and multiple books. And still the question remains: what if? What if the posts had not been square? What if one of those two cursed attempts at goal had gone in? What if Saint-Étienne had won? What might that have meant for the players, for the club, for the city, for football in France as a whole? To mark the 30th anniversary of the match, *So Foot* magazine commissioned a ballistics study in 2006 that found that had the Hampden crossbar been cylindrical, Bathenay and Santini's efforts would have bounced down on to the goal-line and into the back of the net. Proof, at long last? Or scientifically assisted nostalgic fantasy? Either way, it did not change much in the eyes of the players. 'The ball didn't go in and I think, quite simply, that it wasn't supposed to go in,' says Jean-Michel Larqué, who captained Saint-Étienne in Glasgow. 'I'm pretty fatalistic. People look at them and take photos of them. I've seen them [at the museum] and I think it's just one of those things. Maybe if the ball had been slightly less inflated, it would have gone in! I don't know. But it's part of the legend of *Les Verts*. And I think that maintaining the legend, maintaining the story, gives life to the club.'

———

When the mythological structure of post-war European football was being hewn into shape in the 1950s, French hands were frequently at the chisel. France invented the competitions that would provide a framework for the European game in the second half of the 20th century – and beyond – and to begin with, French teams played a leading role within them. The European Cup (later to become the Champions League) was the brainchild of a Frenchman, *L'Équipe* editor Gabriel Hanot, and the leading French club side of the time, Stade de Reims, reached two of the competition's first four finals, going down to Real Madrid in the inaugural decider in Paris in 1956 and again in Stuttgart in 1959. Reims lent both their celebrated coach, Albert Batteux, and many of the era's most famous players – Raymond Kopa, Just Fontaine, Roger Piantoni, Robert Jonquet – to the French national team. *Les Bleus* finished third at the World Cup (another French creation) in Sweden in 1958 and fourth as hosts of the first European Championship (invented by, you guessed it, a Frenchman) in 1960.[2] But over the following decade, French football vanished from the map.

Hamstrung by small crowds, sparse television coverage and competition from other popular sports such as cycling and rugby union, French clubs remained small-town outfits, typically owned by provincial businessmen who had no means of competing financially with the giants of the continental game. Between 1959 and Saint-Étienne's run to the last four in 1975, France failed to produce a single European Cup semi-finalist. As the stars of the late 1950s bowed out, the national team slumped too, making only a single World Cup appearance between 1958 and 1978 and going 24 years without qualifying for the European Championship finals. 'Since 1958 and the great France team of Just Fontaine

———

2 FIFA's French president Jules Rimet was the driving force behind the organisation of the first World Cup in Uruguay in 1930. The idea for the European Championship (initially known as the European Nations' Cup) came from former French Football Federation general secretary Henri Delaunay.

and Raymond Kopa, there had been nothing,' said Saint-Étienne goalkeeper Ivan Ćurković. 'And then, in the middle of the 1970s, a team from a little mining town came along and woke up a whole country.'

Saint-Étienne's domination of the French domestic game began in the 1960s under the presidency of Roger Rocher, a permanently pipe-smoking former miner turned civil engineering boss, who took charge in 1961. The club from the Loire won five league championships and two Coupes de France between 1963 and 1970 with Jean Snella and then Batteux as coach. The path to continental renown began to truly take shape in July 1972 with the appointment as coach of the club's 33-year-old midfielder Robert Herbin, an intense, tracksuit-clad figure with a shock of frizzy ginger hair whose tight-lipped personality earned him the nickname *Le Sphinx*. Drawing inspiration from Johan Cruyff's Ajax, Herbin dramatically ramped up his players' fitness work and set them out on the pitch in a muscular 4-3-3 system. The bulk of his squad came from a gilded generation of players recruited by sporting director Pierre Garonnaire, whose job as a leather goods salesman, driving around France in a white Peugeot 404, enabled him to scout the best young talent in the country. Including goalscoring brothers Hervé and Patrick Revelli, attacking midfielder Santini, imposing sweeper Christian Lopez and loping left-winger Christian Sarramagna, they lived together, trained together, socialised together and even did their compulsory military service together, giving the first indication of their footballing potential by winning the Coupe Gambardella – France's equivalent of the FA Youth Cup – in 1970. Together with Serbian shot-stopper Ćurković, skipper Larqué and wing wonder Rocheteau, they would capture the hearts of the nation.

Saint-Étienne was a dark, grimy place; its buildings blackened by soot from the city's slag heaps and the smoke belched out by the narrow brick factory chimneys that towered over Stade Geoffroy-Guichard. When shaggy-haired centre-back Osvaldo Piazza first arrived from Argentinian club Lanús in 1972, he made sure that his wife got her first look at the city at night so that she would not be dismayed by what she saw. As the mid-1970s approached, the town found itself in the grip of economic decline. The last mine closed in 1973, historic local mail order firm Manufrance was heading towards bankruptcy and the city's state-owned arms manufacturing plant was a fading force. Amid the gloomy context, the players saw it as their duty to produce effort commensurate with the city's working-class values and put smiles back on the faces of the ailing local population. 'The region was losing its industrial identity,' says Larqué. 'You went through the same thing in England. The only standard-bearer was the football. The supporters felt pride in their club and it helped them to forget all the misfortunes that had befallen them.'

The team's legend was born through a series of stunning fightbacks in European ties, made possible by Herbin's exacting fitness work, which would pave the route to France's first European Cup final appearance in 17 years. In the autumn of 1974, Saint-Étienne were soundly beaten 4–1 by Hajduk Split in the away leg of a European Cup second-round tie, only to roar back and win 5–1 in the return leg courtesy of a late brace from substitute Yves Triantafilos. The furious din created by the 26,381 fans packed inside Geoffroy-Guichard, Saint-Étienne's boxy, boisterous, English-style stadium, earned the ground a new nickname: *Le Chaudron* (The Cauldron). The following season, Herbin's men lost 2–0 away to the mighty Dynamo Kyiv in the first leg of their European Cup quarter-final and were being held 0–0 in the return fixture when Oleg Blokhin, the reigning Ballon d'Or, found himself clean through on goal. But he hesitated, allowing Lopez to tackle, and after Piazza had carried the ball out of defence with a characteristic surge, Patrick Revelli flicked on for his brother, Hervé, to score. In an atmosphere of wild-eyed delirium, Larqué levelled the tie from a free-kick before Patrick Revelli cut the ball back for Rocheteau – reduced to the role of spectator by cramp for the previous half an hour – to sweep home a famous extra-time winner.

Ćurković's acrobatics helped Herbin's men to advance past PSV Eindhoven in the semi-finals and when the Saint-Étienne squad advanced upon Glasgow for the final a month later, it was with a green-clad horde of 25,000 supporters in tow. In a phenomenon that France had never previously experienced, green fever gripped the country. Singer-songwriter Jacques Monty penned a song called 'Allez les Verts', which sold four million copies and stayed at number one in France for 10 months. Rocheteau said that he received fan mail 'worthy of a rock star'. *Les Verts*' European adventure dominated the national press and when TV viewers switched on TF1 to watch Yves Mourousi deliver his lunchtime news bulletin on the day of the game, they discovered that the camera had been fitted with a filter that bathed the studio in a green glow.

Obliged by broadcasters to play in unfamiliar black shorts, which some players saw as a bad omen, Saint-Étienne had a lucky escape inside the first two minutes at Hampden when Gerd Müller had a goal incorrectly ruled out for offside. The fateful encounters with the woodwork came within six minutes of each other towards the end of the first half, Bathenay crashing a shot against the bar from 25 yards and Santini seeing a header come back off the frame of the goal after flinging himself at a cross from Sarramagna (Hervé Revelli tamely heading the rebound straight at Sepp Maier). Franz Roth drilled Bayern in front from a free-kick shortly before the hour and despite a sparkling late cameo from the patched-up Rocheteau, who had been unable to start due to a thigh injury, Saint-Étienne's legendary powers of recovery finally deserted them. Carried for so long by a sense of purpose and momentum that had seemed irresistible, Herbin's players were bereft. 'I shed every tear in my body,' said Santini. It was only upon returning to Paris that the squad could appreciate the true extent of their new nationwide popularity. Thousands flocked to see them paraded down the Champs-Élysées in a fleet of cars (Rocher and Herbin leading the way in a green Renault 5), after which they were received at the Élysée Palace by President Valéry Giscard d'Estaing. 'It was incredible how many people were there on the Champs-Élysées,' says moustachioed wide forward Patrick Revelli, the younger of the two Revelli brothers. 'It was unimaginable, especially as we'd lost.'

Herbin's tenure would yield a total of four league titles and three Coupes de France (to go with the five league titles and three Coupes de France he had previously won with the club as a player), earning him a place in the pantheon of France's greatest coaches. But the Saint-Étienne story would not conclude with a happy ending. In the early 1980s, Rocher was found to have creamed off around 20 million francs from the club's coffers to make illicit under-the-table payments to players in a scandal that became known as *L'affaire de la caisse noire* (The Slush Fund Affair). Disgraced, he spent four months in prison, while Saint-Étienne sank into the second tier. Having fallen agonisingly short in pursuit of European glory, only to overreach and be consumed by scandal, *Les Verts* had unwittingly established a template that a succession of leading French clubs would find irresistible.

———

Saint-Étienne's European Cup heroics in 1976 placed them firmly within a well-established French sporting tradition: that of the gallant runner-up. There had been middleweight boxer Marcel Cerdan, fighting valiantly with a dislocated left shoulder against Jake LaMotta throughout a June 1949 world title fight in Detroit before being forced to retire in the 10th round.[3] There had been distance runner Michel Jazy, who led the men's 5,000m final with 100 metres remaining on a rain-soaked dirt track at the 1964 Olympics in Tokyo, only to run out of steam in the home straight and finish fourth. Most famously of all, there had been Raymond Poulidor, the Limousin cyclist whose long, fruitless quest for Tour de France glory against his rival Jacques Anquetil earned him the nickname *L'Éternel Second*. Anquetil was an imperious rider who won the Tour five times, often dominating the race from start to finish, but French cycling fans overwhelmingly preferred Poulidor, fondly known as 'Poupou', for his modest, slightly bumbling demeanour and courageous attacking approach. French historian Michel Winock dubbed the phenomenon *le complexe Poulidor*, positing that in the lean-faced Anquetil, with his textbook bike posture and machine-like efficiency in time trials, the French glimpsed a troubling harbinger of the country's industrialised future, whereas in Poulidor's weather-beaten features and ragged riding style, they saw reminders of a simple bucolic past that was vanishing before their eyes.

As a population, in a wider sense, the French were not accustomed to celebrating victory. France had emerged on the winning side from the hell of World War II, but carrying the deep pain of four years of occupation by Nazi Germany and the complicated shame of collaboration. Although France bounced back in economic terms after the war, experiencing a 30-year period of continuous

3 Cerdan was renowned French singer Édith Piaf's lover. He died in a plane crash in the Azores four months after the LaMotta fight, while flying from Paris to New York to visit her.

growth that came to be known as *Les Trente Glorieuses* (The Glorious Thirty), the country found itself diminished culturally and politically on the global stage, swamped at home by the arrival of American consumer culture and mass media, weakened abroad by the collapse of its colonial empire.

Sport in France had long taken its cue from the credo of Pierre de Coubertin, the French aristocrat who founded (there they are again) the Modern Olympic Games: 'The important thing in life is not the triumph, but the fight. The essential thing is not to have won, but to have fought well.' French football resisted the arrival of professionalism for longer than any other major European nation, not taking the plunge until 1932, and its clubs continued to be run according to amateur ideals – the kindly paternal chairman, the supportive local mayor, the cheerful Corinthian players – for decades. The advancement of the sport was not helped by certain factors particular to France. The late onset of urbanisation in the country, where it did not take off until the 1950s, meant that relatively few cities possessed the kind of large populations needed to support thriving professional clubs (hence the complete absence of French towns or cities with more than one major team). High tax rates, meanwhile, made it significantly more complicated for French clubs to offer the kind of salaries available in Europe's other leading football countries. When the Bosman ruling[4] was passed in 1995, France's leading talents left the league in droves. France also regulated its football clubs more strictly than its continental neighbours, having in 1990 become the first country to set up an independent financial watchdog – the Direction Nationale du Contrôle de Gestion (National Directorate of Management Control), known as the DNCG. It was arguably not until the 1980s and the arrival of ambitious, business-minded presidents such as Bordeaux's Claude Bez, Marseille's Bernard Tapie and Lyon's Jean-Michel Aulas that the French club game truly shifted to a professional footing, bringing with it a ruthlessness in pursuit of victory that meant any notions of 'fighting well' went out of the window. That ruthlessness often came accompanied by an impatience,

---

4 In a case brought by Belgian footballer Jean-Marc Bosman, the European Court of Justice abolished restrictions on the number of foreign players from EU countries allowed to play in European leagues and enabled players to move clubs without a transfer fee at the end of their contracts.

a chafing against France's burdensome taxes and tight regulatory guidelines, which would leave several high-profile club directors the wrong side of the law.

The French men's national team underwent its own mindset shift in the 1980s and 1990s, spurred by the influence of players like Michel Platini, Didier Deschamps and Zinédine Zidane who left the country to play in Italy. When they returned to France on international duty, they came equipped with a newly acquired win-at-all-costs mentality that would ultimately enable *Les Bleus* to shake off their tag as international football's nearly men. It was as if, for France to finally prevail on the international stage, something fundamentally French needed to be discarded first. 'The French mentality obliges you to diminish yourself, almost to self-flagellate,' said Youri Djorkaeff, who triumphed with France at the 1998 World Cup while on the books at Italian giants Internazionale. 'Culturally, we weren't used to winning. We were programmed to think that success must belong to others. Why not to us?' The national team's triumphs around the turn of the millennium revealed the Bosman ruling to have been a double-edged sword: French clubs lost their best players, rendering the national league weaker and less attractive, but those players made the national team stronger with the experience and professionalism that they had acquired overseas.

Where the national team led, however, the club sides did not follow. At the start of the 2023–24 season, of the 161 major UEFA trophies that had been up for grabs in men's football since the launch of the European Cup in 1955, only two – remarkably – had found their way into French hands.[5] It means that French clubs have won less continental silverware than their counterparts in each of Belgium, Ukraine[6] and Scotland, not to mention the Netherlands and Portugal, which have both regularly outperformed France despite having much smaller populations. Collectively, the entire country has won as many major European honours in men's football as Nottingham Forest. For a nation that has

5 The competitions are the European Cup/UEFA Champions League, the UEFA Cup Winners' Cup (now defunct), the UEFA Cup/UEFA Europa League and the UEFA Conference League. Marseille won the Champions League in 1992–93 and Paris Saint-Germain won the Cup Winners' Cup in 1995–96.
6 This includes Dynamo Kyiv's two victories in the Cup Winners' Cup, both of which were won beneath the banner of the Soviet Union.

produced footballers as incontrovertibly brilliant as Platini, Zidane, Jean-Pierre Papin, Éric Cantona, Thierry Henry, Karim Benzema and Kylian Mbappé, it is an extraordinary state of affairs.

If French football has not yet figured out how to win, at least in the club game, it also remains deeply conflicted regarding the question of how to play. Batteux's great Reims team of the late 1950s were renowned for the vibrant quality of their football, known as the *jeu à la rémoise*, which relied upon rapid passing exchanges and individual expression. Michel Hidalgo, who played under Batteux at Reims, embraced the same principles during his time as national coach in the late 1970s and early 1980s. Built around the fabled *carré magique* (magic square) midfield of Platini, Alain Giresse, Jean Tigana and Bernard Genghini, his dashing team won the admiration and sympathy of the entire footballing world when they lost to West Germany in cruel fashion in the semi-finals of the 1982 World Cup. Hidalgo's side were known as 'The Brazilians of Europe' and they turned French football into a byword for technical brilliance, creative ingenuity and courageous, front-foot play. But the influence of the players schooled in Italy meant that when France durably took up residence among the world's leading national sides from the late 1990s onwards, it was with teams in which defensive solidity was prioritised over attacking flair. Embodied by Deschamps, who led France to World Cup glory as captain in 1998 and then as coach in 2018, the modern French style is an altogether more pragmatic, reactive affair. And for all that it has turned France into one of the most successful teams in the international game, with appearances in four of the last seven men's World Cup finals, it has not been enough to spare Deschamps from reproaches that he could – or should – be doing more with the talent at his disposal.

These days, France are criticised for winning ugly. They used to be celebrated for losing beautifully. Saint-Étienne's bruising encounter with the Hampden goalposts created a blueprint for valiant defeat. And there was no defeat more beautiful, more bewitching and more brutal than the one that befell *Les Bleus* in Seville.

1

LES BLEUS

ONE NIGHT IN SEVILLE

'Before Patrick's injury, there were 11 of us. After his injury,
there were 55 million.'

Jean-Luc Ettori

Patrick Battiston lies flat on his back inside the West Germany penalty area, his head lolling limply to the left, his left hand, clenched in a grotesque spasm, mechanically lowering itself to rest on his stomach. Gérard Janvion, Dominique Rocheteau and Didier Six are the first France players on the scene. Cradling Battiston's head and seeing his lifeless expression, Six turns towards the dug-outs and frantically indicates that medical attention is required. More blue shirts appear at Battiston's side – Marius Trésor, Jean Tigana and Michel Platini, his roommate, whose anguish is palpable. France team doctor Maurice Vrillac races on to attend to the stricken player, now obscured behind a scrum of bodies save for his red socks and black Adidas boots. The Saint-Étienne defender's motionless body is loaded on to a stretcher and carried from the field, Platini tenderly touching his cheek and holding his drooping right hand as he departs. All the while, the man responsible for Battiston's condition, German goalkeeper Harald 'Toni' Schumacher, stands impassively chewing gum inside his six-yard box. Informed later that his victim had been left with concussion, a fractured vertebra and three missing teeth, he sneered: 'If it really pleases him, I'll pay his dentistry bills.'

Having raced on to a lofted pass from Platini, Battiston had just managed to steer a shot towards goal before Schumacher slammed into him, the goalkeeper

1

leaping into the air and turning his body squarely to the left so that his right hip crashed into the Frenchman's face with sickening force. Dutch referee Charles Corver neither awarded a penalty nor showed a card to Schumacher, who restarted play with a goal-kick. At the moment of impact, some of Battiston's teammates had instinctively feared that he was dead. 'Yes, we did think that,' says Maxime Bossis, who had slipped the ball to Platini seconds before the fateful collision. 'Especially because we knew Battiston wasn't the type to make a meal of it. If he was on the ground, it was serious. And it *was* serious. And it could have been even more serious. When Schumacher came out, he was miles late. It was a deliberate and dangerous foul. Battiston could have lost his life. But no penalty, no card, nothing. It was incredible what happened. Crazy.'

It was a sultry July evening inside Seville's Estadio Ramón Sánchez-Pizjuán and the score was 1–1 with half an hour remaining in the second semi-final of the 1982 World Cup. Pierre Littbarski had drilled West Germany in front in the 17th minute. France had levelled through a Platini penalty. The Germans, reigning European champions, had sought to impose themselves physically from the start. 'You have to play hard against the French,' former skipper Franz Beckenbauer had said before the game. 'They hate physical play.' Schumacher seemed keyed up from kick-off and was told by Platini to calm down after hurling himself on top of Six while claiming a cross late in the first half. But as play resumed following Battiston's withdrawal, every German touch now copiously whistled by the French and Spanish spectators in the crowd, it was France who took control. French defenders Trésor and Bossis strode confidently into German territory with the ball; French midfielders Platini, Tigana and Alain Giresse exhibited their technical mastery with an endless parade of neat first-time passes, deft volleyed lay-offs and casual outside-of-the-foot flicks. In the first minute of stoppage time, left-back Manuel Amoros picked up possession on the left and let fly with a 25-yard effort that cannoned against the crossbar. 'Before Patrick's injury, there were 11 of us,' said goalkeeper Jean-Luc Ettori. 'After his injury, there were 55 million.'

Extra time brought no respite for the Germans. Three minutes in, Giresse's free-kick from wide on the right flicked off Paul Breitner in the two-man wall and fell for Trésor to hook a thumping volley into the top-right corner.

Moments later, Six laid the ball off to the edge of the German box and Giresse drove an exquisite shot in off the left-hand post with the outside of his right foot before tearing down the touchline in celebration, his eyes squeezed shut and his fists clenched tight in ecstatic disbelief. 'We're in the World Cup final,' he says, 40 years later, reliving the thoughts that popped inside his head like fireworks as he watched the ball nestle in Schumacher's net. 'My head explodes. What I did was totally spontaneous – it was unplanned, unforeseeable. There's an explosion. Boom! I'm running and I'm thinking: "We're in the World Cup final! We're in the World Cup final! It's not possible, we're in the World Cup final, fucking hell!" We all went crazy. And that's what wasn't good, because we didn't control things.'

The three minutes and four seconds that followed represent one of the most endlessly discussed passages of play in French football history. In the popular imagination, France continued to attack, continued to throw caution to the wind, and paid a fatal price. The reality is more nuanced. As the Germans looked to build attacks following their kick-off, France put every player behind the ball. Klaus Fischer had a header ruled out for offside. Platini saw a free-kick saved at the second attempt by Schumacher. 'I don't think the Germans believe any more,' said Thierry Roland on Antenne 2. 'So much the better for us!' replied co-commentator Jean-Michel Larqué, the former Saint-Étienne captain. But then France did leave themselves exposed. Giresse and Platini were both victims of fouls that went unpunished high up on France's right flank and when Bossis lost possession on the halfway line, Littbarski had time and space to curl in a cross from the left that substitute Karl-Heinz Rummenigge jabbed home at the near post. West Germany, revitalised by Rummenigge's entrance, equalised three minutes into the second half of the extra period when Fischer volleyed in. After one squandered spot-kick apiece (Uli Stielike for West Germany, Six for France), the subsequent penalty shoot-out lurched the Germans' way when Bossis' scuffed effort was parried by Schumacher, diving low to his right. Horst Hrubesch scored and back home in France, the hearts of 30 million television viewers sank. Bossis never took another penalty again.

The desolation could be read on the faces of every single France player. Amoros stood on the touchline with his hands on his hips. Tigana stared into the middle distance. Platini, disappointment etched across his features, stalked off the pitch with a white German shirt bunched in his hand, a gold chain bouncing against his bare chest. Upon returning to the changing room, the players were informed that Battiston had regained consciousness and been transferred to hospital. But their relief was no match for their despair. 'There were 30 of us, players and officials altogether, who cried like kids,' said Trésor. Michel Hidalgo said the scene reminded him of a 'kindergarten class when the mums leave'. Too distraught to move, Six had to be bundled into the showers in his kit. When the German players, led by Stielike, knocked on the door asking to swap shirts, they were angrily chased away. French fury over Corver's officiating intensified hours later when they found him sharing jokes with the German squad at Seville airport, Tigana having to be physically prevented from confronting him. In a third-place play-off that none of the players had the heart to play in, a much-changed France were beaten 3–2 by Poland. In the final, West Germany lost 3–1 to Italy. 'JUSTICE IS DONE!' crowed *France Football*.

As they nursed their disappointment over the summer weeks that followed, France's crestfallen players came to realise that something fundamental had changed over the course of that epic, excruciating, electrifying evening in Andalusia. They had played the football that they wanted to play – brave, positive, brimming with flair and artistry – and they had come close to beating one of the best teams in the world. Not only that, but their compatriots, for so long indifferent towards their sport, had lived the match with them in the most intense way possible; had raged over Schumacher's unpunished brutality, had exalted over Trésor and Giresse's goals, had wept at the bitter injustice of the end result. 'Everyone remembers where they were that day,' Bossis says across the table of a café in a modern hotel complex just outside Caen. 'On holiday with their parents, at a family party, wherever it was . . . Thirty million people in front of their televisions. Theatre companies have staged plays about that match, there are 15, 20, 30 books about it. It's really stayed in people's memories. We like sport in France, but it isn't a religion like it is in England. That day it was. And for a very long time we'd had a real inferiority complex, both at club level and in the national team. That game showed that we could stand up to a Germany team that was among the two or three best in the world.' Tigana said the match was the regret of a lifetime. Platini, who came to realise that he had taken part in a game of singularly captivating drama, called it the most beautiful moment of his career.

———

Hidalgo had taken charge of the national team in November 1975, stepping up from his role as assistant following the departure of former Ajax coach Ştefan Kovács, whose attempts to teach Total Football to the French had yielded mixed results.[7] In Hidalgo's first game in charge, a 2–2 draw with Czechoslovakia in a March 1976 friendly, he awarded senior debuts to two promising 20-year-olds: a rangy centre-back from Nantes called Bossis and a goalscoring midfielder from Nancy called Platini, the latter daintily curling in France's second goal at the Parc des Princes from an indirect free-kick. His first competitive game, away to Bulgaria in World Cup qualifying the following October, was another 2–2 draw featuring another Platini free-kick. The game is chiefly remembered for the moment when Roland, exasperated by Scottish referee Ian Foote's error-strewn officiating, raged from the commentary box: 'I'm not afraid to say it – Mr Foote, you are a bastard!'

France qualified for the 1978 World Cup, ending a 20-year wait, but the tournament in Argentina was fraught and forgettable. The day before the squad were due to fly to Buenos Aires, Hidalgo and his wife, Monique, escaped an attempted kidnapping by armed activists opposed to the Argentinian military junta while driving towards Bordeaux (Hidalgo wrestling a revolver – which he later discovered was not loaded – from one of the couple's two assailants). Preparations were further disrupted by a stand-off between the squad and kit provider Adidas. Unhappy with the bonuses they were being offered by the German firm, France's players threatened to black out the brand's white stripes on their boots in protest. Although they did not carry through with their threat, the episode became known as *L'affaire des chaussures* (The Boots Affair). Successive 2–1 defeats against Italy and the host nation condemned *Les Bleus* to elimination after only two games and their tournament ended in farcical circumstances when

———

7 P15 W6 D4 L5. The Romanian left with the parting advice that French football put too much emphasis on 'aesthetics' and needed to adopt a more rigorous, professional approach.

a colour clash obliged them to borrow a kit from local club Atlético Kimberley for their final match, a 3–1 win over Hungary. It remains the only time a France team have taken to the field in vertical green and white stripes.

On the morning of France's defeat by Argentina, Hidalgo started crying while being interviewed by journalist Jacques Chancel on his France Inter radio programme *Radioscopie*. For all the strain that he was under, it was not an uncommon occurrence. A short, sturdy man with a kind, open face, Hidalgo was, by his own admission, 'naturally sensitive'. He would cry when France won important games. Sometimes he would even cry during pre-match team talks (an exercise at which he excelled), pumping his players so full of purpose and belief that he himself succumbed to the emotion that he was generating, his bright blue eyes abruptly filling with tears. He constantly sought new ways to inspire his squad, on one occasion urging them to play for the women who had sewn the French cockerel badges on to the breasts of their blue jerseys. 'It was a delight to listen to him because he always came up with something fantastic in his team talks,' says Henri Émile, who served as team manager for a succession of France coaches. 'I remember him taking the players to an Adidas factory to show them the people who made their boots. He wanted to show them the labourers whose work allowed them to express themselves.' Hidalgo was close to his players and encouraged dialogue, regularly sounding out trusted senior figures for feedback on the mood in the camp or thoughts on the best approach to a forthcoming game. He allowed some of the players to address him using *tu*, the informal French word for 'you', as opposed to the formal *vous*, which was the norm.

As a coach, he did not possess hard and fast tactical principles, but he held strong convictions about the kind of football he wanted his sides to play. Hidalgo had played under Albert Batteux at Reims and Lucien Leduc at Monaco, both of whom were proponents of slick, possession-based attacking football, and he saw it as his calling to try to emulate them. He described his preferred style as 'light, lively, pleasant football', which for him was *'football à la française'* ('French-style football'). He said that to play good football was 'to carry dreams' and that 'living on the pitch with cowardice' was 'worse than dying'. And from early on in his tenure as France coach – as early, in his recollection, as 1977 – he became

6

convinced that the best way to get his team playing the way that he wanted was to squeeze as many playmakers into his starting XI as physically possible.

Platini was the first piece of the jigsaw. A mainstay of the side from the moment he first donned the blue shirt, the swaggering midfielder was appointed captain in 1979 at the age of just 24. The tireless Tigana, who was said to have 'three lungs', made his senior debut in May 1980 and quickly became a strong contender for a place in the first XI. After two and a half years in the international wilderness, diminutive Bordeaux playmaker Giresse was given an opportunity to resurrect his France career at the age of 28 after catching the eye in a World Cup qualifying defeat against the Netherlands in March 1981. When Genghini, the elegant Sochaux number 10, impressed alongside Giresse and Tigana in a 3–2 qualifying win over Belgium the following month, in place of the injured Platini, he staked a claim for a starting berth too. In the 2–0 win over the Netherlands in November 1981 that all but secured France's place at the 1982 World Cup, Hidalgo played with a three-man midfield composed entirely of number 10s in the form of Platini, Giresse and Genghini. But although Hidalgo's vision was taking shape, the fans remained unconvinced. In a poll published by *L'Équipe Magazine* prior to the victory over the Dutch, only 3 per cent of respondents said that he deserved to remain in place beyond the World Cup.

Come the tournament itself, Hidalgo continued to tinker with the configuration of his midfield. Platini played as a false nine in France's opener, a 3–1 defeat by England in sweltering Bilbao, but lined up alongside Giresse and Genghini in midfield for their 4–1 win over Kuwait and 1–1 draw with Czechoslovakia.[8] Tigana failed to make the starting XI for any of the first three matches. But when Platini was given a dead leg by Antonín Panenka (he of the immortal penalty) against the Czechs, it prompted a rethink. Tigana took the skipper's place for the opening game of the second group phase, a 1–0 win over Austria in Madrid, and France played so fluently that *L'Équipe* dared to ask: 'Are *Les Bleus* better without Platini?' Hidalgo knew the answer to that one. For the

8 The victory over Kuwait in Valladolid was memorably interrupted when a Kuwaiti prince, Sheikh Fahad Al-Ahmed Al-Jaber Al-Sabah, stormed down to the pitch and successfully argued for a goal by Giresse to be disallowed because the Kuwaiti defenders had been distracted by a whistle blown in the crowd.

next game against Northern Ireland at Atlético Madrid's Estadio Vicente Calderón, he aligned Platini, Giresse, Genghini and Tigana together at kick-off for the first time and in the baking Spanish sunshine, France soared, winning 4–1 to book a place in the semi-finals for the first time since 1958. The *carré magique* was born.

'We combined well, because there was technical quality and playing intelligence,' says Giresse, who scored two of France's goals against Northern Ireland. 'You had Bernard Genghini and his left foot, Jean Tigana and his ability to win the ball back and play it forward and then Michel, who was always going to produce that little bit extra. And I combined in the middle of that, to provide balance. When Michel dropped deeper, I went a bit higher. If Michel went higher, I went deeper. *Voilà*. We made little adjustments as we went, depending on the circumstances of the match.' Hidalgo considered it the match in which he saw his team 'find their style'. 'Until then, over six years, they'd been looking for it, with successes, trial and error, doubts, setbacks,' he wrote in his autobiography, *Les buts de ma vie* (The Goals of My Life). 'On this late afternoon, they shine. My joy is immense.'

The *carré magique* was retained for the ill-fated semi-final against West Germany, with Six slotting in wide on the left when France were out of possession and Rocheteau dropping in from time to time on the right. But if Hidalgo had finally found the perfect balance in midfield, the same could not be said of his substitutes' bench. Curiously, he chose to leave the only other central midfielders in his squad, Bordeaux's René Girard and Saint-Étienne's Jean-François Larios, sitting in the stands.[9] When Genghini was forced off by a bruised calf five minutes into the second half, Hidalgo replaced him with Battiston, who had spent the previous season playing at right-back. And when Battiston's participation was viciously curtailed by Schumacher, his place went to the Saint-Étienne sweeper Christian Lopez. 'I was a bit disappointed not to be on the team sheet against Germany,' says Girard. 'It could have helped with the balance of the team when Patrick went off. But we'll never know.'

9 Larios had a strained relationship with Platini, his Saint-Étienne clubmate, over allegations that he'd had an affair with Platini's wife, Christèle.

For Hidalgo, France's performances in Spain proved that it was possible to play his kind of football – *football à la française* – and succeed. 'An ID card specific to French football now exists,' he confidently told *France Football* after the tournament. No sooner had French supporters finished drying their tears than thoughts turned to the 1984 European Championship, which France was set to host. After the disappointment of Glasgow and the agony of Seville, it was time for the French game to transform the shimmering football into silverware.

A landmark moment in the development of French football occurred six weeks before the 1982 World Cup when Platini boarded a Cessna private jet at Lyon Satolas Airport one April morning and flew to Turin to sign a two-year contract with Juventus. He was about to turn 27 and had become the most coveted footballer in Europe thanks to his match-winning exploits in the green of Saint-Étienne and the blue of the national side. In plumping for Juve, Platini turned down offers from Paris Saint-Germain, Arsenal and Tottenham Hotspur, later explaining that he had spurned the overtures of the two north London clubs because he was concerned about English football's heavy schedule and lack of a winter break. But more than that, Turin was a choice of the heart. His paternal grandfather, Francesco, had emigrated to northeastern France from the Piedmont region at the end of World War I, setting up a sports bar, the Café des Sportifs, in the small town of Jœuf, which he decorated with pictures of Italian football stars like Sandro Mazzola, Gianni Rivera and Gigi Riva. Platini's wife, Christèle, also had roots in northern Italy, her parents having grown up in Bergamo. Joining Juve brought Platini into a changing room that boasted six of the players who would start for Italy in the World Cup final[10] and introduced him to a championship renowned around the world for the meticulousness of its tactics and the miserliness of its defending. The knock-on effects of his exposure to Italian football culture would be game-changing for the French national team, to such an extent that he

---

10 Dino Zoff, Claudio Gentile, Gaetano Scirea, Antonio Cabrini, Marco Tardelli and Paolo Rossi.

came to believe that had he moved to Serie A at a younger age, France would never have had their hearts broken by West Germany in Seville.

Born in Jœuf on 21 June, 1955, Platini inherited a love of football from his father, Aldo, a promising amateur player who taught mathematics at a local college. His mother, Anna, was also of Italian heritage and had been a talented basketball player. When Platini was seven, the family moved to a house on a cul-de-sac in Jœuf called Rue Saint-Exupéry, where the young Michel and his friends could practise hammering shots against his wooden garage door without having to worry about passing traffic. Platini was short for his age and was nicknamed *Ratz*, a local expression that was short for *rase-bitume*, meaning 'asphalt-scraper'. He hated it. As he got older, he drew encouragement from the way that Johan Cruyff managed to dominate games despite his slender physique. But his first football hero was Pelé. Platini used his boyhood kickabouts, and later his matches with the town team AS Jœuf, to imitate the Brazilian's driving runs and would sign his school textbooks 'Michel Peléatini'. Aged eight, he went to watch an exhibition match at Stade Saint-Symphorien, home of local club FC Metz, and was enthralled by the performance of the great Hungarian striker László Kubala. At one point in the game, Kubala controlled a high ball on the left flank and then, without letting it bounce, volleyed a pinpoint pass to a teammate on the other side of the pitch. Platini said the incident 'kind of changed my life', making him realise that a player with faultless technique and a good awareness of his teammates' positions could unlock any door on the pitch. His dreams of joining Metz were crushed when, aged 17, he failed a breathing test during a medical examination at the club and was erroneously deemed to have a weak heart by the team doctor. Fortunately for him, his father's football connections enabled him to secure a trial at the region's other major club, AS Nancy-Lorraine, and this time he was taken on. He made his first-team debut in a 2–1 win over Nîmes in May 1973 and scored his first two goals in professional football in a 4–1 defeat of Lyon nine days later.

Over the seasons that followed, Platini succeeded in capturing the imaginations of French football fans in a manner not seen since Raymond Kopa's heyday. Slim and sideburned, the shorts of Nancy's all-white kit hitched high on his thighs, he was not especially quick and he was not a great dribbler, but he possessed immaculate technique, exceptional vision, impeccable ball-striking ability and an innate sense of timing that turned him into one of the greatest goalscorers of the era. Platini was famed above all for his pinpoint free-kicks, but he found the net in all sorts of other ways as well: from brave headers, flashing volleys and scrappy poacher's goals to ice-cool one-on-one finishes, clever lobs and long-range piledrivers. He scored 127 goals in 214 appearances for Nancy, captaining *Les Chardons* (The Thistles) to Coupe de France glory in 1978, and 82 goals in 145 games for Saint-Étienne. Debates raged throughout his time in France as to whether he might be better off playing at centre-forward, but although he judged himself on his scoring returns, he always preferred the greater freedom afforded by the number 10 role.

Troubled by the thought of seeing Platini leave the country, French football supporters responded enthusiastically when he opted to join Saint-Étienne after leaving Nancy in 1979. Club president Roger Rocher was still dreaming of European Cup glory and made a bold statement of intent that summer by recruiting both Platini and celebrated Dutch winger Johnny Rep, who arrived from Bastia. But Platini's three-year spell in green would prove only a partial success. Although it yielded the only French league title of his career in 1981, *Les Verts* made it no further than the European Cup quarter-finals during his time at Stade Geoffroy-Guichard and his spell at the club ended amid the shame of *L'affaire de la caisse noire*.[11]

Leaving France for Italy in 1982 took Platini's career to the next level, turning him into a global superstar and three-time Ballon d'Or winner and filling his trophy cabinet with silverware. But in the context of the national team, perhaps the greatest legacy would be the impact that playing in Serie A had on his conception of the game. Platini was already a fiercely determined competitor; joining Juventus taught him what it looked like when every single component of a sporting institution was minutely geared towards achieving success. Victory was all that mattered in Italy and as he explained in vivid terms in his 1987 autobiography, *Ma vie comme un match* (My Life as a Match), co-written with

---

11 Convicted of receiving illegal payments from Rocher, Platini and 10 of his Saint-Étienne teammates were given suspended four-month prison sentences that were later annulled.

Paris Match journalist Patrick Mahé, Platini found a visceral thrill in the knife-edge tension that that mindset engendered. 'Here, football is sacred, it's the *corrida* (bullfight) of the Italians,' he wrote. 'There's a putting to death in the defeat of a team. And I feel close to that. When, aged 15, I saw the dribbles of Pelé and the passes of Cruyff, I already felt everything that is sacred, that is religious, that is tragic in the putting to death of the beaten team. That taste of blue blood, of noble blood, hasn't left me since. And it's here, on the burnt ground of my ancestors, that I've rediscovered it, intact, on the lips of all the players and their *tifosi* (fans).'

It was that primal hunger for victory that Platini brought to the France squad. In consultation with Hidalgo, he introduced various subtle tactical adjustments to the team's approach. France began to spend more time allocating roles at set-pieces before games (Platini had observed that Italian defenders watched their man and not the ball). There was a concerted collective effort to prevent opposition free-kicks from being taken quickly. Prior to matches, Platini would visit his teammates' rooms for individual pep talks and convene informal meetings between players, to which the coaching staff were not invited, where they would discuss how to contain and confound their opponents. Above all, through his words and his actions on the training pitch, the hatred of defeat that he conveyed in every single exercise and the narrowing of the eyes that set in whenever a big game appeared on the horizon, he helped to instil a winning mentality that the French game had long considered itself to be lacking. 'He communicated that thirst for victory to us,' says Bossis. 'Because at Juventus, they had to win. In Italy, it's victory that counts: if you play well, so much the better, but it's winning that counts. It was important that he went over there [to Italy]. He could tell us that we were playing well, that we weren't far away, but that now, it was time to win.'

It undoubtedly helped, as far as winning was concerned, that Platini was about to have the tournament of his life.

───────

By the time the 1984 European Championship came around, 'Platoche' had entered a new dimension as a footballer. Two years into his Juve career, he had just collected winners' medals in the league and the European Cup Winners' Cup, finishing as top scorer in Serie A with 20 goals, and had won the first of what would prove to be three consecutive Ballons d'Or the previous December. He was also, crucially, fully fit. The France captain had been bothered by a groin problem throughout the 1982 World Cup and would go into the next World Cup, in Mexico, nursing a painfully swollen Achilles tendon, but in 1984 there was nothing holding him back. 'He was winning everything – and when I say everything, I mean everything,' said France striker Bernard Lacombe. 'No joke. He played cards, he won. Rummy, same thing: he won every hand. He went to the Font-Romeu Casino and played the slot machines, *brrrrring*, jackpot! It's the truth! He won everything, everything. I said to Michel: "If you set up as an umbrella salesman in the desert, it would rain every day!"'

As the host team, France were able to prepare for the competition in optimal conditions. Hidalgo arranged a pre-tournament training camp at altitude in Font-Romeu in the French Pyrenees, where the players ramped up their fitness by going on runs, hikes and mountain bike rides in the surrounding forest. The squad's base during the tournament was a tranquil converted priory in the sleepy village of Saint-Lambert-des-Bois in the Yvelines, 20 miles southwest of Paris.

From a footballing perspective, the chief novelty was a change to the personnel who made up the *carré magique*. The original quartet of Platini, Giresse, Genghini and Tigana made only one further appearance in the same configuration after the 1982 World Cup, lining up for a 1–0 friendly win over Hungary at the Parc des Princes the following October. Young PSG midfielder Luis Fernandez made his France debut a month later and Hidalgo quickly decided that with his fizzing industriousness, his tigerish ball-winning and his furious will to win, he possessed a skillset that could 'rebalance' the French midfield. In a symbol of France's steely-eyed post-Seville focus, Fernandez took over from Genghini; a number 10 giving way for a number six. Where the original *carré magique* had been a loose diamond – Tigana at the base, Platini at the tip, Giresse and Genghini either side – its new iteration was something closer to a modern box midfield, with Fernandez and Tigana patrolling the space in front of the back four, allowing Platini and Giresse even greater freedom further up the pitch. 'When Michel Hidalgo put it in place the first time, there was

Genghini, Giresse, Tigana and Platini,' Fernandez tells me in a (Covid-enforced) Microsoft Teams call from the beIN SPORTS studios in Paris, where he works as a television pundit. 'It worked, but maybe they also needed someone to stabilise the midfield a bit, someone who'd be a ball-winner and do the work in the shadows. My role was to stay in my position, win the ball back and pass it on as quickly as possible.'

A deflected 78th-minute strike by Platini at the Parc des Princes secured a 1–0 win over an obdurate Denmark team in France's opening game. Wary of the threat posed by next opponents Belgium, Hidalgo made a tactical adjustment for the match in Nantes, bringing Genghini back into midfield and moving Fernandez to a marauding right-back role to counter the menace of Belgian left-winger Franky Vercauteren. The 51,359 fans in attendance at a sun-soaked Stade de la Beaujoire witnessed one of the stand-out performances of the Hidalgo era, a France team clad in a white change kit whitewashing Belgium 5–0. Platini scored a perfect hat-trick[12] – a left-foot drive, a right-foot penalty and a powerful header – with Giresse and Fernandez completing the rout. Two years earlier, in Spain, France had felt their way into the tournament game by game. On home soil, two years later, they hit their stride early. 'It was a symphony,' smiles Giresse. 'It was a philharmonic orchestra playing the most beautiful music in the world. If you wanted to take a photograph of that team and what it was all about – *tac*, that's it.' Returning to his old stomping ground of Stade Geoffroy-Guichard, Platini plundered *another* perfect hat-trick in a 3–2 win over Yugoslavia (close-range finish with his left foot, brilliant diving header, curling free-kick with his right foot) to send France sailing into the last four.[13]

The semi-final against Portugal at a characteristically raucous Stade Vélodrome in Marseille was an instant classic. Establishing a tradition of improbable French goalscorers in major semi-finals, left-back Jean-François Domergue put Hidalgo's side ahead midway through the first half when he blasted a free-kick into the top-left corner. But future Bordeaux winger Fernando

---

12 It was also the first hat-trick of his professional career.
13 The match was overshadowed by the death of Yugoslavia team doctor Bojeda Milenović, who suffered a heart attack while attending to a player early in the second half and died in hospital.

Chalana crossed for Rui Jordão to level with a looping header 12 minutes from the end of full-time and the same pair combined again for Jordão to volley Portugal in front in extra time. Domergue stabbed home his second goal to equalise with six minutes remaining and then, with penalties looming and memories of Seville thudding in the French players' heads like a particularly insidious bassline, birthday boy Tigana drove to the byline on the right and pulled the ball back for Platini to fire a heart-stopping 119th-minute winner into the roof of the net.[14]

The final against Spain at the Parc des Princes had particular significance for the players in the France squad with Spanish roots. Fernandez was born in Tarifa in Andalusia and moved to the Lyon region with his family when he was seven, while Amoros' parents were both Spanish and Giresse's mother hailed from Salamanca. Spain's players targeted Fernandez with taunts of *'Renegado!'* ('Traitor!'), along with other choice expressions, throughout the game. Prior to kick-off, Platini instructed his teammates to fix their eyes on the Henri Delaunay Trophy during the pre-match protocols so as to focus their minds on the task at hand. A combination of nerves and fatigue meant that France produced their least convincing display of the tournament and even Platini needed a helping hand, his tame 57th-minute free-kick somehow being allowed to smuggle its way into the net by Spanish goalkeeper Luis Arconada. It was his ninth goal of the competition – a record that still stands. After centre-back Yvon Le Roux had been shown a second yellow card with five minutes remaining, reducing France to 10 men, Tigana freed Bruno Bellone to dink a shot over Arconada and make it 2–0. Two years on, the ghosts of Ramón Sánchez-Pizjuán had been exorcised. As a grinning Platini lifted the trophy above his head in front of President François Mitterrand, the fans in the stadium chanted simply: *'On a gagné!'* ('We have won!') It was the first continental-level team success in French sporting history.

The players and staff celebrated with a dinner in the basement dining room at the French Football Federation (FFF) headquarters on Avenue d'Iéna. Although thousands of jubilant supporters flocked to the Champs-Élysées,

---

14 Tigana was not the only person celebrating a birthday at the Vélodrome that night: Zinédine Zidane, who turned 12 the same day, was in attendance as a ball boy. His future France teammate Youri Djorkaeff watched the game from the stands.

tooting their car horns and waving their *Tricolores*, there was no parade down the famous avenue, but it suited the players just fine. 'We all felt a lot of joy,' says Bossis. 'We celebrated. But we had set ourselves that goal and once we'd achieved it, there was perhaps less jubilation than there would have been if we'd achieved something we hadn't expected to. If we'd made the final in Spain [in 1982], I think the joy would have been greater because we'd never expected to reach the final.'

At six o'clock the following morning, having struggled to find sleep, Fernandez went out to his local newspaper kiosk on Avenue de Wagram in Paris' 17th arrondissement and bought every paper he could find. The reports were unanimous: nothing would ever be the same again. 'That team left a mark because it was an expansive France team that had ambition and played *football à la française*, which was the football that we loved,' Fernandez says. 'It was creative football, spectacular football, played with desire and lots of enthusiasm. The first title always leaves a mark. It will remain forever. There might be world champions or European champions that come later, but you needed to have that first team to show the way.'

After Hidalgo stepped down, former Nantes captain Henri Michel steered France to another semi-final showing at the 1986 World Cup in Mexico. Following a breathlessly high-quality quarter-final victory over Brazil on penalties in Guadalajara, *Les Bleus* came unstuck against West Germany in the last four once again, losing 2–0. Only this time, although there was disappointment, there was no wailing and gnashing of teeth, no changing room awash with weeping players, no distraught millions back at home. This time, France had a trophy on the mantlepiece already. This time, they knew they belonged.

2

GESTE TECHNIQUE

LE COUP FRANC À LA PLATINI

The signs that Michel Platini would turn into one of the finest free-kick takers that the game had ever seen were there early on. As a boy, he always had a ball at his feet and would challenge himself to hit random targets – a tree branch, a tin can sitting on a fencepost – in the streets around the family home in Jœuf. They were innocuous, playful exercises, but at the same time, his small stature quickly brought it home to him that if he was going to get the best of his schoolmates in their furiously competitive after-school kickabouts, it would be through finesse rather than force. His father, Aldo, nourished his enthusiasm for technical practice, putting on impromptu individual coaching sessions for him on idle afternoons. A 'devilish' free-kick taker in his own right, according to Michel, Aldo used to challenge his son to score directly from corners during junior matches on small-sized pitches in a bid to further improve his accuracy. Long before the floodlights of France's top-flight stadiums began to beckon, the young Platini had acquired a reputation for the remarkable power and precision with which he struck a stationary football.

Platini's recruitment by Nancy at the age of 17 presented him with the opportunity to hone his craft in systematised fashion. He joined the club at the same time as a young goalkeeper called Jean-Michel Moutier, who would become Platini's faithful lieutenant in his quest for set-piece perfection. On a daily basis after training, the future France captain would take upwards of 50 free-kicks from a variety of angles against Moutier on Nancy's mud-splattered training pitch, with the loser in their wagers treating the victor to a grenadine *diabolo* in the club bar. Noticing Platini's dedication to his craft and appreciating the fruits of it in the first team's matches, Nancy president Claude Cuny presented him with a makeshift wall of defenders: a set of four man-sized foam figurines with square heads and V-shaped bodies, anchored in buckets full of concrete. Confronted day after day by this line of faceless foes, Platini became renowned for his ability to get the ball to curl over the wall before dipping viciously towards goal. 'When Michel took a free-kick, we'd be already lining up in our own half,' said his former Nancy teammate Olivier Rouyer.

Platini's favoured position for free-kicks was 20 to 25 yards from goal, slightly to the left of centre. His trademark technique was a *frappe brossée* – a 'brushed' shot with the inside of his right foot. Regardless of where he was aiming for, certain details of his shooting action remained the same: head over the ball, back straight, right arm held straight down by his side, left arm swinging across his body as he made contact. 'Explaining what I do is a bit like telling you how I walk,' he told Nancy club magazine *Chardon Rouge* in September 1976. 'I shoot by reflex, placing the ball or hitting it with power depending on the position of the goalkeeper. I certainly have a few little tricks but I prefer not to speak about them so I can pull off a few more. But the essential thing is training. It doesn't come on its own.'

Over and above any technical considerations, what particularly appealed to Platini about the exercise – indeed, what made him such a thorn in the side of opposition goalkeepers – was the psychological aspect. He knew that he could put the ball broadly where he wanted to, but he always tried to throw the goalkeeper off the scent as much as possible too. 'It's the goalkeeper against me, me against the goalkeeper,' he told a *L'Équipe Explore* documentary in 2017. 'It was a real game of bluff between me and the keeper. I had to anticipate what he was going to do.' In the first instance, Platini would try to obscure the ball, often by instructing a teammate to stand in the keeper's line of sight. Perhaps his greatest strength, as a set-piece expert, was his ability to wait until the very last moment before deciding where to aim for, giving him the opportunity to make a last-minute recalibration if he spotted the goalkeeper inching in a particular direction as he advanced upon the ball. A frequent observation during Platini's career was that because of his high success rate, free-kicks awarded to his team were effectively the same as penalties; in terms of his duel with the opposition goalkeeper, he approached them as if they were.

Dino Zoff, Platini's future Juventus teammate, fell victim to the Frenchman's adaptable approach in a February 1978 friendly match between Italy and France in Naples. Shortly after the hour, Platini whipped a picture-book *coup franc* (free-kick) into the top-left corner, only for Spanish referee Ángel Franco Martínez to rule it out because he had not yet blown his whistle. Fifteen minutes later, Martínez whistled for an Italy foul in an almost identical position and with everyone in the stadium expecting Platini to repeat the trick (not least Zoff, who took a huge step to his right as the France skipper converged upon the ball), he nonchalantly swept a shot into the bottom corner on the opposite side of the goal to earn *Les Bleus* a 2–2 draw.

Platini netted armfuls of free-kicks for his three club teams, Nancy, Saint-Étienne and Juventus, but the ones that have lingered longest in the memory in France are, inevitably, the ones he scored in the colours of the national side (11 from a total of 41). He scored three goals in his first six international appearances and all came from indirect free-kicks. On Platini's debut against Czechoslovakia in March 1976, France captain Henri Michel was standing over an indirect free-kick just inside the Czech area when the 20-year-old newcomer sidled up behind him and said: 'Give it to me and I'll stick it in.' Michel duly obliged and Platini duly obliged. Two of his free-kicks, four years apart, sent France to World Cups: one against the Netherlands in November 1981 and one against Yugoslavia in November 1985.[15] Ironically, his best remembered dead-ball strike for France was probably his worst: the tame effort in the Euro 84 final that Spain goalkeeper Luis Arconada allowed to squirm beneath his body, which remains the only direct free-kick to have been scored in a men's European Championship final. But if anybody had earned the right to a bit of good fortune from the free-kick gods, it was Platini.

---

15 On both occasions, direct free-kicks by Platini opened the scoring in 2–0 wins at the Parc des Princes. The victory over the Netherlands in 1981 did not guarantee France a World Cup place, but left them needing only to beat whipping boys Cyprus in their final match to qualify (which they did).

3

BORDEAUX

VICTORY AMID THE VINEYARDS

'He was very clannish: you were either with him or you were against him.
But if you were with him, it was until death.'

Bernard Lacombe on Claude Bez

Alain Giresse was very particular about his football boots.

'Firstly, I was the only one who was allowed to look after them,' he says. 'We didn't have all the staff that there are today who look after the boots. But even today, I still don't think I'd give my boots to the staff. I find it so personal, your boots, because when they're on your feet, you have to feel them. I don't like it when people call them "tools". Because they're more than tools: they're jewels. To play football, you need a certain degree of sensitivity [in your feet]. When the ball arrives and you take it with you, it's because you feel good, because you have the right boots on. And I had boots that were like *that*.' He traces his index finger around the outline of his hand. 'You wouldn't have got a cigarette paper between my foot and the leather of the boot. I had a whole gallery of boots – I must have had 40-odd or 50-odd pairs. I still have them. I waxed them before every game. And they *shone*.'

We are sitting beside a table football table in the clubhouse of Balma Sporting Club in the eastern Toulouse suburbs, where Giresse's youngest son, Arnaud, plays in the amateur football section. It is a cold, damp January evening and in the wintry drizzle outside, a few hardy runners in hats, gloves and waterproof tops are completing laps of the sodden red athletics track. Giresse, his grey hair parted at the side, is wearing a black gilet over a blue and white checked shirt. If he talks about his boots like a painter might discuss his favourite paintbrushes, it is because for the duration of his 18-year playing career, he turned the football pitch into a canvas. Short (5'4") and powerful, his muscular thighs and calves the legacy of a childhood spent cycling up and down the hillsides of his native Gironde, Giresse hit the ball with a rare combination of force and accuracy, danced between defenders with beguiling ease and picked out teammates with pinpoint passes that most players could not even see. His France teammate Michel Platini said that he was 'capable of dribbling and scoring with his eyes closed'. Hailing from the village of Langoiran, 15 miles southeast of Bordeaux, Giresse has played more games (592) and scored more goals (179) for *Les Girondins* than anyone else and tops the table for the most appearances by an outfield player (587) in the history of the French top flight.

During his time at Bordeaux, Giresse's fastidiousness with regard to his boots (Adidas Copa Mundial, UK size 5) extended to always banging them against the wall in the same area of the Parc Lescure tunnel. 'I'd go down, *tac-tac*,' he says. 'And because the boots had been waxed, it left a trace – a little bit of wax. *Tac-tac-tac* and then right, I was off. Before every match.' The tunnel at Lescure stretched nearly 150 metres in length, making it the longest in European football. It was one of several quirky features of the art deco stadium, which was rebuilt to stage games at the 1938 World Cup.[16] The players accessed the tunnel by crossing a courtyard outside the changing rooms known as *le paddock*. A double doorway plunged them down a steep, spiralling concrete ramp, with red handrails on either side, and into the main body of the tunnel: a long, cramped, subterranean passageway with a low roof, whitewashed concrete on both sides and a strip of electric lights overhead. Short straight bit, left turn, curve round to the right, long straight bit, left turn, up a set of steps, two sharp right turns and then out into the glare of the arena. Legend has it that Bordeaux's players would allow their opponents to make their way down the tunnel first before thundering up behind them in a portentous rumble of studs. It was on this long, winding

16 The stadium was known as Parc Lescure until 2001, when it was renamed Stade Chaban-Delmas in honour of former Mayor of Bordeaux Jacques Chaban-Delmas.

journey to the pitch that the home side's hard men – Raymond Domenech, René Girard, Gernot Rohr – would set the tone for what was to follow. 'I saw it, yes. There'd be ears being pulled, little [menacing] signs, all sorts!' laughs Giresse. 'There weren't any big skirmishes, but it enabled you to create an atmosphere.'

In the mid-1980s, Bordeaux's opponents had plenty to fear as they trooped down the Lescure tunnel, and not just in a physical sense. Under provocative club president Claude Bez, the team from southwest France dominated French football, winning three league titles, two Coupes de France and reaching two European semi-finals, as well as providing the backbone of Michel Hidalgo's celebrated France team. But their demise would be even more vertiginous than their rise.

Giresse made his league debut for Bordeaux aged 18 in a 1–1 draw at Nîmes in October 1970. The club finished fifth in Division 1[17] at the end of his maiden campaign, but it was to prove a false dawn. *Les Girondins* were a stubbornly mid-table side throughout the 1970s and repeatedly flirted with the drop, finishing just a point above the relegation places in 1974 and 1978. Bez had joined the club as treasurer in 1974 and became president four years later when Jean Roureau, a local wine merchant, stepped down. Thickset and sporting a spectacular walrus moustache, Bez had achieved professional success as the director of a local accountancy firm and quickly made it known that his ambitions for Bordeaux had no limits. He was fiercely proud of his local roots, enjoyed the good life that could be had in Gironde and was determined to turn the football club into a beacon for the region.

'He was a *bon vivant*,' says Giresse. 'A real southwest man, a man of the land, a pure *girondin*.[18] We sometimes travelled by train on away trips and we'd see him when we were eating our meals. He liked good food. We'd be eating sandwiches and he'd say: "Sandwiches? No, that's not right." He wanted to take things into a different dimension in terms of what could be put in place in a professional,

---

17 The French top flight was known as Division 1 until 2002, when it was rebranded as Ligue 1.
18 A *girondin* is a person from the French department of Gironde.

sporting sense. With ideas that were quite strict: commitment to the club, respect for the colours. And straight away, he said: "We're going to aim for Europe." We looked at him like: "We spend our time fighting to stay up and he's talking about Europe?" But then he started to bring international players into the club: Marius Trésor, [Patrick] Battiston, [Jean] Tigana, [René] Girard. And Bordeaux inevitably started climbing.' Centre-back Alain Roche graduated from the Bordeaux youth system in the mid-1980s and remembers the high sartorial standards to which Bez held his players. 'The president ruled that the players had to wear suits when we went to away games,' he says. 'It was a very English approach. Bordeaux was a bourgeois city, there was the wine, the close connections with England.[19] We always had shirts with club ties, suits; most of the players and directors had duffel coats with nice loafers. Claude Bez set a lot of store by that. He thought we were representing the club when we travelled and he wanted to see an exemplary attitude from everyone.'

Bringing his accountant's eye to Bordeaux's financial affairs, Bez targeted players who were out of contract and could therefore be acquired more cheaply. He immediately sought to establish a close relationship with Jacques Chaban-Delmas, the long-standing mayor of Bordeaux, by explaining that *Les Girondins* could serve as ambassadors for the city and help to attract investment to the region. Bez had hospitality boxes installed at Parc Lescure, where local bigwigs and visiting businessmen could be schmoozed and entertained. In return for the publicity that the city of Bordeaux got from its increasingly successful football team, Chaban-Delmas granted the club low-interest loans and boosted municipal funding. Bez struck lucrative sponsorship deals with international firms such as German car manufacturer Opel. He set up an official supporters' club, an official club shop, even an official club hotel. But his biggest contribution to the commercialisation of French football was his pioneering role in the development of television rights agreements. French broadcasters were accustomed to showing football matches for free and Bez saw no reason why other companies should make money off his back, even going so far as to physically block camera crews

19 England has imported wine from Bordeaux since the 12th century. The city spent three centuries under English rule after Henry II, husband of local noblewoman Eleanor of Aquitaine, became King of England in 1154.

from entering Lescure. He led the negotiations on behalf of the clubs when the major French broadcasters began to take an interest in broadcasting matches and his efforts helped to spark a bidding war between rival TV companies Canal+ and TF1,[20] bringing more money into the coffers of France's leading sides and helping them to become more competitive at European level.

Bez was outwardly flamboyant – rolling around town in a navy-blue Bentley with a white roof – but privately reserved. He spoke with a stammer and when he addressed the players before matches, he kept things brief. 'Good evening my lords,' Bez would say after knocking on the changing room door. 'Hope everything goes well. See you later.' When Bordeaux won, even by a handsome margin, he would offer a succinct post-match verdict: '*Assez bien.*' ('Quite good.') A formidable negotiator, he was known as a man of his word, sealing every agreement with a handshake that was in his eyes irrevocable. 'He was very clannish: you were either with him or you were against him,' said former Bordeaux striker Bernard Lacombe. 'But if you were with him, it was until death. He gave his word and never betrayed it. Ever.' Bez respected his coaches' expertise, never meddling in tactics or team selection, but would ask for significant footballing decisions to be explained to him. His influence gave him considerable sway within the French Football Federation and the Ligue de Football Professionnel. In 1988 he played a central role in Platini's appointment as coach of *Les Bleus*. He typically arrived for meetings in Paris carrying piles of folders that he would ostentatiously spread out on the table before him, later confiding to one associate that they were simply old files that he would grab from the shelves of his accountancy firm before leaving Bordeaux.

Bez was also power-obsessed, ill-tempered and capable of reacting explosively if he felt that Bordeaux had been treated unfairly. When eccentric Serbian goalkeeper Dragan Pantelić was banned for a year after assaulting a linesman in the tunnel at Lescure, Bez expressed his displeasure by sending his team out without a recognised keeper for their final game of the 1981–82 season at Nantes. Giresse, the smallest player in the side, donned the team's red goalkeeper kit, but

20 Canal+, Europe's first subscription channel, launched in France in 1984, while public broadcaster TF1 was privatised in 1987.

it was centre-back Trésor who played between the posts, albeit without being able to use his hands. 'We put a system in place that meant that I would go in goal at corners,' recalls Giresse. 'There was a corner. The ball was cleared, [Nantes player Thierry] Tusseau hit it and I just heard: whoosh! And the ball was in the back of the net. I went to get the ball out of the net and I said to myself: "Is this what being a goalkeeper is, getting the ball out of the back of the net? No thank you." It was so stupid.' Bordeaux lost 6–0.

One of Bez's first moves when he became Bordeaux president in 1978 was to appoint Luis Carniglia as head coach. The venerable Argentinian had steered the great Real Madrid side of Alfredo Di Stéfano and Raymond Kopa to two European Cup successes in the late 1950s, but his methods had become outmoded and the Bordeaux players found his training sessions too light. When a poor start to the 1979–80 campaign left Bordeaux sitting in the relegation zone after 13 matches, Bez sacked Carniglia and replaced him on an interim basis with Belgian coach Raymond Goethals, who had led Anderlecht to glory in the European Cup Winners' Cup a year earlier. Goethals engineered a turnaround that saw Bordeaux finish the campaign in sixth place, but a pall was cast over the season in April 1980 when France international midfielder Omar Sahnoun suffered a heart attack during a training-ground jog and died at the age of 24.[21]

Goethals' departure left Bez with a vacancy in the dug-out and on Lacombe's recommendation, he turned to an up-and-coming 38-year-old coach called Aimé Jacquet. The future mastermind of France's 1998 World Cup triumph, Jacquet had worked with Lacombe at Lyon, first as his teammate, then as his coach, and had impressed the striker with his calm professionalism and his skill for working with young players. In Jacquet's recollection, during his first meeting with Bez in Paris, the Bordeaux president told him: 'You have three years to build a team who'll qualify for Europe.' But for all his bombast, Bez allowed Jacquet to

---

21 Sahnoun's son, Nicolas, who was born after he died, became a professional footballer and started his career at Bordeaux.

work in peace and gave him the means to build a trophy-winning side by assembling a squad that was packed with experienced internationals. Giresse, bulldozer centre-forward Lacombe, attacking right-back Jean-Christophe Thouvenel and German utility man Gernot Rohr were already at the club prior to Jacquet's appointment, while Trésor and midfield enforcer Girard arrived the same summer. Over the years that followed, Bez and sporting director Didier Couécou brought in France internationals Raymond Domenech, Thierry Tusseau, Jean Tigana, Léonard Specht, Patrick Battiston and Dominique Dropsy (the world's most unfortunately named goalkeeper), along with prolific German striker Dieter Müller and dazzling Portuguese winger Fernando Chalana.

Jacquet prized good football, once summing up his coaching philosophy as '*le jeu, le jeu, le jeu*' ('the game, the game, the game').[22] As a player at Saint-Étienne, he had played under legendary French coaches Jean Snella and Albert Batteux, both of whom prided themselves on putting technique at the centre of everything they did. Jacquet had fond memories of four-hour training sessions with Snella, during which the players would play barefoot, focused purely on developing their technique. He displayed similar attention to detail at Bordeaux. 'When I was 18, he worked with me on my cross-field passes,' says Roche. 'He had me stay out wide and hit 10 with my left foot and 10 with my right, over 20 to 40 metres. I was extremely grateful, because repetition is important in football, just like rehearsing in music. He had other things to think about, but he spent that time with me because he really wanted me to make progress. He loved his job and he loved to transmit his passion.' Jacquet encouraged dialogue between his players and created an environment of mutual respect by showing faith in their professionalism. 'He made us accountable,' says Giresse. 'There were days when you arrived and it was: "OK, today you're free. You can choose what you want to do, individually. And we'll respond to your demands." I'd say: "Mémé, I don't really want to touch the ball. I need to get hungry for the ball." He'd say: "OK, OK." There was a little wood at Le Haillan [the Bordeaux training ground]. He'd tell me: "Go and find me some acorns and mushrooms." Things like that.

---

22 The notion of *le jeu* (the game) has specific connotations in French football. A coach who prioritises *le jeu* is someone who advocates for expansive, possession-based, attacking football.

There's mutual respect there and at the same time, there's trust. And then, day of the game – I'll show up. I have to respond and give back.'

Aided by former Bordeaux goalkeeper Bernard Michelena, who doubled up as a fitness trainer and a dedicated goalkeeping coach, Jacquet brought new rigour to the team's physical preparation. Every summer, Michelena would lead the squad through sapping pre-season running drills in the eastern spa town of Aix-les-Bains, equipping them with the base-level fitness that would carry them to the end of the campaign. It gave Jacquet a blueprint for the rest of his coaching career. 'I can say today, I took to the France team everything that I'd done at Bordeaux, with the same principles, the same philosophy, the same determination and the same respect for the players,' he said. 'I was never vulgar with them, but always ruthless on work and preparation. We were very strong on preparation. I owe it to Bernard Michelena.' Jacquet also succeeded in persuading Bez to leave the club's rustic training pitches at Rocquevielle and set up an ultra-modern facility at Le Haillan, a sprawling 11-hectare site northwest of the city centre set around the handsome 19th-century Château Bel-Air. By the time Bordeaux took up residence there in 1986, they were already the best team in France.

Bordeaux came third and fourth in Jacquet's first two seasons, before a runners-up finish behind champions Nantes in the 1982–83 campaign confirmed their title credentials. The arrival from Nantes of the versatile and indefatigable Tusseau in the summer of 1983 gave *Les Girondins* a balance that would prove critical to the success that followed. Prefiguring the manner in which he would construct his World Cup-winning France team around Zinédine Zidane, Jacquet aligned a hard-working midfield trio of Girard, Tigana and Tusseau, which enabled Giresse to operate in a free role behind strikers Lacombe and Müller.

Jacquet's men took control of the Division 1 title race from the start in 1983–84 and completed league doubles over both Nantes and Saint-Étienne, the latter being thrashed 7–0 in a memorable game at Lescure in late March in which Müller plundered a 13-minute hat-trick. They ceded top spot to Monaco after losing 2–1 at Stade Louis II in their next game, but wins over Paris

Saint-Germain, Auxerre and Bastia got them back on track. When Monaco could only draw at Toulouse on the season's final day, Bordeaux's 2–0 win at Rennes – courtesy of goals in each half from Lacombe and Müller – gave the club a first league title in 44 years.

Bordeaux has a reputation as a bourgeois, dispassionate city, a world away from the exuberant excesses of Marseille, but the 1984 title win sparked scenes of wild celebration. 'It sent Bordeaux into a frenzy,' recalls Giresse. 'We come back from Rennes, we land and then, at Mérignac airport . . . wow. People everywhere. The hall of the airport was rammed. It was madness. That took us up a level in terms of the club's popularity. There was lots of pride. And I felt it even more. I'd been following *Les Girondins* since I was a little kid, I'd been through a period where we only ever played to stay up and now we were champions. That settled us. It gave us even more maturity, experience, control. That's why the year after, the second title didn't cause us any problems.'

The following season, Jacquet's Bordeaux reached the peak of their powers. Five of his players – Battiston, Tigana, Giresse, Tusseau and Lacombe – had become European champions with France over the summer and they carried that momentum into the league campaign. Exuding an air of total authority, *Les Marine et Blanc* (Navy Blue and White) beat closest rivals Nantes home and away once again, finished the season with both most goals scored (70) and fewest conceded (27) and wrapped up the title with two games to spare.

The club's European Cup campaign that season captured Jacquet's imagination. Prior to important European matches, he would take his players to a family-run hotel in a little rural village called Belin-Béliet, 30 miles south of Bordeaux, so that they could prepare in perfect tranquillity. His attention to detail was such that he was able to provide the squad not only with comprehensive tactical breakdowns of how their next opponents played, but photographs of all the opposition players – brought back with him from his scouting trips – so that they would all know what their opposite numbers looked like. 'We knew our opponents from A-Z, even their faces, despite having never encountered them,' midfielder Girard tells me in a phone call from his native Gard. 'He was a very precise person, very attentive. We were warned about everything that was coming our way.' After narrow wins over Athletic Bilbao and Dinamo Bucharest in the early rounds, Bordeaux had to come through a chaotic trip to Soviet side Dnipro Dnipropetrovsk in the quarter-finals. Bordeaux's delegation was held up in Kyiv for 24 hours due to fog and after arriving only a few hours before kick-off (Bez having angrily rejected a proposal by the Soviet authorities for the squad to travel by sleeper train), they discovered that the pitch was frozen.[23] A late equaliser by Tusseau sent the tie to penalties and Bordeaux prevailed when the left-footed Chalana settled the shoot-out by planting the decisive spot-kick in the top-left corner . . . with his right foot. Jacquet's men lost 3–0 to Juventus in the first leg of their semi-final tie (Platini having supposedly unsettled them by breezily popping into their changing room before kick-off to say hello), but in the second leg, *Les Girondins* came within a hair's breadth of pulling off one of the most improbable comebacks in European Cup history.

In the days building up to the return fixture in April 1985, the Bordeaux squad's temporary home in Belin-Béliet was deluged by cards and letters from supporters and well-wishers urging the players to keep faith. When tickets for the game went on sale, hundreds of supporters slept on the pavement outside the ticket office overnight in the hope of getting one. Come the night of the game, they packed into Lescure in their thousands, brandishing their blue and white banners, flags and scarves and setting a stadium attendance record of 40,211 that still stands.

In addition to Platini, then the world's pre-eminent footballer, Juventus also boasted Polish great Zbigniew Boniek and several members of the Italy team – Gaetano Scirea, Antonio Cabrini, Marco Tardelli, Paolo Rossi – that had triumphed at the 1982 World Cup. But Bordeaux flew at them from the start, reducing the arrears in the 25th minute when Müller swivelled to score from Lacombe's cut-back and making it 2–0 on the night with 10 minutes remaining when Battiston let rip from 30 yards with a devilishly swerving shot that crashed into the net via the right-hand post. Lescure was now a maelstrom of noise and fury – Lacombe said the players 'could almost feel the stadium physically pushing us' – and Tigana had a late chance to send the game to extra time, only for his thunderous effort to be boxed away by Luciano Bodini. Just like Reims in the

---

23 The game took place at Stadion Metalurh in Kryvyi Rih, central Ukraine because foreigners were not allowed to enter Dnipropetrovsk at the time due to its close proximity to Soviet missile factories.

late 1950s, just like Saint-Étienne in 1976, just like Bastia in 1978, beaten by PSV Eindhoven in the UEFA Cup final, French football had been on the brink of a breakthrough in a European club competition, only to come up just short.

———

There were three minutes remaining in extra time of the 1986 Coupe de France final and Bordeaux were drawing 1–1 with Marseille when Tigana broke into space on the right flank and clipped a cross into the box. Waiting at the back post, about 15 yards from goal, Giresse controlled the ball with his left instep, allowed it to bounce and then lifted an impossibly delicate lob over Joseph-Antoine Bell and into the net. *Les Girondins* had finished third in the league, behind PSG and Nantes, but Giresse's exquisite goal at the Parc des Princes allowed them to end a run of five successive defeats in Coupe de France finals. Unbeknown to anyone in the stadium – least of all Giresse himself – it was to prove his last significant kick in Bordeaux blue.

Giresse, then nearing his 34th birthday, was out of contract and his relationship with Bez had badly deteriorated. Returning to Bordeaux after the 1986 World Cup, he began to feel that he was no longer held in the esteem that he deserved. He had turned down one approach from Bernard Tapie earlier in the year, but when the newly installed Marseille president called him again, Giresse said yes, stimulated by the prospect of resurrecting his partnership with Hidalgo, who had been appointed OM's general manager months previously. The news landed in Bordeaux like a bombshell. Giresse, *le petit prince de Lescure*, was a child of the club, had risen through the ranks to become captain, had taught new recruits about the local wine culture, had led the team from the ignominy of relegation scraps to the summit of the French game, and now he was leaving for their biggest rivals. Bez was livid, accusing Giresse of having betrayed the club for money. 'For me, someone who goes back on their word is no longer a man,' he said. 'The *salopard* (bastard) is him and not me.' When Giresse returned to Lescure with Marseille the following April, his picture in the match programme was replaced with a question mark and Rohr was sent off for hacking him down midway through the first half. 'He was the kind of player who you couldn't see at any other club than the one where he'd come through, but Gigi ended up going to Marseille,' says Girard. 'It took the wind from our sails.'

Bordeaux's squad was evolving. Trésor, Domenech, Müller and Tusseau had also left by then, Lacombe was nearing retirement and a group of younger players – led by talented France internationals Jean-Marc Ferreri, Philippe Vercruysse and the livewire José Touré – was taking command. Reinforced by the mid-season arrival of 22-year-old striker Philippe Fargeon, who scored 20 goals between early December and the end of the campaign, Bordeaux claimed the club's first league and cup double in 1986–87, finishing four points clear of Marseille in Division 1 and beating the same opponents 2–0 in the final of the Coupe de France.[24] But if Bez was winning the battles, Tapie would prevail in the war.

After finishing second to Arsène Wenger's Monaco in 1987–88, Bordeaux slumped to 13th a year later – Jacquet having been summarily sacked in the meantime – as Marseille secured the first league title of the Tapie era. The title battle between Marseille and Bordeaux that dominated the following season would be one of the most bitter in French football history. Tapie and Bez were poles apart – one a brash, smooth-talking TV personality, the other a shy, grouchy outsider – and they made no secret of their mutual antipathy, regularly trading insults and allegations of off-pitch skulduggery. Tapie said that before entering football, Bez had been 'nothing'. Bez branded Tapie 'a cancer for football'. The fans and the French sports media lapped it up. When Bordeaux travelled to the Stade Vélodrome for a pivotal fixture in the title race in April 1990, Bez provocatively thumbed his nose at Tapie and the baying locals by being driven right up to the stadium perimeter in a midnight blue Cadillac with a '33' Gironde number plate. But Bordeaux lost 2–0 and OM finished the season as champions again. 'Bez didn't like this expressive, expansive person, who talked a lot,' says Roche. 'He was the opposite of him. What was difficult for Bez was when he had to accept that he no longer had the means to fight with Tapie. Bez didn't have the means any more and Tapie squashed everyone with his success.'

---

24 Bordeaux also reached the semi-finals of the European Cup Winners' Cup, losing on penalties to Locomotive Leipzig after a 1–1 aggregate draw.

Bez's downfall was dizzying. He had gambled on continued success in European competition, but an early exit from the European Cup in the 1985–86 season and failure to qualify for Europe at all in 1988–89 left the club in serious financial difficulty. Mayor Chaban-Delmas had consistently bailed Bordeaux out over the years, but debts of 320 million francs represented a hole too vast for municipal aid to fill. When journalists reporting on Bordeaux's financial difficulties turned up at Le Haillan in September 1990, Bez flew into a rage, throwing punches, wrestling cameras from the arms of startled cameramen and furiously ordering the reporters to leave.

Worse was to follow when tax inspectors discovered an unaccounted shortfall of 10 million francs in the club accounts related to renovation work undertaken at Le Haillan. After being charged with fraud and forgery offences, Bez resigned as president in late November 1990. Despite Bordeaux finishing 10th in Division 1 at the end of the 1990–91 season, French football's newly created financial watchdog, the Direction Nationale du Contrôle de Gestion (National Directorate of Management Control), relegated the club to the second tier due to their financial problems.[25] Bez was imprisoned for two months in 1992 as part of an investigation into illegal payments relating to player transfers. In March 1995, he was sentenced to a further three years in prison (with two years suspended) by Bordeaux's Court of Appeal over the renovation of Le Haillan but would spend only three months behind bars on account of ill health. He died from a heart attack at the age of 58 in January 1999.

The pride of Bordeaux, the shame of Bordeaux; a beacon become a distress flare. Bez dreamed big, spent big and won big, bringing European glamour, national glory and international renown to Lescure, only for his footballing empire to be reduced to rubble in a matter of months. He was not the first French club president to fly too close to the sun. He would not be the last.

---

25 Brest (who finished 11th) and Nice (14th) were relegated for the same reasons. Bordeaux were promoted back to Division 1 at the first attempt.

4

MARSEILLE

TAPIE'S TAINTED TRIUMPH

'I see who the two bosses of French football are: [Monaco president] Jean-Louis Campora and Claude Bez. By pinching Giresse from Bordeaux and Papin from Monaco, I made them understand that from now on, I was the boss.'

Bernard Tapie

'I closed my eyes when it suited me.'

Marcel Desailly

Bernard Tapie stands in the shade at the side of the Stade Vélodrome pitch, master of all he surveys. It is May 1993 and Olympique de Marseille are about to take on Paris Saint-Germain in their penultimate match of the season. If they avoid defeat, they will claim an unprecedented fifth consecutive French league title. Three days previously, they beat the great AC Milan 1–0 in Munich courtesy of Basile Boli's first-half header to become the first French team to lift the European Cup. The following evening, amid scenes of unfettered delight, around 20,000 fans flocked to the Vélodrome to acclaim their returning heroes. There are over twice as many supporters in for the visit of arch-rivals PSG, who must win to stand any chance of denying Marseille the title. It is a balmy, early summer evening, the sun just beginning its slow descent behind the Tribune Jean-Bouin, and the stadium is awash with happy faces. Wearing a light-grey suit jacket over a light-blue shirt and diamond-patterned tie, his hands stuffed into the pockets of his navy-blue trousers, Tapie shoots the breeze with two television executives on the touchline as the stadium fills around him, oblivious to the swarm of cameramen and photographers who scrutinise his every gesture. Stocky and sun-bronzed, his thick, brown hair swept across his forehead, he is a picture of relaxation and success.

The players emerge from their changing rooms in the bowels of the stadium – Marseille in their all-white home strip, PSG in a royal blue change kit – and clatter along a concrete corridor in their boots towards the pitch. A television reporter snatches a word with 24-year-old Marseille captain Didier Deschamps. 'We can't allow ourselves to be carried away by the atmosphere,' warns Deschamps as he trots up the steps leading to the pitch. 'We want this fifth title.' As is customary, the opening bars of 'Jump' by the American rock band Van Halen are the cue for the players to leave the mouth of the tunnel, which sends a roar rippling around the ground. Behind the goal at the opposite end of the pitch from the tunnel, the fans on the top tier of the Virage Sud wave blue, white and red flags to create a giant French *Tricolore*. The bottom tier is a sea of flags and white pom-poms. 'The Stade Vélodrome is absolutely superb,' purrs Canal+ commentator Charles Biétry. 'The sun is out for what is sure to be a party.'

Marseille are caught cold in the eighth minute when Vincent Guérin pounces on a rebound to put PSG ahead. But Rudi Völler equalises from Franck Sauzée's knock-down and in the 36th minute the home side take the lead with a goal so absurdly spectacular it could have been lifted straight from the pages of a comic book. Boli, the hero of Munich three days earlier, breaks up a PSG attack 10 yards inside his own half by heading the ball upfield to Abedi Pelé. With his back to goal, the Ghanaian forward cushions the ball on his chest and then showily lifts it over Daniel Bravo's head with his left thigh. Jean-Philippe Durand takes over, controlling the ball on his chest, flicking it back over the unfortunate Bravo and adroitly volleying a pass infield to Boli, who has continued his run down the middle of the pitch. '*Oh la la*, it's a recital!' exclaims Biétry from the commentary box. 'The Brazilians are in white!' Boli plays a pass out to Pelé on the left and when the OM number 10 digs out a cross to the edge of the area, Boli hurls himself through the air and meets it with a flying header that catapults the ball into the top-left corner via the underside of the crossbar. 'Fabulous goal by Basile Boli! Fabulous move by Marseille, worthy of the European champions!' yells Biétry. 'A diving header into the top corner. I don't know if there's been a more beautiful goal in French football.' Boli sprints in celebration towards the touchline, his face contorted by emotion. The entire stadium is on its feet.

There is genuine bad blood between the two sides – December's foul-strewn reverse fixture in Paris, won 1–0 by Marseille, came to be known as *La Boucherie* (The Butchery) – and the tackles really start flying in during the second half. But a third goal for Marseille, thundered home by Alen Bokšić, makes the game safe and even the sorry sight of PSG's travelling fans firing smoke bombs into the home supporters' seating sections cannot dampen the spectacle. The final whistle sounds on a 3–1 win and the pitch floods with people: ball boys in matching teal-coloured tracksuits, photographers and cameramen in yellow bibs, besuited club officials, a few enterprising supporters. Fabien Barthez blows kisses to the crowd at the base of the Virage Sud. Arm in arm, Deschamps and Marcel Desailly embark on a jig down the touchline in front of the Tribune Ganay, a flaming red flare held aloft in Deschamps' right hand. Marseille and their giddy, disbelieving supporters are on top of the world.

And yet OM's downfall is already afoot. The sands are already shifting, the thread that will cause the entire club to unravel has already come loose. A week previously, Valenciennes defender Jacques Glassmann had accused representatives from Marseille of offering him and two of his teammates cash to 'go easy' during a league game between the clubs shortly before the Champions League final. *L'affaire VA-OM*[26] will send shockwaves through French football and leave Marseille on their knees, banned from the Champions League, relegated to France's second tier and stripped of the league title that they have just won by beating PSG. Six people will receive

---

26 VA (pronounced vey-AH) is Valenciennes' nickname and refers to the club's former name of Union Sportive Valenciennes-Anzin. Anzin is a suburb of Valenciennes that was incorporated into the club in 1929.

judicial convictions, Tapie will spend nearly six months in prison and the image of the game in France will be left in the mud.

French football had never before risen so high. It would never again fall so low.

It does not take long, when you are in Éric Di Meco's company, to appreciate what it means to have played for the only French club to have won the Champions League. We are sitting outside a restaurant just around the corner from Notre-Dame de la Garde, the spectacular Neo-Byzantine basilica built upon a limestone outcrop that towers over Marseille's bustling Vieux Port. It is a warm spring afternoon and the busy square beside the restaurant buzzes with the sound of car horns, screeching tyres and kids whooshing by on motorised scooters. Di Meco hails from nearby Vaucluse and was one of *Les Minots*,[27] the name given to a celebrated group of youth-team players who were parachuted into the first team after OM went into liquidation in April 1981 and who prevented the club from going under. The only player in the 1993 Champions League-winning side to have graduated from Marseille's perennially neglected youth system, he can scarcely go 10 minutes without someone shouting a greeting or coming over to shake his hand and grab a selfie. 'It's a marker, even for people who aren't interested in football,' Di Meco says. '"Oh look, that's the guy who won the Champions League." I live in the city and there's not a day that goes by without someone talking to me about it.'

It is nearly 30 years since Di Meco reached the summit of European football with OM. Gone is the shaggy black mane of his playing days, but although his closely cropped hair is grey and his beard white at the chin, he is tanned and trim. Wearing a black gilet over a khaki-coloured hoodie, he looks like he could easily launch himself into a two-footed challenge should an opposition winger unexpectedly come dribbling around the corner. He has swapped the full-blooded tackles for no-nonsense punditry on radio station RMC Sport these

---

27 'The Kids' in the local Provençal dialect.

days, but in the lilting, gently rhythmic accent characteristic of this part of the world (they call it a *chantant* or 'singing' accent in France), he remains an ardent and outspoken defender of all things OM.

Founded in around 600 BC by settlers from the ancient Greek city of Phocaea, Marseille is France's oldest city. Shimmering in the hot Mediterranean sunshine, it fizzes with a vibrancy born of centuries of trade and inward migration. It is a port city; a gritty, chaotic city; a city that countless outsiders – from Italy, Armenia, Corsica, Algeria and beyond – have come to call home. It is a fiercely proud city and a place where football is lived with unique intensity. Patrick Delamontagne, a quiet, elegant playmaker from Brittany, spent one season at Marseille in the late 1980s and was horrified by the intrusions that the club's fans permitted themselves. 'I needed peace and quiet and I had guys coming to my house to leave notes on my windscreen,' he told *L'Équipe* in 2017. 'They even stole a shirt that was drying in the garden. You arrived at training and you signed 200 autographs. The day after, the same ones came back!' During the Tapie years, players were known to have been driven out of the Vélodrome in the boots of their cars so as to avoid unhappy supporters waiting for them outside. Desailly felt that one season at Marseille was worth 'three or four at any other club'. The suffocating local context has traditionally made it difficult for homegrown players to make names for themselves. There have been exceptions – Di Meco, Samir Nasri, Boubacar Kamara – but for a club of its size and huge local reach, only a vanishingly small number of locally born players have ever made the grade. OM's inability to produce its own homegrown talent has meant that, more than any other major French club, it, too, has long been synonymous with outsiders.

I ask Di Meco if he can sum up what OM means to the city. He puffs out his cheeks. 'Here in Marseille, it's more than a football club,' he says. 'OM is more of a social vector. It serves as a vessel for that idea that Marseille is unloved, that there's always been this antagonism [between Marseille and Paris]. I don't know what the equivalent would be in England – maybe Liverpool and London? It's the working-class city, the poor city, which the capital drags along. We've always held on to that, but through football, we've been able to affirm our differences. It's a special city: a poor city, a city of immigrants, but a city of bourgeois districts too. And everywhere you go, the local trademark is the [OM] jersey, the tracksuit, the cap, the scarf.'

As the year 1985 approached its close, the club was stagnating. Di Meco and *Les Minots* had secured promotion from Division 2 in 1984, but having avoided relegation by only two points in their first season back in the top tier, OM were locked in another battle to avoid the drop. Beset, once again, by financial difficulties, they had gone 14 years without winning a league title and nearly 10 years without lifting the Coupe de France. The Vélodrome needed a spark. It would arrive, naturally enough, in the form of an outsider.

Paris, October 1985. Elected leader of the Soviet Union six months previously, Mikhail Gorbachev was visiting the French capital to ask his counterpart François Mitterrand for assurances that France would not sign up to American president Ronald Reagan's proposed missile defence system known as the 'Star Wars programme'. During a dinner staged in Gorbachev's honour at the Embassy of the Soviet Union, an imposing Soviet-style building in the 16th arrondissement that backs on to the Boulevard Périphérique, an encounter occurred amid the clinking glasses and tinkling cutlery that would set OM on a radical new footing. Gaston Defferre, the Socialist mayor of Marseille, was in attendance in the company of his wife, writer Edmonde Charles-Roux, who found herself sitting at the same table as a charismatic Parisian businessman called Bernard Tapie. When conversation at the table moved on to the subject of football, Tapie voiced his opinion that OM were crying out for a new owner and that, backed by the club's wildly passionate fans, there was an opportunity to build something special there. Charles-Roux left the table to tell her husband about the exchange and by the time the coffees came round, he and Tapie were deep in conversation.

Then aged 42, Tapie had already tried on multiple careers for size before setting his sights on the world of elite sport. Born into a modest family in the northeastern Paris suburbs – his father, Jean-Baptiste, a milling machine operator turned refrigeration mechanic; his mother, Raymonde, a healthcare assistant – Tapie tried his hand as a television salesman, shopkeeper, healthcare entrepreneur, actor and pop star before finally finding his calling in the late 1970s: turning around failing companies and selling them on for millions. The firms he took over, many at the cost of a symbolic franc, included household goods manufacturer Terraillon, cycling equipment company Look, health food chain La Vie Claire, weighing machines manufacturer Testut, electrical battery producer Wonder and sportswear firm Donnay. Tapie made his first sporting acquisition in 1982 when he bought the sailing yacht *Le Phocéa*, on which he would break the world record for the quickest Atlantic crossing in a monohull in June 1988. In 1984 he set up his own cycling team, sponsored by La Vie Claire, which won the Tour de France with Bernard Hinault in 1985 and again with Greg LeMond in 1986. In OM, he saw an opportunity to restore one of French sport's sleeping giants to former glories and simultaneously create a local support base that would help to advance his ambitions to enter politics.

Mindful of his outsider status in football, Tapie spent the months leading up to his acquisition of Marseille meeting top-level coaches, players, administrators and agents in a drive to expand his knowledge of the game. In his first major coup, he succeeded in convincing Michel Hidalgo, amiable architect of France's watershed triumph at Euro 84, to be the club's general manager (the French sports media dubbing the pair's collaboration 'Tapidalgo'). After a protracted and tetchy takeover process, Tapie eventually completed his acquisition of OM in April 1986, paying a trademark one franc to become the financially imperilled club's new owner. Jean-Pierre Papin was one of the first players to sign up for Tapie's project and remembers meeting him for the first time at his opulently furnished offices on Avenue de Friedland in Paris, a stone's throw from the Arc de Triomphe. 'The first thing that I remember was the huge model of *Le Phocéa* that he had in his office. It was larger than life, magnificent,' Papin tells me. 'At the time, he was very young. He had that self-assurance that he could have anything. He said: "In three or four years, I want to be European champions." It's his ambition that attracts you. And then he puts in the resources you need for that. When you leave his office, it's hard to say no.'

Tapie was already a well-known figure in French public life. His business success had opened the door to regular appearances on television talk shows and the more viewers saw of this attractive, confident and unapologetically ambitious

40-something with the expensive suits and the easy manner, the more they liked him. But beneath the charming exterior, Tapie was an uncompromising workaholic who ran his business affairs at 100mph and expected his collaborators to approach their work with the same unyielding intensity. He boasted of needing only four hours' sleep, would abruptly cancel meetings if someone was more than five minutes late and used to assail his staff with phone calls at all times of the day and night. His business associate Patrick Le Lay, the former president of commercial TV network TF1, described him as 'a Ferrari without brakes'.

Jean-Pierre Bernès was a childhood Marseille fan who had grown up watching games at the Vélodrome with his father and who joined the club as general secretary in October 1981. Kept on when the takeover went through, the 28-year-old was quickly swept into Tapie's turbulent orbit. With Tapie detained in Paris during the week due to his business and TV commitments (he had begun presenting a Friday night show called *Ambitions* on TF1 in February 1986), Bernès became his eyes and ears on the ground. According to Bernès, Tapie expected him to be available to take his phone calls '24 hours a day'. 'I no longer saw my daughter, my wife, nor my parents,' Bernès recalled in his book, *Je dis tout : les secrets de l'OM sous Tapie* (I Tell All: OM's Secrets Under Tapie). 'I started to turn down invitations to dinner, to evenings out – I was too scared that he wouldn't be able to get hold of me.' But if working for *Le Boss* was exhausting, maddening, overwhelming and all-consuming, it was also thrilling. 'I think that Tapie's great strength, when you work with him,' Bernès said, 'is that it makes you feel alive.'

When Marseille's fans turned up at the Vélodrome for the first game of the 1986–87 season, the club's transformation was already well under way. Over the summer, Tapie had installed a new state-of-the-art sound system and erected a giant video replay screen on the Virage Nord. The players emerged from the tunnel to the springy synth intro of Van Halen's 'Jump', which has been played before OM home games ever since. After a 3–1 win over Monaco, in which Papin scored a debut brace, the supporters were treated to a spectacular laser show and firework display. Only 14,950 spectators had attended Marseille's final home game of the previous season against Le Havre. For the first match of the new era, the attendance shot up to 46,411.

Tapie was busy behind the scenes too. Drawing on his experiences in elite cycling and what he had learned about the practices at the era's leading football clubs, he increased the size of the players' medical team, improved the quality of the food that they were served and arranged for them to fly to away matches rather than travel by bus or train. He also had a pizza restaurant, Le Maracana, built beneath the Vélodrome's Tribune Jean-Bouin to give the players (as well as VIP guests and sponsors) somewhere to eat after matches.[28] But he made his biggest splash in the transfer market, bringing in peerless German centre-back Karlheinz Förster from Stuttgart and pulling off two major coups by signing Papin and France playmaker Alain Giresse. By then 34, Giresse was more Bordeaux than red wine, but his relationship with *Girondins* president Claude Bez had become strained, while 22-year-old Papin had been on the brink of joining Monaco after a breakthrough season in Belgium with Club Brugge. Tapie was determined to send out a message. 'When I arrive, I'm not an idiot,' he later explained. 'I see who the two bosses of French football are: [Monaco president] Jean-Louis Campora and Claude Bez. By pinching Giresse from Bordeaux and Papin from Monaco, I made them understand that from now on, I was the boss.'

Giresse quickly found his feet and was named French Footballer of the Year by *France Football* for a third time in 1987, but it took Papin a little longer to get going. He scored only 13 league goals in his first season, prompting OM's impatient fans to declare that his 'JPP' initials stood for *J'en peux plus* or 'I've had it'. It moved Papin to take a decision that would transform his career. 'I started working in front of goal,' he says. 'That's the only thing that changed. I was sick of the criticism from the fans. When the next season started, every day I'd do 45 to 60 minutes of shooting practice. And during the five years that followed, I did that every day.' Buoyed by his work on the training pitch and a new determination to shoot at the earliest opportunity, Papin would finish as the French top flight's leading scorer for the next five seasons in a row. OM came second in Tapie's first

---

28 In later years, when Marseille began to qualify regularly for Europe, Tapie would bring the kitchen staff from *Le Phocéa* to cater for the squad in the build-up to important Champions League games.

campaign and sixth the following year before things fell into place in season three. When his side began the campaign by drawing at home to Montpellier and losing at Lille, Tapie sacked Gérard Banide as head coach and replaced him with inexperienced academy director Gérard Gili.[29] In spite of his rookie status, the moustachioed Gili succeeded in creating a relaxed, positive atmosphere and with Papin and feared German striker Klaus Allofs banging in 50 goals between them in all competitions, the club claimed their first league title since 1972. A 4–3 victory over Arsène Wenger's Monaco in the Coupe de France final, in which Papin scored a magnificent hat-trick, was the cherry on the cake.[30]

Marseille failed with an audacious attempt to sign Diego Maradona from Napoli in the summer of 1989,[31] but the prospect of a tilt at the European Cup enticed several other stellar names to the Vélodrome: tough-tackling Brazilian centre-back Carlos Mozer; France internationals Jean Tigana, Manuel Amoros and Alain Roche; regal Uruguayan playmaker Enzo Francescoli. And a stoop-shouldered winger from Gateshead called Chris Waddle. Looking for a striker to replace Bordeaux-bound Allofs, Tapie started scouting Tottenham Hotspur striker Paul Walsh, only to be blown away by his teammate Waddle's free-spirited dribbling and eye for the spectacular. It cost a French-record 45 million francs to prise the 28-year-old away from White Hart Lane, which made him the third most expensive footballer of all time, but although his new teammates were

29 Gili was initially appointed as an assistant to Hidalgo, only for the former France coach to decide after one game – a 0–0 draw with Sochaux – that the job was not for him. Gradually frozen out by Tapie, Hidalgo switched his focus to the club's plans to set up a permanent training base at La Commanderie.

30 Éric Cantona arrived from Auxerre for a French-record transfer fee of 22 million francs in the summer of 1988, but his first season at OM – the club he had supported as a boy – made headlines for all the wrong reasons. The flamboyant 22-year-old striker received a 12-month ban from representing France for likening national coach Henri Michel to a *sac à merde* (bag of shit) on live TV after not being selected for a friendly against Czechoslovakia. When he angrily removed his shirt and tossed it at the referee after being threatened with an early substitution during a charity match against Torpedo Moscow in Sedan in January 1989, a furious Tapie immediately farmed him out on loan to Bordeaux.

31 Hidalgo met Maradona at his Naples villa and felt that he was genuinely open to the possibility of joining Marseille. But news of the meeting leaked to the media, effectively torpedoing the transfer, after Hidalgo's whereabouts were revealed when he took a call from *France Football* journalist François de Montvallon, thinking it was Tapie. Maradona later met Tapie in secret at the Grand Hotel Brun in Milan, but Napoli refused to countenance the player's departure.

sceptical at first glance ('He was as red as a beetroot!' recalls fellow new recruit Roche), he would go on to become one of the club's greatest players. 'What did he bring to the team? Fantasy,' says Papin. 'We were already pretty good. Chris brought fantasy. And effectiveness at every set-piece. He did things in training sometimes and you said to yourself: "He's an extra-terrestrial."' With sweeper keeper Gaëtan Huard in goal, Amoros, Mozer, Forster, Roche and Di Meco at the back, Sauzée, Tigana, Deschamps (a November signing from Nantes), Philippe Vercruysse and Bruno Germain in midfield and a spectacular Papin-Waddle-Francescoli attack, this side is considered by some observers as the finest to have worn the club's colours.

Marseille finished as champions again in 1990, but for all the team's success, they remained a ramshackle outfit. They had no permanent training centre, obliging the players to train on local municipal pitches.[32] At Luminy, where Marseille shared a playing field with the sports science faculty of Aix-Marseille University, former players recall having to dodge javelins hurled by student athletes. Waddle was amazed to discover that he and his teammates were expected to wash their own kit. And yet in spite of that, the players from that period remember it with immense fondness. 'It was like Club Med,' says Di Meco. 'I remember training sessions that went to the dogs completely. You'd have Carlos Mozer playing centre-forward, Chris [Waddle] as a *libero* . . . It was all about having a laugh and taking the piss out of each other. I remember Papin playing jokes, calling the stadium announcer from the changing room and asking for announcements with made-up names. Nobody fell out with anyone or took themselves for somebody else. They were my best years.'

But Marseille's age of innocence would not last.

———

On their return to the European Cup in the 1989–90 season, Marseille successfully eliminated Brøndby, AEK Athens and CSKA Sofia to set up a semi-final meeting with Sven-Göran Eriksson's Benfica. Tapie's men dominated the

32 Marseille did not move to their current training base, La Commanderie, until July 1991.

first leg at the Vélodrome, but with Francescoli in particular squandering a number of chances, they only won 2–1. The return leg in Lisbon was poised at 0–0 with seven minutes remaining when Angolan striker Vata used his hand to punch Valdo's corner from the Benfica left into the net. To Marseille's horror, Belgian referee Marcel Van Langenhove allowed the goal to stand, sending Benfica through on away goals. In his comments to the media after the game, Tapie suggested that Marseille had been punished for their lack of status on the European stage and for having failed to cosy up to the match officials before the game. 'It's not the defeat of the players but the OM directors,' Tapie said. 'It will never happen like this again.' The episode is commonly held to have marked the beginning of a new, darker level of intensity in Tapie's stewardship of the club.

His first move, in September 1990, was to appoint Franz Beckenbauer in a hybrid technical director/head coach role. Beckenbauer had just led West Germany to glory at the 1990 World Cup in Italy and Tapie felt that his appointment would serve 'to give my club the prestige that it didn't have', but although he was praised for bringing a new level of professionalism to Marseille's approach and for his skilful squad management, the German struggled with the language barrier and quickly tired of Tapie's interfering in team selection. By Christmas he had been withdrawn to an advisory role.

Enter Raymond Goethals. The 70-year-old Belgian coach was well known to Marseille fans, having spent the previous season at the helm of a Bordeaux team who had fought OM tooth and nail in the title race. With his shabby dress sense, unkempt hair and habit of mispronouncing players' names in his strong Brussels accent, Goethals had the bearing of a shambolic grandfather, but he was renowned for being a football obsessive with a sharp eye for tactical detail (earning him the nickname *Raymond la science*). Goethals believed in picking a starting XI and sticking to it, dismissively addressing players on the fringes of his squad as '*Chose*' ('Thingy'). He exhibited greater delicacy in his handling of his demanding boss, putting up with the middle-of-the-night phone calls and warding off the threat of tactical meddling by strategically sharing his ideas with Tapie so that the Marseille president would think of them as his own. 'I had to listen to him and give him the impression that the idea had come from him,' Goethals wrote in his autobiography, *Le douzième homme* (The Twelfth Man). 'I didn't say to him: "This is my team." I'd say to him on Tuesday: "How about if we did this . . .?" On Wednesday, he'd call me and he'd say: "We're going to do this!" The idea that I'd whispered to him the day before had become *his* decision.'

In Goethals' first game in charge, OM demolished Lyon 7–0, with Papin scoring four times. Two weeks later they put six unanswered goals past Nantes. The European Cup quarter-final draw paired Marseille with Arrigo Sacchi's fêted Milan team of Franco Baresi, Paolo Maldini, Ruud Gullit, Frank Rijkaard and Marco van Basten. It was the most daunting assignment in world football, but Goethals decided to play the defending champions at their own game with a high defensive line and an aggressive offside trap. A mix-up between Mozer and Bernard Casoni allowed Gullit to put Milan in front in the 14th minute of the first leg at San Siro, but OM quickly equalised when Papin slammed home from Waddle's expertly curled pass. Two weeks later at the Vélodrome, Waddle crashed in a right-foot volley from Papin's flick-on to put OM 2–1 ahead on aggregate with 15 minutes to play.[33] After a floodlight failure in stoppage time, Milan's players left the pitch and refused to return despite Swedish referee Bo Karlsson declaring that there was sufficient light to finish the game. Marseille were awarded a 3–0 win and Milan were suspended from European competition for a year. Disappointment followed in the final when Marseille were beaten on penalties by Red Star Belgrade after a desperately poor game in the Italian city of Bari, but OM were now clearly contenders.

Marseille were French champions again in 1991 and 1992, but the European Cup had become an obsession. When OM crashed out against Sparta Prague in the second round in November 1991, Tapie proclaimed that his team had reached 'the end of its cycle'. Come the end of the season, Papin left for Milan, Mozer went back to Benfica and Waddle returned to England with Sheffield Wednesday. Völler, Desailly, Barthez, playmaker Jean-Marc Ferreri and defensive midfielder Jean-Jacques Eydelie all came in, while Bokšić was integrated into the squad after

---

33 Left concussed after a clash of heads with Maldini minutes earlier, Waddle did not even remember scoring. (Not that his friend Paul Gascoigne, who had to come to watch the match, could jog his memory: after the game, the OM players found the England midfielder blind drunk at Le Maracana.)

a fruitless loan spell at Cannes. Temporarily sidelined when his assistant Jean Fernandez was promoted to the role of head coach, Goethals returned to the dug-out in the autumn of 1992 and succeeded in steering Marseille to the final of the inaugural Champions League against old foes Milan. Two years on from the heartbreak of Bari, the dream was within touching distance again.[34]

By now, the city of Marseille had taken Tapie to its heart. OM fans were thrilled by his ambition, his truculence and his commitment to defending the club at any cost. Here, at last, was somebody prepared to stand up to the central powers in Paris and if it took a little bending of the rules for him to achieve his goals, well then so be it. OM's success had helped to bring Tapie the political legitimacy he had long craved – he was elected to parliament as a Socialist MP in 1989 and became Minister for Cities at President Mitterrand's behest in 1992. To his close associates, he made no secret of his dream of becoming mayor of Marseille. There was even talk that he might run for president. He carried on expanding his business empire too, having acquired Adidas in 1990 for nearly 1.6 billion francs. But he remained a control freak and continued to maintain a state of perpetual tension at Marseille in the belief that it was the best way of driving the club forwards. While Tapie possessed exceptional powers of motivation – Boli, a 1990 signing from Auxerre, describes him as 'the greatest communicator that I've ever met' – some felt worn down by the constant tub-thumping. 'He doesn't tolerate the merest sign of relaxation,' said Goethals. In the words of former OM coach Gili, Tapie 'puts you in a syringe and presses all the way down'.

It was also clear by now that Tapie had his own unique interpretation of football's moral code and that there were few levers he was not prepared to pull

---

34 The 1991–92 season ended in tragedy when a hastily assembled temporary stand collapsed prior to Marseille's Coupe de France semi-final against Corsican side Bastia at the Stade de Furiani, leaving 18 people dead and 2,357 injured. It remains France's worst stadium disaster. Tapie received praise for his heroic response, having helped to pull several people free from the wreckage. The final was cancelled as a mark of respect.

in pursuit of success. He would harangue and goad his players to breaking point, pressuring them to play when injured, ferociously upbraiding them for sloppy displays and accusing them of having been paid off by their opponents if they underperformed. Coming to play at the Vélodrome became an ordeal for visiting players, who reported being woken up by mysterious phone calls to their hotel rooms in the middle of the night. Opposing coaches complained of provocation and intimidation, of one-sided refereeing and phantom penalties. Journalists who fell foul of Tapie were berated and threatened. Several clubs even accused Marseille of having covertly drugged their players prior to heavy defeats at the Vélodrome by spiking their orange juice or serving them doctored tea.[35] In a book released in 2019, Marc Fratani, a former parliamentary aide and personal assistant to Tapie, said that OM had indeed surreptitiously drugged their opponents, using 'ultra-thin needles' to inject an anaesthetic called Haldol into their plastic water bottles. Tapie rubbished his claims.

There were suspicions about doping too, although no player was ever revealed to have failed a drugs test during Tapie's tenure. Following a 2–2 draw at Nice in December 1988, Di Meco and Germain were summoned for a random post-match doping test, only for Papin and full-back Philippe Thys to show up in their place. Marseille's directors explained that Di Meco and Germain's shirt numbers – three and six – had been sloppily scribbled down on a piece of paper that was then read upside down, making them look like the numbers two and nine belonging to Thys and Papin. In his 2002 autobiography *Capitaine*, Desailly said that prior to Marseille's league game at PSG in December 1992, Tapie instructed his players to swallow tablets that – according to the defender's recollection of what it said on the bottle – could be considered an illegal substance for elite athletes if taken in high doses. Desailly added that he felt no effects from the tablets, which prompted him to wonder if they were in fact 'a kind of placebo intended to make us feel like we were unbeatable'. Waddle revealed in December 2003 that he had received injections 'all the time' while at Marseille, but that

---

35 The clubs pointing the finger included Lech Poznań (beaten 6–0 in the European Cup in November 1990), Rennes (beaten 5–1 in Division 1 in December 1991) and CSKA Moscow (beaten 6–0 in the Champions League in March 1993).

they had no effect on him.[36] Eydelie alleged that 'several' members of the Marseille starting XI were given injections in their bottoms before the 1993 Champions League final (which Völler angrily refused) and that players were once handed 'white pills' at half-time of a league game against Nantes. Tapie sued him for defamation and lost.

From early on in his Marseille tenure, Tapie became convinced of the need to mollify referees in the hope of receiving preferential treatment. 'Tapie understood it as soon as he arrived in football,' said Bernès, who became OM director general in 1990. 'Straight away, he wanted to give himself the means to win. And in particular, he understood that a European Cup couldn't only be won on the pitch. Everything has to be controlled: the environment, the relationships with the referees, the officials.' In practices that were not wholly uncommon at the time, referees visiting Marseille for European games would be wined and dined at swanky restaurants, offered tours of the city, given gifts and provided with prostitutes.[37]

Accusations of match-fixing, meanwhile, were swirling around the club long before L'affaire VA-OM came to light: players told to ask former teammates for favours when they played against Marseille; opponents promised moves to the Vélodrome in exchange for sub-par performances against OM; bonuses paid to clubs for beating Marseille's title rivals; opposing players rolling their socks down to show which of them had been 'bought' in certain games; off-the-books payments to mysterious intermediaries.[38]

Tapie's response to such accusations was always the same: there was no proof, there were never any convictions, it was all part of a plot, mounted by the football

---

36 Tony Cascarino played under Tapie at Marseille from 1994 to 1996 and told me that he received injections of what he suspected to be illegal substances during his time at the club. 'I said to the doctor: "What are we taking?" And he said: "An adrenaline boost." I never knew 100 per cent, but it was pretty clear . . . If you put all the jigsaw together, it's pretty obvious that things were not as they should have been.'

37 Bez admitted to having offered similar 'favours' to referees at Bordeaux.

38 Set up in April 1990 to investigate accusations of corruption made against each other by directors from Marseille and Bordeaux, French football's National Disciplinary Commission suspended Tapie from football activities for 12 months (of which four were suspended) in January 1991 for threatening and trying to intimidate referees. Bernès was suspended for six months. However, citing an absence of 'external witnesses or objectively irrefutable material proof', the commission said that it had not proven allegations of corruption and cheating.

authorities and facilitated by the jealous Parisian media, to prevent him from succeeding. For his defenders, even if he crossed the line on occasion, he was doing nothing worse than what any of the other major European clubs were doing at the time. The players, caught in Tapie's web, had to square things with their own consciences. As Desailly put it: 'I closed my eyes when it suited me.'

———

Marseille's players had spent the days leading up to the 1991 European Cup final cloistered away inside an ultra-secure hotel in Bisceglie, 40 miles outside Bari. Stuck in their rooms with nothing to do but think about the biggest game of their lives, many found the atmosphere oppressive. Two years on, Tapie had learned his lesson. For the final in Munich, the Marseille delegation stayed at the picturesque Hotel Bachmair beside Lake Tegernsee in the Bavarian countryside. This time, the doors to the outside world were flung open. A team of journalists from TF1 were present to document the squad's preparations and frequently found themselves on the receiving end of the players' pranks. Waddle spent a few days with the squad and was allowed to join in with training, which took place on a rustic pitch in a nearby village. The players ate their meals in the sunshine at an outdoor buffet. It felt like a summer camp. Barthez, then aged 21, stayed up watching TV in his room until five o'clock in the morning on the night before the final and then stunned Tapie by peacefully snoozing through the coach journey to the Olympiastadion.

Goethals stuck with the 5-2-3 formation that had become OM's default shape in Europe: Barthez in goal; Eydelie, Jocelyn Angloma, Boli, Desailly and Di Meco across the back; Sauzée and Deschamps, who had been appointed captain only a few months previously, in midfield; Pelé, Völler and Bokšić in attack. On the Milan bench, Papin took his place among the substitutes. Seeking to win the trophy for the third time in five years, Fabio Capello's side settled quickly, with Barthez obliged to save from Van Basten and Daniele Massaro in quick succession. But within the Marseille ranks, belief began to take root. 'Lots of players will tell you that you often have an idea of what's going to happen in a match,' says Di Meco. 'Of course, you don't know. But quite quickly, I felt that they weren't going to beat us. When Fabien makes the first two saves, a bit miraculously, you tell yourself: "They're not going to get there. They're not going to score any goals. Maybe we'll go to penalties, but they're not going to score."' Boli injured his knee in the first half and indicated to Goethals that he would have to come off, but Tapie – sitting in the stands – grabbed his walkie-talkie and insisted to Bernès, who was sitting in the dug-out, that he stay on.

Two minutes before half-time, Marseille won their first corner of the game on their right side. Pelé had told Boli before the match that, fearing Milan's height advantage at the back post, he would aim his corners towards the near post. Pelé curled the ball in with his left foot and Boli held off Baresi and Rijkaard to glance a header past Sebastiano Rossi. Capello quickly introduced Papin in the second half, but the nearest he – and Milan – came to an equaliser was a hooked volley that bounced wide with 12 minutes remaining. '*Et c'est fini!*' cried TF1 commentator Thierry Roland at the final whistle as the Marseille dug-out erupted and the bow-legged Goethals set off on a shambling victory dash across the pitch in his ill-fitting black suit. 'Olympique de Marseille have won the European Cup! The curse of the last 38 years is over: a French club has finally won a European cup!'

Boli had broken down in tears after the 1991 final in Bari and his sobbing face became a symbol of the club's dismay. Now he was the hero. He marched straight over to the OM fans behind Barthez's goal and traced imaginary tears running down his cheeks before demonstratively wagging his finger and shouting: '*Non! Non! Non!*' Tapie consoled a distraught Papin in the middle of the pitch and could be seen wiping away tears with the back of his hand as he walked away. 'It's stupid, because we shouldn't put ourselves in this state,' he told TF1's Pascal Praud in a hoarse croak as the players caroused around him. 'But who cares. We're not going to pretend – it's brilliant!'

Back home, a TV audience of 17 million people watched as Deschamps hoisted the famous trophy into the Munich sky. In Marseille, tens of thousands of supporters streamed down to the Vieux Port for a party that would last for days. *L'Équipe* took its cue from *La Marseillaise* the following morning, calling it '*LE JOUR DE GLOIRE*' ('THE DAY OF GLORY'). Regional newspaper *La Provençal* said simply: '*ON L'A!*' ('WE'VE GOT IT!') For the players and staff, a whirlwind few days followed: triumphant return to Marseille, title-sealing win over PSG, presidential reception at the Élysée Palace. But the headlines quickly took on a very different tone.

News of the allegation that Marseille had attempted to fix their league game against Valenciennes was already public knowledge in the days building up to the final. The previous weekend, Jacques Glassmann – the Valenciennes defender turned whistle-blower – gave an interview to TV station France 2 in which he said that on the night before the game, he and his teammates Christophe Robert and Jorge Burruchaga were at Hôtel du Lac in Condé-sur-l'Escaut, the northern club's usual pre-game retreat, when they received a phone call from Marseille midfielder Eydelie, with whom they had all previously played.[39] Eydelie passed the phone to Bernès, who promised the three Valenciennes players money if they agreed to take it easy in the following day's game, which OM won 1–0.

Any hopes that Marseille might have harboured that the affair would blow over thanks to their Champions League triumph were dashed on 8 June – 13 days after the final – when Noël Le Graët, president of France's Ligue de Football Professionnel (LFP), filed a legal complaint with Valenciennes city prosecutor Éric de Montgolfier. Two weeks later, investigators discovered an envelope containing 250,000 francs buried in the garden of Robert's aunt's home in the Dordogne. The money was traced to Marseille after notes with the same serial numbers were discovered during a raid on the club offices the following week. On 6 September, Marseille were expelled from the Champions League by UEFA. On 22 September, they were stripped of their 1992–93 league title by the French Football Federation (the title remaining unattributed). The following April, while on course for a second-place finish behind PSG in Division 1, the club was punitively relegated to the second tier.

---

39 Eydelie had played with Robert and Burruchaga at Nantes and with Glassmann at Tours. Burruchaga is principally known for scoring the winning goal for Argentina against West Germany in the 1986 World Cup final.

The plot had been set in motion on *Le Phocéa*, 10 days before the Champions League final and beneath the noses of the TF1 film crew, who were filming on board at the time. In an explosive 2006 book in which he made allegations of widespread corruption at Marseille, Eydelie said that he, Deschamps and Desailly were summoned to 'a huge sitting room with smoked glass windows and deep pastel-coloured divans' at the back of the boat by Tapie and Bernès and told to tell their former teammates at Valenciennes to go easy on them in their last game before the final. After the Marseille squad had arrived at the Valenciennes Novotel on the evening before the match, Bernès told Eydelie to come to his room. It was there, in Room 234, that the fateful call was placed at around nine o'clock. Afterwards, Bernès gave Eydelie a brown envelope containing the cash, which he handed to Robert's wife, Marie-Christine, in the hotel car park. Appalled by Bernès' proposal, Glassmann informed Valenciennes coach Boro Primorac of what had happened shortly before the game. At half-time, with OM leading 1–0 through a scruffy Bokšić goal, the VA directors lodged a complaint with the match referee that an attempt to fix the game had been made. The allegation did not create a huge splash initially, but within weeks it would be the leading item on every news bulletin in the country.

Marseille's response was to assert that it was Primorac, whose side were fighting for survival, who had proposed fixing the game. Primorac told the investigating magistrate, Bernard Buffy, that during a meeting at Tapie's office in Paris in mid-June, the OM president had offered him financial incentives and promised him future job opportunities if he agreed to say that it was he who had spoken to Bernès on the night before the game rather than the three Valenciennes players.[40] Tapie denied having ever met Primorac and said that at the time their encounter was supposed to have taken place, he was in a meeting at his office with the Socialist MP Jacques Mellick. But days later, a municipal newsletter published a photograph showing that when Mellick claimed to have been with Tapie in Paris, he was actually attending a function in the northern city of

---

40 The envelope full of cash having not been discovered at this point, the only material proof of any attempted corruption was the record of the phone call from the Novotel to the Valenciennes team hotel on the night before the game.

Béthune, where he was the local mayor. Mellick subsequently claimed to have travelled to Béthune from Paris *after* his meeting with Tapie, but the journey would have required him to travel at exceptional speed and there was no record of his chauffeur-driven Renault 25 TX having passed through any motorway toll gates. The episode earned him the nickname 'The Fastest Mayor in France' and a one-year suspended sentence for false testimony.

Bernès had stubbornly denied any wrongdoing, but when the VA-OM trial finally came to court in Valenciennes in March 1995, he sensationally changed tack, admitting that on Tapie's orders, he and Eydelie had attempted to fix the Valenciennes match and that 'all the OM players' had been aware of what was happening. On 15 May, 1995, two years after the affair began, the Valenciennes Criminal Court convicted Tapie of bribery and witness tampering, sentencing him to two years in jail with one year suspended. Bernès, Eydelie, Burruchaga and Christophe and Marie-Christine Robert all received suspended sentences. Tapie's effective prison term was reduced to eight months on appeal, but in February 1997, having been smuggled out of his Paris home in the boot of his son Stéphane's car in order to avoid the scrum of journalists waiting outside, he was incarcerated. Tapie saw out most of his sentence at Prison de Luynes near Aix-en-Provence and would spend a total of 165 days behind bars.[41] In an infamous remark during the trial, he had said: 'I lied, but it was in good faith.'

It was not until May 1997 and the start of another trial concerning allegations of financial malpractice at OM that Tapie confessed that the club had attempted to fix the match against Valenciennes. He would later explain that he was motivated purely by a desire to avoid the fate that had befallen Saint-Étienne in 1976, when Gérard Farison and Christian Synaeghel were both ruled out of the European Cup final against Bayern Munich after being injured during a physical league

---

41 Tapie was twice convicted of tax fraud, in 1997 and 2005, but avoided further jail time. His imprisonment over the VA-OM affair brought an end to his political career and when he left jail, he went into acting, returning to OM in 2001 for a short spell as sporting director.

game against Nîmes. The accounting trial would lay bare the full extent of corruption at Marseille during the Tapie years, with Bernès making the shocking confession that 'a sum of five to six million francs per year left the OM accounts via fictitious invoices to fix matches' in both domestic and European competitions.[42]

And yet in spite of that, many of those involved have sought to muddy the waters over the ensuing years, emboldened by an admission attributed to De Montgolfier, the VA-OM prosecutor, that 'had it not been Tapie, he would never have gone to prison'.[43] For OM's partisans, Tapie paid the price for the isolated mistake of having wanted to protect his players ahead of a vital game and everything else is just noise. Papin, for whom Tapie was 'like a father', points the finger at the LFP. 'The league could have just postponed the [Valenciennes-Marseille] match until after [the final],' he tells me. 'And there would have been no VA-OM affair. Because regardless of what happened, I don't think Tapie wanted to pay off the Valenciennes team. He didn't care about Valenciennes. He wanted to protect his players.' But when people look back at that Marseille team now, the trophies and the corruption allegations are synonymous. What does that change for him? He looks at me impassively, blows out his cheeks twice. 'Nothing,' he says. 'Absolutely nothing. I know Bernard Tapie well and I know that what he did was just to protect his players.'

Over the years, some of Tapie's most outspoken critics have come from the Monaco team that was twice beaten to the title by Marseille during his tenure. Di Meco spent four years at Monaco after leaving Marseille in 1994 and he offers a provocative rebuttal of their complaints. 'I was at Monaco and I know how serious the players were compared to what we were doing [at Marseille] and unfortunately it's an easy excuse for hiding your own incompetence or your own shortcomings,' he says. 'I witnessed the professionalism of the players at Monaco

---

42 'I was dishonest for four years,' Bernès said. 'Multiple matches were bought. I saw a TV show where they said that Monaco had had two titles stolen from them and it's accurate. There are 45 French players who might be in question. I don't want to say their names. It's possible that I said in Valenciennes [during the VA-OM trial] that only the VA-OM match had been bought. It was difficult for me to say anything else so as not to disappoint people . . . I screwed up for four years, I recognise it.'

43 De Montgolfier has clarified that it was his belief that if Tapie had not been a former government minister, he would probably have received a more lenient sentence.

and I know the effort you have to put in and the sacrifices you have to make to be at the top level. And I know that over there [Monaco], they didn't always make them. The guys who were crying at the time [over the VA-OM affair], I saw them at work every day and they didn't have the dedication of the top level.' He is in characteristically bullish mood. Surely, I suggest, the memories of what he achieved at Marseille must have been tarnished by all the suspicions? 'Oh, no. For me, never,' he replies. 'It's the story of football. The great Saint-Étienne team were suspected of doping.[44] I think that even in England there must be stories about clubs that dominated. In Italy it was the same. There are true stories and there's what have become urban myths, but which I accept were generated by our own stupidity [with regard to *L'affaire VA-OM*]. It's recurrent in the history of French sport. When you win, there's always a doubt. The French are never legitimate winners because they don't have the rigorousness, they don't have whatever. That's the story. It doesn't bother me any more.'

Not everyone has found it so easy to turn the page. As a young player, Emmanuel Petit was a stalwart of the Monaco team that was repeatedly edged out by Tapie's Marseille and has long been an outspoken critic of his regime. In his uncompromising 2008 autobiography, *À fleur de peau*,[45] Petit spoke of the 'disgust' he felt over the matter and revealed that Wenger once confided to him that he suspected certain Monaco players of having been paid off prior to a 3–0 defeat by Marseille in April 1992. Fifteen years have passed since the book's release when I meet Petit at his apartment in central Paris on a grey and blustery January afternoon in 2023, but his anger has not subsided. 'I had trophies stolen from me,' he says. 'Myself and my teammates.' Petit says that when he was first starting out in the France senior team in the early 1990s, he was 'threatened' by some of the Marseille players in the squad for having spoken out about the accusations against their club. When Petit went on to achieve glory with France

---

44 Rumours about doping dogged the great Saint-Étienne team of the 1970s, without ever being substantiated. Former Saint-Étienne midfielder Jean-François Larios said that he had taken the amphetamine Captagon during his time at the club in his 2017 autobiography *J'ai joué avec le feu* (I Played With Fire). Several of his teammates dismissed his claims.
45 Literally meaning 'on the surface of the skin', the expression *à fleur de peau* is used to refer to someone who is extremely sensitive and easily provoked.

at the 1998 World Cup and the 2000 European Championship, it was alongside some of the Marseille players – notably Deschamps and Desailly – who were alleged to have had knowledge of the VA-OM plot. Was that difficult to set aside, I wonder? He tilts his head back and points at his throat. 'It's still there today,' he says. 'It's still stuck in my craw. The implication of certain people, the repeated lies over three decades. Even today, some of them are still in complete denial. When you start bringing up the story, fucking hell, you get the impression you're talking about . . . What's he called, the guy in Harry Potter? Voldemort? "You mustn't say his name!" Is that still where we are? Woah! It's over, guys, there are statutes of limitations! You can't go back in time. But I don't even blame the players, because they were puppets. They were used. I blame the people above them who were pulling the strings.'

———

Tapie has been dead for six months by the time I visit his grave at Marseille's Cimetière de Mazargues in April 2022. The tall Cypress trees that demarcate the cemetery's southern periphery are still and the sky overhead is blue and marked only by airplane trails. Somewhere in the trees, a Eurasian collared dove gently coos its three-note call. Tapie's rectangular concrete tomb stands on its own plot in a quiet corner of the graveyard, with fading pale blue fabric stretched across it. A collection of bouquets stands on top, wrapped together in a light-blue Marseille scarf. There are candles, faded photographs of Tapie in his pomp and a blue OM pennant held down by stones. Fans have stuck stickers to the exposed concrete at the front of the tomb: *MARSEILLE 1899, ALLEZ L'OM!, NOTRE BOSS À JAMAIS.*[46]

Tapie died aged 78 in October 2021 after a long, public battle with stomach and oesophageal cancer. He had once predicted that at his funeral 'there will be more people crying than people who are happy' and the great and good from the worlds of football, politics and the arts came out in force to show their respects. France's First Lady Brigitte Macron, former French President Nicolas Sarkozy, film director Claude Lelouch, post-war songstress Line Renaud and Olympique

46 OUR BOSS FOREVER.

Lyonnais president Jean-Michel Aulas were among the mourners at his funeral mass in Paris, where Papin and Boli acted as pallbearers. French President Emmanuel Macron (an OM fan) said that in spite of 'the shadows of his legal sagas', Tapie's 'ambition, energy and enthusiasm' had been 'an inspiration for generations of French people'. Around 5,000 supporters from all over France attended a subsequent memorial service at the Vélodrome and they were present again outside Marseille's hulking Cathédrale de la Major the following day, flags and flares held aloft, when Tapie's life was celebrated for the final time. 'Bernard, you have come home forever,' said Jean-Louis Borloo, former mayor of Valenciennes and Tapie's business lawyer and friend. 'You weren't mayor of Marseille, but you were Marseille.'

It is thanks to Tapie that Marseille's fans will always be able to celebrate being *à jamais les premiers* (forever the first), the shorthand by which OM's status as France's first ever European club champions has come to be remembered. In recent years, that status has been treasured with all the more relish in light of PSG's recurrent shortcomings in the Champions League. The stars may have graced the Parc des Princes, but the star – the one, true star, coveted by all of European football – resided at the Vélodrome.

For many, the 1993 Champions League triumph will always be tarnished by its association with *L'affaire VA-OM* and the various other allegations that hung over Marseille during the Tapie years. In their eyes, it is not a star that sits above the OM crest but an asterisk. Yet for many of the players who ascended to the summit of European football on that dizzy May night in Munich over 30 years ago, Tapie's impact on the game – not just in Marseille but in France as a whole – deserves to be celebrated. 'It wasn't until long afterwards that I understood the extent to which that first European victory for a French club – and, what's more, in the Champions League – had changed everything for the future of French football,' Deschamps said after captaining France to victory at the 1998 World Cup. 'It had uninhibited, liberated a whole generation of footballers by showing that it was finally possible for us, Frenchmen, to win a major trophy. I've already said it and I repeat it, at the risk of disturbing some: if France are world champions today [after the 1998 World Cup], they owe it also and above all to Tapie.' A world champion with France as captain in 1998 and as coach in 2018,

Deschamps has advanced through the bulk of his career guided at least in part by Tapie's relentlessness in pursuit of victory. He has also done so, since 2009, with Bernès in his corner, Tapie's former lieutenant having become a leading football agent after his lifetime ban from the game, imposed by the FFF, was overturned by FIFA in 1996. Though disgraced and imprisoned, scorned as a cheat and a charlatan, Tapie's legacy lives on.

All is calm at the graveside. From beyond the walls, the distant sound of traffic rumbling past. A cemetery worker in his 50s, wearing blue overalls and with straggly grey hair, pauses to inspect Tapie's grave while passing by and then continues on his way. He may be gone, *Le Boss*, but love him or loathe him, he will not be forgotten.

5

GESTE TECHNIQUE

LA PAPINADE

PAPINNNNNN!!!

Has a name ever rhymed so resonantly with scoring goals? Or seemed so perfectly suited to soundtracking the moment the ball hits the net? Five letters, two syllables; PAP like the ball exploding off a striker's foot, AHN as it nestles in the netting. It is a name like a whip crack, a name like a Batman sound effect. A name to be screamed at the top of your lungs.

Football commentators across France and Europe became very accustomed to screaming Jean-Pierre Papin's name in the late 1980s and early 1990s. From 1986 onwards, as the spearhead of Bernard Tapie's insatiably ambitious Marseille team, the firecracker striker established himself as one of the sharpest and most spectacular goal-getters in the game, racking up 182 goals in 275 appearances, finishing Division 1 top scorer for five seasons running and firing OM to four consecutive league titles. When he won the Ballon d'Or in 1991, he became only the third French player to have done so after Raymond Kopa and Michel Platini.

Papin's rise was a case of practice makes perfect. Derided for his clumsiness in front of goal after a mixed first season at the Vélodrome, he set about honing his craft with dead-eyed dedication: hour after hour after hour on the Marseille training pitches, shot after shot after shot, volley after volley after volley; a hapless reserve goalkeeper between the sticks, the grass illuminated by the headlights of his car whenever the groundsman switched the floodlights off. Before long, blistering volleys had become his trademark and in May 1988, they were given a name. After watching Papin smash in a volley against Niort, Alain Pécheral, a football writer from regional newspaper *La Provençal*, realised that it bore a striking resemblance to a goal that the

OM number nine had scored against Racing Club de Paris two years previously. Pécheral decided to call such goals *papinades*. His coinage referred to a particular type of volley – struck powerfully across the goalkeeper from the right side of the penalty area – but the word came to stand for any memorable Papin strike.

I met Papin in late February 2022 at his home in Chartres, a cathedral town 50 miles southwest of Paris, during his two-year spell as coach of the local football club, C' Chartres. Early spring sunshine streaming through the sitting room window, his Ballon d'Or trophy glinting proudly on a low table between us, he talked me through the shooting techniques that turned his name into a byword for jaw-dropping goals.

I read somewhere that it was your father, Guy, who taught you how to strike a football.
'Yes. By the age of five, I had a perfect shot.'

And what is a perfect shot? What are the key ingredients?
'For me, the perfect shot is the force you put into it and the position of your standing foot. I think the most difficult thing for me was where to put my standing foot. But when you're little, you learn quickly and it's something I learned very quickly. Every time, I kept progressing. When I was 11, I was in *pupilles* [Under-12s] and I played in *minimes* [Under-15s] because the goalkeepers were this big [raises hand to chest height] and I was the only one who could put the ball over them from 30 metres. I wasn't big, so I was playing against kids who were bigger, but every time I took a free-kick, it went in.'

How did you work on your shooting with your father?
'My parents were divorced, so I only saw my father in the summer. Every morning we'd go down to the beach, in Boulogne-sur-Mer. And he'd get me to take shots. Shots, shots, shots. Hundreds of times. And for as long as it wasn't perfect, I carried on shooting!'

How does a perfect shot feel? Are you even seeking perfection in the first place?
'I once saw a report about the All Blacks rugby player Dan Carter. His father [Neville] taught him how to kick, because his father had been an All Black too, and built a set

of posts in the garden. He explained that he practised every day. Every day, every day. And he became one of the best penalty-kickers in the world. I think that with stories like that, whether it's mine, whether it's his, whether it's [Jonny] Wilkinson's, which was the same, if you're not stubborn enough to want to do that, you'll never achieve perfection. For me, my shot was perfect from the start. But the *papinades* became an instinctive thing [clicks fingers]. The only thing that I understood before everyone else was that you didn't have time to take a touch. For me it was clear. Today it's even more the case than before. You don't have time to take a touch. When you're able to give yourself that advantage, it's only half a second, but it's enough [slaps one hand against the other]. You unleash and it's over. The goalkeeper doesn't have time. At the time, they knew, because they could see it all the time on TV, that I'd arrive *here* and I'd put the ball *there*. They knew it. But they couldn't do anything. Because it was surgical. And today, when I work with my players, I tell them: "You have to hit the zone." And the zone, for me, is just inside the post [indicates a gap of about two feet]. Same on the other side. I've shown them, by doing it into an empty goal, with a mannequin beside the zone. I make them do 10 shots, 10 dead balls. Ten shots right-hand post, 10 shots left-hand post. Then five shots right, five shots left. Today their success rate is 85 per cent. Football is a question of repetition and precision. And when you have that, you have a big advantage!'

When you started doing extra work on your finishing in 1987, what was your routine?
'The routine was 200 shots, 200 volleys. Per day. After every training session. Split up into sets of 20: 10 from one side, 10 from the other. And I'd do that 10 times. But it was just fun. It wasn't even work. You, the goalkeeper, two crossers and you take shots for 45 minutes. When I started, I'd score four [out of 20], then three, then four. Sometimes I'd water things down and take a touch so as to be able to score. But six years later, it was 17/20 and I wasn't taking a touch or anything. I'd shoot and it'd be in the net.'

Where did the idea to work like that come from?
'When I was little, I used to play *Goal à goal* (Goal to Goal). You have two goals 20 metres apart and you're goalkeeper and striker at the same time. That's all I

did when I was little, with my friends. When I started to doubt myself, I remembered what I'd done when I was little. And it worked well because I scored a load of goals. So I started doing that and I carried on. And after one or two months, you realise that the ratio in games is changing. You have as many chances, but you score more goals. You see? When you realise that it works, you carry on. And I carried on for seven or eight years. Even at Milan, I still did it. I stopped at Bayern because I got injured.'

And among those 200 shots, how many were with the right foot and how many with the left foot?

'It was just the right foot. With the left foot, there weren't many! My father always told me: "You're better off having one good foot than two average feet!"'

When did you hear the word *papinade* for the first time and what did you think?

'I didn't think anything. I was just happy that Alain Pécheral had invented a name for that [type of] shot that had my name in it. He came up with it in '88. I think the first one was in a match against Racing Paris and the goalkeeper was [Pascal] Olmeta, who was my big mate. I scored a crazy goal. I should never have played that match because I'd just had an ankle operation! The doctor told me: "I'm going to operate on you tomorrow." The day after, I woke up, I was in a cast and it no longer hurt. So I took a bread knife and I opened my cast and took it off. And I went training. The doctor was beside himself. "What are you doing?" But then he said: "The talofibular ligaments in your ankle are damaged, but the tendons are holding everything together. So you just need to work on your tendons." So I strengthened my tendons and I never had a sprain again. That day, I shouldn't have played. But I took my cast off, I scored one of my best goals and that's where the word *papinade* came from!'

Let's imagine you're on the pitch, near the edge of the opposition penalty area. The ball is in the air on its way towards you – when do you decide you're going to attempt a volley?

'From the moment it leaves the foot of the player crossing it. When you've scored as many as I did, over six years [at Marseille], it enabled me to have a head-start. The only person who could potentially bother me was the goalkeeper. Because he works every day as well on the movements of the ball etc. But for me, from the moment the ball left the foot, I knew where it would arrive. So I had that advantage. I knew whether I needed to be in front of the defender or the other side. Doing it every day means that at some point, it becomes natural. The ball's kicked and straight away, you go where you need to be. The defender, when the ball's kicked, has lost a second – the time it took for you to move. And he'll never get that second back.'

When you're taking in visual information, while the ball is in the air, what are you looking at?

'I only look at the ball. To hit a perfect volley, you have to watch the ball the whole way through. It's like in tennis or golf. Have you ever played golf? When the guy does that [stands up and mimics a golfer teeing off], when the guy hits the ball, his head is still there [mimics golfer looking down at the end of their swing]. In football, it's exactly the same. Until the last moment, you have to watch the ball.'

Which part of your foot were you trying to use? Or does it depend? Let's take the example of the *papinade* against Racing.

'Against Racing, the ball comes in like that [mimes ball coming in from deep on the left] and I arrive like that [mimes moving down inside-right channel]. And I hit it with my instep. The other one was against Niort. The ball came from behind, I arrive at top speed and I hit it with my side-foot into the other corner. Then there's the one against Belgium [a brilliant mid-air volley from just inside the area in a March 1992 friendly at the Parc des Princes]. Basile [Boli] crosses and there's a Belgian defender in front of me. I took one step backwards, he stayed there and I put my foot up here [sticks hand into the air] and I put it right in the top corner. Then there's Spain [in a Euro 92 qualifier at the Parc des Princes in February 1991], where the ball comes in from [Manuel] Amoros and it's deflected. I'm ahead of the ball, so I go like that [mimes getting ahead of the ball] and the ball arrives there [behind him]. So I turn like that and I hit it. It goes very quickly.'

What's the perfect cross for a volley?

'There isn't one. They can all be perfect. It's your technique that has to be perfect, not the cross. Often, when the cross is perfect, you want to hit it too well. You think: "This is arriving so nicely." So you have to adapt a little bit. But it happens so quickly. We're talking about things that happen in a second. You have to decide. And I don't even know if you decide. It's instinct. "In this scenario, you do this." And I'd done so many that I didn't even ask myself questions. I knew that I wasn't going to take a touch.'

Who were the best crossers of the ball you played with?
'Chris [Waddle] is among them. Klaus [Allofs]. Alain Giresse. Canto [Éric Cantona]. And [Roberto] Donadoni. At [Bayern] Munich there weren't many!'

Perhaps the most difficult question: which was the best *papinade*?
'The one against Belgium [in 1992]. Why? Because for me, it was the most improbable. It seems impossible at the start. But for me, it was natural. I was beaten, because I couldn't control it anyway, so I tried it. We were losing 3–2, so you never know.'

As far as volleys are concerned, were there other players who impressed you in terms of their technique?
'Sylvain Wiltord. Because he could do it right foot, left foot. Not acrobatic, just classic volleys. And another one who was very impressive was Jean-Philippe Durand. And then, apart from French players, Marco [van Basten]. We used to have competitions [in AC Milan training]. It was amazing.'

Which volley scored by another player would you have liked to have scored?
'The Van Basten one against Russia [in the Euro 88 final]. I scored others, different ones, but that one, at that moment, from that angle, I would have really liked to have scored. Scoring that goal, in the final of the European Championship, it's magnificent.'

Final question: is your shot intact?
'My shot is intact. Because even today, from the edge of the box, if I aim for the top corner, I get within a metre of it. If I hit 10 shots from the same spot, they'll all be within a metre of that. So you don't lose it. But with overhead kicks, the problem now is when you land!'

6

LES ROSBIFS

LIVING THE DREAM

'The training was hard and the diet was as close to perfect as it
could be. It was the best thing that happened to me in my club
career by a country mile.'

Tony Cascarino

A red Porsche 911 Turbo speeds along a winding hillside road above Monaco in
glorious summer sunshine, green vegetation flashing past on the roadside, the
azure waters of the Mediterranean sparkling in the distance below. A young
English footballer called Mark Hateley is at the wheel – roof down, music
blaring from the speakers – and he is thrilled by the speed he is generating,
hurling the powerful car around the tight corners and making the engine roar
out of every bend. Sitting beside him in the black leather passenger seat is
another, slightly older English footballer called Glenn Hoddle. It is the summer
of 1987 and both men have recently signed for Monaco. The club's training
centre sits in a former quarry in La Turbie, a hillside village that overlooks the
principality of Monaco, and Hateley has offered to drive Hoddle home after
training. When the car reaches the bottom of the hill, Hoddle swears that he is
never going to accept a lift from Hateley again. 'He was that colour when he got
out!' Hateley laughs, holding up a white paper napkin, as he recounts the scene
in an Italian restaurant in Glasgow 35 years later. 'I did it on purpose probably.
Turned the music up and away we went. Glenn would have put Neil Diamond
on or something like that. I'd have had AC/DC or something. I was a fast driver

back then, as a young lad, and that car was the most dangerous car ever. It was a death trap. But it was great fun.'

As transplants from English football in the late 1980s, Hateley and Hoddle lived the dream on the French Riviera. They and their families resided in the same luxurious seafront apartment building, the Houston Palace, on Avenue Princesse Grace. They had children of similar ages and the families spent lots of time together. Racing driver Ayrton Senna was one of their neighbours. Boris Becker lived nearby. The England teammates played tennis at Monaco Tennis Club, once taking part in a game of doubles with Ilie Năstase and the Dutch former tennis professional Tom Okker. Hateley befriended Prince Albert of Monaco and would occasionally meet him for a drink at a local bar. Hateley's first wife, Beverly, became friendly with Prince Albert's sister, Princess Caroline, and would take the children for walks with her on the promenade. It was a peaceful, sun-kissed existence of beach days, al fresco meals, leisurely shopping trips and visits to Monaco's open-air cinema. And the football was not bad either.

A tall, mobile, physically imposing centre-forward, Hateley was 25 and had been looking for a new challenge on the continent after falling out of favour at AC Milan. Monaco offered the promise of regular football, an escape from the day-to-day claustrophobia of life in Milan and the opportunity to play for an up-and-coming 37-year-old coach called Arsène Wenger. Hoddle, who was nearing his 30th birthday, had decided to leave boyhood club Tottenham Hotspur and had been in talks to join Paris Saint-Germain. But Hoddle's agent, Dennis Roach, also represented Hateley, who tipped Wenger off that discussions with PSG had stalled. Wenger called Roach as he and Hoddle were preparing to fly to Paris and managed to re-route them to Monaco. Hoddle, by his own admission, had 'never heard of Arsène Wenger', but he was seduced by the blissful setting and enthused by the bespectacled young coach's plans for him on the pitch. 'It was like trying to find a new house,' Hoddle said. 'You can see 100 houses before you find the right one or you can find it straight away. It wasn't long before I knew that Arsène was the perfect manager for me.'

British footballers were spreading their wings in the 1980s. Several of the era's leading players had been lured to Italy during the first half of the decade – Trevor Francis and Graeme Souness joining Sampdoria; Luther Blissett, Ray

Wilkins and Hateley heading to Milan – and the ban on English clubs playing in Europe imposed by UEFA after the 1985 Heysel stadium disaster only served to enhance the appeal of football on the continent.[47] Only two English players had graced France's top flight in the 30 years prior to Hateley and Hoddle's arrival at Monaco in 1987: Bristolian forward Jantzen Derrick, who made three appearances for PSG in the early 1970s, and former Real Madrid winger Laurie Cunningham, who spent the 1984–85 season at Marseille.[48] That would quickly change. Income from sponsorship and television deals was on the rise in France, several stadiums had been either built, rebuilt or extensively renovated for Euro 84 and the buccaneering exploits of the national team served to paint the country as a place where football was played the right way (not least as, with the sole exception of Michel Platini, every player in *Les Bleus'* squad still played on home soil). Whereas attendances were plummeting in England in the 1980s, in France they were climbing.

A steady stream of players from Britain and the Republic of Ireland headed over the Channel in the final years of the decade, including Mo Johnston (Nantes), Clive Allen (Bordeaux), Graham Rix and Mark Stein (Caen), Simon Stainrod (Strasbourg), Frank Stapleton (Le Havre), Mick McCarthy (Lyon) and, most memorably of all, Chris Waddle (Marseille). Down in Monaco, Hateley and Hoddle (or 'Attleh' and 'Oddeul', as their names were pronounced by French commentators) were the first to get their hands on some silverware.

———

It was at half-time of a pre-season friendly against Red Star Belgrade that Hoddle began to realise how playing in France was going to revolutionise his career. Playing in England had programmed him to systematically track back when his team lost the ball, but Wenger told him to stay high up the pitch and leave the dirty work to the players behind him. As the team's number 10, he was finally

47 English clubs were banned from European competition for five years (and Liverpool for six) after a charge by Liverpool fans prior to the 1985 European Cup final against Juventus at Heysel Stadium in Brussels left 39 people dead.
48 Ray Wilkins joined PSG from Milan in 1987 but left for Rangers a few months later.

being given the liberty – and creative responsibility – that he had always craved. 'It was music to my ears,' Hoddle wrote in his autobiography, *Playmaker*. 'I realised that I should have been playing with that freedom since I was 17. The number 10 role didn't exist in England, but it was so important in France. It was like being a quarterback in an NFL team.' Hateley found French football more physical and 'a lot quicker' than its Italian equivalent, but the opposition defences were not quite as difficult to crack as those he had encountered during his three years in Serie A. With Hoddle supplying the bullets, he racked up eight goals in his first 10 league games. 'It worked absolutely brilliantly,' Hateley tells me between forkfuls of chilli prawn spaghetti. 'Because the awareness of space that I'd learned in Italy was creating space for Glenn. And I wasn't just running in behind defences either. Sometimes Glenn would go beyond me and I'd drop a little bit deeper or come on to a different angle. He says that he scored more headers than he had in his whole career in that first year with me.'

With former France goalkeeper Jean-Luc Ettori between the posts, Patrick Battiston unflappably marshalling the back four and Marcel Dib and Jean-Philippe Rohr bossing central midfield, Wenger's team boasted rock-solid foundations. Monaco led from the front and secured the title with two games to spare. In their final home match, a 3–2 win over Auxerre, Hoddle scored one of his most famous goals in a Monaco shirt, twice feinting to cross from wide on the left before curling an audacious shot inside Bruno Martini's near post with his right foot. Hateley netted the winner from the penalty spot to take his tally for the campaign to 14, which left him third in the top scorer standings behind Marseille's Jean-Pierre Papin and Saint-Étienne's Patrice Garande. During a champagne-soaked title party at an exclusive Monte Carlo nightclub called Jimmy'z, the two Englishmen toasted becoming league champions for the first time in their careers.

Nine years before Wenger's arrival at Arsenal, Hoddle and Hateley got a sneak preview of the transformative methods that he would bring to English football. Physical preparation was radically different to what they had known in England, with more running, extensive stretching sessions (sometimes with the aid of a ballet barre), targeted recovery work, massages, siestas and regular blood tests. Before joining Monaco, Hoddle had never even done a warm-down.

Wenger always wore a tracksuit and always had a stopwatch around his neck. Every element of every training session was meticulously timed. He issued strict dietary guidance, neatly typed out on A4 paper, detailing what his players were allowed to eat in the days leading up to games. They were told exactly how much of each foodstuff they could consume per day – 300g of bread, 60g of cheese, 150g of fruit – and given advice on how to maximise the body's absorption of vital nutrients (no drinking during meals, for example, or eating green vegetables and potatoes separately). Hoddle felt fitter than he ever had and many of the other players who moved to France from Britain at the time reported similar improvements to their overall health. Within months of arriving at Bordeaux, Allen had lost a stone in weight.

Former Republic of Ireland striker Tony Cascarino joined Marseille from Chelsea a few years later and credits his move to France with enabling him to continue playing until a few days shy of his 38th birthday. 'The training was hard and the diet was as close to perfect as it could be,' he tells me. 'It was the best thing that happened to me in my club career by a country mile. On my first day of training at Chelsea in '92, I met all the lads in this caravan on bricks on the Harlington Road and everyone was having full English breakfasts! In France, the day after a game, you'd be in for a warm-down, stretching, massages. Not going to the pub, like in England, and having a roast dinner. It was a complete lifestyle change and it was so good for me. It felt like I'd left school.' A tidal wave was heading towards English football; the players who left England for France in the late 1980s and early 1990s were among the first to feel its swell.

The learning curve was no less steep away from the pitch. The French players of the era preferred wine to beer, drank espressos before training, smoked cigarettes after games and congregated around the dinner table rather than the bar. Hateley and Hoddle were used to having a few pints after getting back from a game, often popping into an Irish pub around the corner from their apartment block, and it brought them into conflict with Wenger. 'I said to him: "This is what me and Glenn do after a game,"' says Hateley. 'We'd be at the back of the plane with a couple of beers and the French boys would all be smoking. Beers weren't part of French culture, cigarettes weren't part of British culture. But he was learning, because we were obviously the first English players that he'd coached. I think it stood him in good stead for Arsenal.' Cascarino, meanwhile, had a rude awakening when he turned up for his first Christmas party at Marseille. 'The year before at Chelsea, we all went out in fancy dress for the Christmas party and I went as Popeye,' he says. 'Bear in mind, we got a three-week break in France, so I go out thinking . . . [rubs his hands together in mock anticipation]. We meet in this pizzeria at about seven o'clock. Glass of wine, pizza, bit of chat and by 10 o'clock, everybody's gone home!'

But life on the other side of the Channel had much to recommend it. Eric Black was 22 when he joined Metz from Aberdeen in 1986 and enjoyed himself so much that he stayed in eastern France for five years, winning the Coupe de France in 1988. 'One of the first coaches I had was a guy called Marcel Husson and he invited me and my wife, Nina, to his house for dinner, along with two of the other players,' Black tells me in a Zoom call from his home in Leamington Spa. 'I thought: "What? The coach has asked you round for dinner?!" We're sitting in his back garden in the sun, his wife's prepared everything and he's got his very favourite bottle of Aloxe-Corton Burgundy wine out. It felt surreal, but it wasn't over there. And the food . . . You would go to somebody's house in Britain, they'd prepare something and you'd just eat it and it was nice. But [in Metz] they'd be: "Oh, you've got to see this lettuce that I found today. And these tomatoes. And the croissants were made here and you got the bread there because he made the best bread. You should go to the cheese shop down there because he has two cheeses and he's the only one in France who does these. You need to taste these cheeses." It was really an eye-opener, the love and the intensity of what they ate and how they ate it and what they ate it with and what they drank with it . . . It was fabulous.'

Black was determined to learn French when he arrived, carrying a little Collins dictionary around with him and hiring a private French tutor. But although the striker quickly got to grips with the language, his linguistic forays were not without mishaps. 'After four or five months, my wife was expecting,' he says. 'In French, expecting is *enceinte*. I remember thinking: "I'd better tell the boys." We were sitting at dinner, pre-match, and I said: "I'd just like to say that my wife is *ancienne*." Ancient! And they all went: "Hey, no problem. You're in France now, no problem."' He erupts with laughter. 'I used to go back and repeat whatever shit I'd heard in the dressing room to my wife and she would use it at dinner parties. People were like: "What? Oh, he's a bastard!"'

———

When Waddle flew in to Marignane Airport after signing for Olympique de Marseille in July 1989, he was quickly accosted by a scrum of journalists. How did it feel to be in Marseille? Was he looking forward to playing at the Stade Vélodrome? Which song was he going to open with? *Erm, sorry?* After some confused exchanges, it transpired that the reporters had mistaken the mullet-haired winger for David Gilmour, frontman of British rock band Pink Floyd, who were playing a concert in the city that evening. The episode encapsulated the local reaction to Waddle's blockbuster £4.5 million transfer from Tottenham: people were simultaneously excited and – footage of foreign championships not being as freely available in the late 1980s as it is today – not entirely sure who he was. 'Nobody knew Chris Waddle,' says Papin, Marseille's then captain. 'I'd seen a few video cassettes of him. When he started at Marseille, we saw some footage of him and you thought: "OK, this could be good." But we didn't know.'

Marseille's squad, reigning league champions and Coupe de France holders, had been in pre-season training for weeks. Waddle had been on holiday in Cyprus. He was unfit, a few kilos overweight and found the heat of a Mediterranean high summer unbearable. 'I'd never experienced anything like it,' he said. Eager to see his new recruit in action, Marseille president Bernard Tapie decreed that the 28-year-old be named on the bench for OM's opening league fixture at newly promoted Lyon. Despite having only a couple of days' training behind him, Waddle came on for Carmelo Micciche at half-time of a 4–1 win and even ended up wearing the captain's armband after Papin pulled his hamstring in the game's latter stages.

Waddle struggled for form in the season's early weeks and issues off the pitch left him worrying that he had committed 'the worst mistake of my life'. Along with his wife, Lorna, and their one-year-old daughter, Brooke, Waddle spent the first few weeks of his Marseille career living in a tatty, mosquito-ridden hotel in nearby Aix-en-Provence called the Amadeus, which did not serve breakfast and had no laundry facilities. The couple had only one car between them and neither of them spoke a word of French. It did not help that Marseille's decision-makers seemed not to know where he preferred to play. Coach Gérard Gili initially deployed him in a central role behind Papin, only for Waddle to explain – using pen and paper to draw a crude tactical diagram – that he would be much more effective cutting in from the right on to his left foot. With Lorna and Brooke struggling to adjust to hotel life, Waddle packed them off back to England for a few weeks and moved in with Papin, who spoke the best English in the squad. The France international striker did his best to teach Waddle some rudimentary French and sensitively glossed over the less than complimentary reviews he was receiving in the national sports media. Towards the end of October, the Waddles finally moved into a place of their own: a secluded rented villa with a swimming pool in Aix that overlooked the sea. 'All of a sudden, I felt a foot taller,' he said.

The catalyst in Waddle's OM career occurred a few days later during a televised Friday night game at home to PSG, who Marseille had pipped to the title the previous May thanks to an ill-tempered 1–0 win at the Vélodrome. There were 11 minutes to go until half-time and the scoreline was blank when PSG cleared a corner and Éric Di Meco hoisted the ball back into the box. Breaking the visitors' offside trap, Waddle raced into the penalty area from wide on the right and leaped to control the ball on his chest before toeing it into the air past the advancing Joël Bats. As the ball descended from the sky, Waddle turned himself side-on and nudged it into the vacant net with a scuffed but sensationally cheeky back-heel. After hurdling a pitch-side advertising board, he stood at the foot of the Virage Nord and spread his arms wide in celebration. 'That goal was shown for weeks and weeks in France,' he said. 'And that was it. That's where my Marseille career took off.' OM won 2–1 and 'Waddle-mania' was born.

Much like his England colleague Hoddle at Monaco, Waddle was encouraged to play to his strengths in a way that he never had been back home. 'The football was slower and more technical and OM had a great system: effectively 5-2-2-1, with me and Abedi Pelé playing on the right and left respectively behind Papin,' he said. 'I had time to think about my game, time that I never had in England playing 4-4-2 at 100 miles an hour.' He felt that it gave him 'the freedom I'd always craved'. Not just in Marseille, but right across France, fans thrilled to his languid, carefree style; his lazy stepovers, his bewitching changes of pace, his habit of beating the opposition left-back and then turning back to beat him again. And again. And again.

Playing in France also served to bring out the showman in Waddle, who became known as 'Magic Chris'. Unable to communicate fluently in the language of his new homeland, he lent into a clownish side to his character – gurning at television cameras, melodramatically flagellating himself for missed chances – that English football fans had scarcely seen. During a break in play in a game at Nancy, he started signing autographs at the side of the pitch. On another occasion, when the referee was taking his time organising the wall at a free-kick during a match against Metz, Waddle lay down, put his head on the ball and pretended to fall asleep. Taken off early in a title decider at Monaco in April 1992, he spent the whole of the second half playing peekaboo with a TV camera beside the dug-out. And French football fans loved it. The Vélodrome was awash with Union Jack flags. Children mimicked his mullet haircut, supporters wept when they met him, schoolgirls chased him through shopping precincts. There were Waddle jeans, there was Waddle wine. He even released a record, a bilingual electropop track called 'We've Got a Feeling', with his Marseille teammate and close friend Basile Boli. When he was stopped for speeding as he drove to training one morning, the police realised who he was, asked him to autograph the ticket they were about to issue him and gave him a blue-light escort to his destination. It was a kind of fandom French football had not often seen and it turned Waddle into an icon. 'There are lots of kids in Marseille who adored Chris Waddle because of his personality and his attitude on the pitch,' says Di Meco, who played with Waddle for three years. 'He brought that thing you find today where youngsters identify with a player, his haircut, his vibe. It was rare at the time. Even though our star was JPP [Papin], you didn't have people with JPP haircuts. Chris brought something extra. Not a showbiz side, because he wasn't like that, but that identification thing. He was a bit of an idol.'

Marseille successfully defended their league crown in Waddle's first season, seeing off closest rivals Bordeaux thanks to a brace of free-kicks from the Englishman in an April 1990 title decider, and finished as champions again in the two seasons that followed. He played a starring role as Marseille eliminated defending champions AC Milan in the quarter-finals of the 1990–91 European Cup, teeing up Papin's equaliser in the first leg at San Siro and then scoring the only goal of the return fixture with a rare right-foot volley, but OM lost on penalties to Red Star Belgrade in the final in Bari (Waddle, scarred by his infamous shoot-out miss for England against West Germany in the 1990 World Cup semi-finals, refusing to take one). OM's second-round elimination by Sparta Prague the following season effectively spelled the end of his time at the Vélodrome, but although he spent only three years on La Canebière, it was enough to earn him a place in Marseille fans' hearts. When the club's supporters were asked to vote for their Player of the Century to mark OM's centenary in 1998, Waddle came second behind Papin. Zinédine Zidane, who watched Waddle on the Vélodrome terraces, said that the Gateshead native 'made me dream'.

Hoddle and Hateley finished empty-handed in their second season at Monaco after Wenger's side came third in Division 1 and lost 4–3 to Marseille in an action-packed Coupe de France final. On a personal level, Hoddle enjoyed one of the most successful seasons of his career, striking up a brilliant partnership with new signing George Weah and finishing joint-second behind Papin in the Division 1 top scorer standings with 18 goals. But an injury to his left knee sustained in a match against Caen in August 1990 brought his time at Stade Louis II to a premature end, while a succession of ankle problems prevented Hateley from recapturing the heights of his maiden campaign. By the end of 1990, both men were back in Great Britain, Hateley signing for Rangers and Hoddle heading to Chelsea to build up his fitness.

The launch of the Premier League in 1992 made leading British and Irish players less inclined to head overseas and come the start of the 1992–93 season, the only footballer from the UK playing in the French top flight was Strasbourg's Northern Irish midfielder Michael Hughes. Over the 30 years since, British footballing expats have arrived in three distinct waves: Scots in the mid-1990s (John Collins, Allan Johnston, Gary Smith, Jamie Fullarton); ageing English midfielders in the early 2010s (Joe Cole, Joey Barton, David Beckham); and, in the early 2020s, either youngsters seeking the top-level playing time likely to be denied them in the Premier League (Stephy Mavididi, Angel Gomes) or older players looking for fresh starts (Aaron Ramsey, Ross Barkley).

For Hoddle and Waddle, in particular, moving to France brought a kind of emancipation. Waddle had been a popular, crowd-pleasing footballer in England, but in France he was adored, his combination of devil-may-care dribbling and cartoonish tomfoolery elevating him to a level of popularity that native players could only dream of. Hoddle, meanwhile, was finally able to play as a number 10, which he called 'the position I had wanted to play all my career'. Back home, his lavish technical gifts had failed to impress a succession of mistrustful England managers, whose reluctance to make allowances for talented individuals restricted him to the relatively meagre tally of 53 international appearances. In France, they knew footballing excellence when they saw it. Platini said that if Hoddle had been French, he would have been capped 100 times. 'I'd seen glimpses of it in training, at international level, but when you were with Glenn every day of the week, training was just . . . pfff,' says Hateley, blowing the air out of his cheeks. 'Players would just stop and applaud him. The different style of football suited him as well. He wasn't getting charged into and chopped up in the air. I think French football was the ideal scenario for him, particularly at his age, because he'd got all the flair and he could deliver a ball with either foot. I think he's really appreciative of the fact that he got the opportunity. In the back of his mind, he might wish he'd done it five years before.'

In a different way, Cascarino's move to Marseille in the summer of 1994 allowed him to transform his career as well. The transfer was a punt for both parties. The lanky former Gillingham and Millwall striker was 32 and out of contract after an underwhelming two-year spell at Chelsea that had been bedevilled by knee problems. Marseille were picking up the pieces in France's second division after being punitively relegated over the VA-OM match-fixing scandal. But Cascarino hit a remarkable 61 league goals in only two seasons, earning himself the nickname 'Tony Goal' and helping Marseille to reclaim their place among the elite, before a switch to Nancy in 1996 allowed him to enjoy an improbable golden swansong. The Irish international fired the Lorraine club to promotion in his first full season, became the oldest player to have scored a hat-trick in French top-flight history[49] and was awarded the city's Médaille d'Or.

'In my final season at Chelsea, I was sub a few times and I'd be in the dug-out,' he says over coffee beside the Thames in central London. 'And every time I got up, there was a guy behind the dug-out, a season ticket-holder, who would shout: "Ah, fucking sit down Cascarino! What are you fucking putting him on for [Ian] Porterfield?" So every time I was about to get out of my seat, I'd be thinking: "Oh, this guy behind me is going to go into fucking raptures now." A year later, I'm "Tony Goal" at Marseille and the fans have turned a whole stand green, white and orange for the Irish flag. I'd go into a restaurant and people would send food over to me and pay my bill. No chance of that in certain parts of my career – they'd be throwing their food *at* me! I sometimes have to remind myself how great it was. I think I'm the longest-serving player from these shores to ever go and play in France. I'm the oldest guy to get a hat-trick in Ligue 1, I got the freedom of the city in Nancy and then I'm "Tony Goal" in Marseille. And it's nice to be loved. I wasn't needy, I'm not a needy person. But it ain't half nice to be loved.'

---

49 Aged 37 years and 31 days, Cascarino scored all three goals as Nancy beat Rennes 3–0 in October 1999.

7

NANTES

THE GOAL THAT CAME FROM SOMEWHERE ELSE

'It's about the pleasure of understanding each other: the pleasure of knowing what you're going to do and knowing that your opponent doesn't know. That's what you go to training for every morning.'

Raynald Denoueix

Three players, four touches, seven seconds. One unforgettable goal that inspired a title triumph and simultaneously encapsulated the ethos of an entire club.

The first half of a televised Friday night game between Nantes and defending champions Paris Saint-Germain in August 1994 was slowly warming up when the home side won a throw-in 10 yards inside the visitors' half on the right-hand side. No sooner had the ball crossed the touchline than Nantes midfielder Benoît Cauet grabbed it in his hands and hurled it down the line towards Patrice Loko. The ball bounced once before reaching Loko, who controlled it on his chest and then, while facing the right-hand corner flag, hooked it over his own head to Reynald Pedros. As the ball descended from the sky and PSG centre-back Alain Roche advanced towards him, Pedros spotted Loko darting into the penalty area from the right. The long-haired Nantes winger leaped into the air, where he seemed to hang suspended for a split-second, and deftly lobbed a left-foot pass over Roche's head to Loko, who converged upon the falling ball before using the outside of his right foot to catapult a stinging volley into the top-right corner. '*C'est fabuleux!*' cried Canal+ commentator Thierry Gilardi as the net bulged. '*C'est extraordinaire!* Goal by Patrice Loko

77

after 18 minutes of the first half. The ball didn't touch the ground and Nantes lead 1–0!' The following day's *L'Équipe* described it as 'a goal that came from somewhere else'. The details of the strike – Nantes' yellow and green vertical stripes, Loko's bouncing dreadlocks, the apologetic left hand that PSG goalkeeper Bernard Lama flailed at the ball as it flew past him – are ingrained more deeply in French football's collective memory than those of probably any other goal in top-flight history.

'Benoît Cauet gets the ball very quickly and that starts it all off,' recalls Pedros during a Zoom call from his home in Orléans. 'Pat runs across me from my left, so I move inside and he gives me the ball in the air. I see Alain Roche in front of me and I can't control the ball because he's close to me. I see the space in behind him, I know what Pat wants to do and I say to myself: "There's only one thing I can do." I jump to play the ball with the inside of my foot so that I can get it over Alain and cushion it enough for Pat to come on to it and take it in his stride, although I'm a bit lucky because it hits my ankle a bit. I put it over Alain and I see Pat arriving and I think: "Well he's not going to shoot [first-time]." So when he shoots with the outside of his foot and scores, I think: "Fucking hell." But it's a question of hundredths of seconds. I don't tell myself: "It's the goal of the season." It's only years later, when people tell you it was one of the best goals ever [that you realise]. It's a brilliant goal and it sums up that team well.'

The goal combined multiple elements of a specific style of play that had been lovingly developed at Nantes for decades. Wordless understanding between teammates. The run triggering the pass. Movement, technical dexterity, one-touch passing, agility, imagination. And devastating speed. Loko described it as 'the emanation of the spirit that propelled our club'. It was, in three players, four touches and seven seconds, the perfect distillation of the *jeu à la nantaise*.

The story begins with José Arribas, a visionary, self-taught Basque coach whose stewardship of FC Nantes between 1960 and 1976 established a methodological framework to which the club from western France would remain faithful until the beginning of the following century. Born in Bilbao, Arribas arrived in France aged 16 in July 1937 after he, his mother and his two sisters were forced to flee the Basque region by the Spanish Civil War. He spent four years playing in midfield for US Le Mans before making his name as a coach with amateur club Noyen-sur-Sarthe, where his adoption of the 4-2-4 system popularised by Brazil at the 1958 World Cup produced spectacular results. Hired by Nantes at the age of 39, he introduced a style of football founded upon movement, teamwork and speed, a game of 'rhythm and liveliness' as he put it, which yielded promotion to the top tier in 1963 and league title glory in 1965, 1966 and 1973.[50] Arribas taught his players to think about their teammates before themselves, engendering a style of play in which everyone worked doubly hard to make themselves available for a pass and learned to anticipate what their colleagues would require in any given game situation. 'It was the collective aspect that was important to him,' says Raynald Denoueix, who joined Nantes in 1966 at the age of 18. 'It was playing with others, playing *for* others. Anticipating your partner, anticipating your opponent. It's about the pleasure of understanding each other: the pleasure of knowing what you're going to do and knowing that your opponent doesn't know. That's what you go to training for every morning.'

One of Denoueix's older teammates was a short, slight defensive midfielder called Jean-Claude Suaudeau. Known as 'Coco' due to his childhood love of eggs (*coco* being an old-fashioned French children's name for eggs), Suaudeau would introduce Arribas' philosophy to the next generation of Nantes footballers, first

---

50 During the 1960s, Arribas found himself at the centre of an ideological battle between *Miroir du Football*, a supplement of the now defunct communist monthly sports magazine *Miroir-Sprint*, and the Amaury Group titles *L'Équipe* and *France Football*. François Thébaud, editor-in-chief of *Miroir du Football*, advocated for the kind of attacking football played by Hungary's 'Magnificent Magyars' in the early 1950s, the Reims and France sides coached by Albert Batteux and Pierre Sinibaldi's attack-minded Anderlecht side of the early 1960s. Arribas, whose Nantes team played with a flat back four, zonal marking, a high defensive line and attacking full-backs, was championed by Thébaud and his colleagues. But at *L'Équipe* and *France Football*, senior journalists Gabriel Hanot and Jacques Ferran vaunted the merits of the defensive approach adopted by Internazionale coach Helenio Herrera (known in Italy and beyond as *catenaccio*, but referred to in France at the time as *le béton* or 'concrete').

as director of the academy and then, from 1982, as head coach of the first team.[51] In addition to what he learned from Arribas, Suaudeau drew inspiration from Rinus Michels' Ajax and Bob Paisley's Liverpool. He spent two weeks watching Liverpool train in 1974 and was struck by the methods Paisley used to encourage movement, such as awarding free-kicks against players who passed or received the ball while standing still. Suaudeau was obsessed with making his players think on their feet ('After training, you should go off less stupid' was one of his numerous maxims) and his training drills, many of which he inherited from Arribas, were specifically designed to exercise their grey matter. During practice matches, he would ban lobbed passes, forcing the team in possession to go the extra yard to create angles for the ball to be played along the ground. There were practice games with an imaginary ball, in which players would play 'passes' by calling out the name of the receiving player. Anticipating a tactic that was later adopted by Pep Guardiola, Suaudeau would divide the attacking zones of the pitch into squares and specify that no square could be occupied by more than one player at the same time. Most fiendish of all was a possession exercise known as *le jeu des couleurs* (the colours game), which involved a team of players wearing bibs of three different colours trying to keep the ball while a team of players in bibs of three other colours attempted to win it off them. Get the colours confused and you were dead.

Players who joined Nantes from other clubs regularly reported needing weeks if not months to get up to speed on the training pitch. 'Suaudeau would stop matches every 30 seconds, every five minutes, and put us back into position because a bad decision had been made or a cross-field pass should have been played and wasn't,' recalls emblematic Nantes defender Maxime Bossis, who played for the club between 1973 and 1985 and again from 1990 to 1991. 'It was really very demanding.' Although Suaudeau's Nantes were renowned for the attractiveness of their football, the insistence on constant movement meant that training sessions had to be physically demanding. 'When I joined Nantes, one of

---

51 Suaudeau had hoped to be appointed first-team coach when Arribas stepped down in 1976, only to be overlooked in favour of former Reims and France left-winger Jean Vincent, who led Nantes to two league titles (1977 and 1980) and one Coupe de France (1979) before leaving to coach Cameroon at the 1982 World Cup.

the first things Raynald Denoueix asked me was: "Do you like running?"' recalls Pedros with a rueful laugh. 'To play the way we wanted, you had to run a lot. You pushed yourself to a limit you weren't aware of.'

Nantes' training ground, La Jonelière, also featured a small, walled pitch, known as *la fosse* (the pit), which would stage intense, small-sided matches in which the ball never went out of play. Occasionally, Suaudeau would use *la fosse* for games where the ball was not allowed to touch the ground, equipping his players with the technical reference points that would one day enable Pedros and Loko to combine for their magical goal against PSG. 'It might sound a bit arrogant, but we scored goals like that hundreds of times in *la fosse*,' says former Nantes striker Nicolas Ouédec. 'It's all we did. Receiving a ball in the air, knowing how to control it, how to weight your pass so that your teammate could hit the ball on the volley. It was all down to spending hours on end in *la fosse*.'

After retiring as a player in 1979, Denoueix returned to Nantes to head up the academy when Suaudeau took over as head coach in 1982 and would go on to launch the careers of future France internationals such as Didier Deschamps, Marcel Desailly, Christian Karembeu and Mickaël Landreau. Suaudeau and Denoueix worked closely, sharing an office at La Jonelière. On Wednesday evenings, Suaudeau would gather all of the club's various age-group coaches together so that they could share ideas, ensuring that every player at Nantes, regardless of age, was being taught to play the same kind of football. His model was to make sure the first XI always featured a nucleus of homegrown talent schooled in the exacting specificities of Nantes' football traditions, supplemented by a handful of adaptable and often more experienced players brought in from elsewhere. Denoueix spent 15 years in charge of the academy and the reserve team before becoming head coach in 1997 when Suaudeau stepped down. When he led Nantes to the league title in the 2000–01 season, 22 of the 27 players in the squad had come through the academy.

In having successfully developed a style of play that was passed down over the generations by a succession of like-minded coaches, Nantes stand alone in the French game as the only club with a footballing heritage comparable in character to the Liverpool Boot Room or the legacies left by Johan Cruyff at Ajax and Barcelona. 'If we were champions in 2001, it was because for 40 years before us, there were players, there were coaches and there was a certain stability, both in terms of the way the club was run and the football that was played on the pitch,' Denoueix tells me. 'There was a transmission of ideas. I'd been immersed in something that made so much sense to me that I wanted to pass those ideas on. But it wasn't a case of defending some kind of football "truth". It was simply about defending our vision of football.' There was no more spectacular manifestation of that vision than the title-winning team of 1994–95.

It was only after straying from their traditions that Nantes would come to appreciate the true value of the *jeu à la nantaise*. French football was going places in the 1980s, propelled by the extravagant spending of Claude Bez's Bordeaux, Bernard Tapie's Marseille and Jean-Luc Lagardère's Matra Racing, and when local retail entrepreneur Max Bouyer became Nantes president in December 1986, he allowed the club to be swept along with the tide. Hello big-name signings (Belgium winger Franky Vercauteren, Scotland striker Mo Johnston), goodbye Suaudeau, dismissed from the dug-out after a 10th-place finish in the 1987–88 season and replaced by Miroslav Blažević, a Croatian coach with no connection to the club. But the new approach failed to work and with results flatlining and the wage bill soaring, Nantes found themselves on the brink of disaster in 1992, saddled with debts of 60 million francs.

It took some creative restructuring by incoming president Guy Scherrer – who made his fortune in the local biscuit industry – for Nantes, now known as FC Nantes-Atlantique, to be able to line up in Division 1 for the start of the 1992–93 campaign, having been threatened with relegation on financial grounds.[52] The economic difficulties obliged Nantes to sell academy graduates such as Desailly and Jean-Jacques Eydelie, both of whom followed Deschamps to Marseille,[53] and prevented the club from bringing in anybody to replace them. But Denoueix's youth-team charges – Loko, Pedros, Ouédec, Karembeu,

52 The club was known as FC Nantes-Atlantique until 2007, when it reverted to its former name of FC Nantes.
53 Deschamps had joined Marseille in November 1989 after four years in the Nantes first team.

Jean-Michel Ferri, Stéphane Ziani – had all got a taste of first-team football by then and with Suaudeau back in the dug-out after being reappointed as head coach in February 1991, the decision was taken to let the youngsters off the leash. 'We found ourselves obliged to promote them because, as we say in French, we had a knife to our throats in an economic sense,' says Denoueix. 'When we started the season, there was obviously a lot of uncertainty. I felt that there was a lot of talent, but when the pressure to get results arrives, you never know.'

Accompanying the Nantes youngsters were two players who had joined the club from elsewhere: a short, furiously industrious right-sided midfielder called Claude Makélélé, who had been plucked from the academy at Brest by sporting director Robert Budzynski, and a tall, effortlessly graceful Chadian playmaker called Japhet N'Doram, recruited from Cameroonian club Tonnerre Yaoundé. Together with the squad's nucleus of youth-team graduates, they gave Nantes a footballing identity that took the best of the club's traditions – the movement, the playfulness, the sense of the collective – but flipped the dial to warp speed. Realising that his fledgling squad did not possess the technical attributes of some of the other teams he had coached in the yellow and green (notably the fêted title-winning side of 1982–83), Suaudeau decided to focus on their other qualities. 'In terms of collective passing technique, they had some shortcomings,' he said. 'So I focused on off-the-ball work. We conceived of attacking football through collective ball recovery.' Nantes hunted for the ball in packs, took one touch where most teams took three or four and flew at their opponents, once in possession, at terrifying velocity. 'We needed very few passes to go from box to box; in just one or two passes, we were capable of advancing 50 yards,' says Ouédec, who partnered Loko up front. 'And with the quality of our movement, with Loko, Pedros, N'Doram, me and Makélélé all moving in every direction, our opponents struggled to position themselves. It was "organised chaos". You uncorked the champagne and the bubbles went everywhere.'

The new-look Nantes finished fifth in the 1992–93 season and lost 3–0 to PSG in the Coupe de France final before coming fifth again the following campaign. A 2–1 win at Guy Roux's obdurate Auxerre early in the 1994–95 season, secured by thumping strikes from Ouédec and Loko, indicated that *Les*

Canaris would be a force to be reckoned with. After late goals from Ouédec secured a pair of 2–1 victories against Caen and Lille, Loko's luminous volley sank PSG at the Stade de la Beaujoire and sent Nantes to the top of the table. A 3–0 home win over long-standing rivals Saint-Étienne in mid-September (in which all three goals arrived in the first 18 minutes) established what became known as the *tarif maison* (house rate): Nantes would score three goals – no more, no less – in a further nine home fixtures, earning them seven wins and two draws. With Karembeu storming forward from right-back, Ferri and Makélélé bossing midfield, Pedros darting infield from the left and N'Doram, *Le Sorcier* (The Sorcerer), stitching things together behind Loko and Ouédec, Nantes fizzed with an irrepressible energy.

By the time they travelled to the Parc des Princes to face Luis Fernandez's PSG in early January, they had a seven-point advantage over their title rivals. The reigning champions boasted a star-studded attack of George Weah, David Ginola and Brazilian playmaker Raí, but despite making a strong start, PSG conceded the initiative midway through the first half when Daniel Bravo was dismissed for a reckless, two-footed lunge on N'Doram. Shortly after, Pedros released Loko to round Lama and open the scoring. Two second-half goals from N'Doram – the first a delightful left-foot lob – completed a resounding 3–0 win. Nantes went 32 games without defeat, establishing a new French record, before their luck finally ran out at Strasbourg, where an attempted header by Frank Lebœuf that looped into the net off his shoulder set them on their way to a 2–0 defeat. But title success was only a matter of time and the club's seventh French league crown was duly secured with two games to spare following a 2–2 draw at Bastia. 'The 1995 Nantes team that won the title kept the *jeu à la nantaise* going,' says Bossis. 'They brought it back after it had been forgotten.' The title party at local nightclub Le Marlowe lasted for three days.

———

In Makélélé's recollection, Nantes' players set off for their summer holidays thinking 'the best is yet to come'. But for the boys of 1994–95, the best had already been and gone. With sad inevitability, the squad's best players began to be picked off one by one, Karembeu moving to Sampdoria and Loko joining boyhood club PSG. The passing of the Bosman ruling in December 1995 only served to expedite the talent drain and by the end of 1997, Pedros, Ouédec, Makélélé and N'Doram had all left too.

As the 1995–96 season approached, the mood in the changing room darkened when Suaudeau discovered that Makélélé had been in a clandestine relationship with his daughter, Stéphanie, for 18 months. That Suaudeau used to enjoy playfully probing his players, and Makélélé in particular, about their love lives only heightened his sense of betrayal. 'I think it really hurt Coco, because everyone knew about it and he was the last person to find out,' says Ouédec. 'He'd known us since we were young, from our academy days, so for one of his players to be going out with his daughter . . . I didn't see any harm in it, personally, but he took it very badly and it created an awkward atmosphere within the squad.' Nantes never threatened to successfully defend their league title and eventually trailed home in seventh place, although the fairy tale continued in the Champions League, where they reached the semi-finals before losing 4–3 on aggregate to Juventus. Suaudeau had already seen his 1982–83 side of Bossis, Thierry Tusseau, José Touré and Vahid Halilhodžić dismantled before his eyes and when the same fate befell the 1994–95 team, it proved too much to bear. After a third-place finish in 1996–97, he abruptly stepped aside for Denoueix on the eve of the following campaign, bringing to an end a largely unbroken 37-year association with the club that had helped to turn Nantes into a byword for courageous, stylish, winning football.

Suaudeau's team could have gone on to enjoy a second lease of life in the colours of the national side, but although that did not happen – at least, not entirely – it was not for want of trying. As he rebuilt after the calamity of France's failure to qualify for the 1994 World Cup, newly installed national coach Aimé Jacquet naturally sought to hitch himself to the Nantes bandwagon. When France played Romania in October 1994 in the first home game of their qualifying campaign for the 1996 European Championship, they lined up with five current or former Nantes players in the starting XI: Desailly at the base of midfield, Karembeu and Pedros either side of him and Ouédec and Loko up front, with Manchester United's Éric Cantona in the N'Doram role. But although Jacquet was greatly enthused by his side's performance against one of the quarter-finalists at the previous summer's World Cup, the game finished 0–0. It was to become a recurring theme: remarkably, four of France's first five matches finished goalless. Ironically, the campaign finally came to life in Nantes, which was the scene of a 4–0 win over Slovakia in April 1995, but with the majority of the Nantes contingent – Karembeu, Pedros and Ouédec – on the bench. By the time the tournament in England came round, Jacquet had settled on a front three of Zinédine Zidane and Youri Djorkaeff plus either Loko or Christophe Dugarry. Jacquet had assured Ouédec of a place in his squad, only for the striker to sustain a muscle tear in the Champions League semi-final second leg against Juventus. Pedros' most notable contribution was a fatally squandered spot-kick at Old Trafford that condemned France to defeat in their semi-final against the Czech Republic.

Deschamps, Desailly and Karembeu would all play key roles in France's World Cup triumph two years later, but none of the Nantes-schooled attacking players made the cut. Whereas defensive-minded players found it easy to slot themselves into new playing systems, the attackers, hardwired to play the kind of intuitive, one-touch football they had been taught at Nantes, struggled. It was a similar story when they cut the apron strings that had tied them to La Jonelière and sought pastures new. Ouédec and Pedros never recaptured the heights they had hit at Nantes, N'Doram's career was cruelly ended by a knee injury at Monaco and after two impressive seasons at PSG, the goals dried up for Loko.

Pedros joined Parma in January 1997, after half a season at Marseille, and remembers being horrified when his new teammate Lilian Thuram advised him to be more selfish in front of goal. 'I replied: "No, I can't do that,"' Pedros recalls. '"If I see that they're in a better position than me and I can pass to them, I'll pass to them." And Lilian said: "OK, but be warned: the forwards here only think about themselves." He made that absolutely clear to me, but I just couldn't get my head around it. I'd always been taught to give the ball to a teammate whenever they were in a better position than me.'

The players left, the coaches too, and when Denoueix departed in 2001, the last vestiges of the *jeu à la nantaise* vanished with him. But the idea endures, somewhere in the ether, along with the memory of a fearless collection of young players who reduced a formidable, pre-Bosman French top flight to ruins with the sheer, iridescent splendour of their football. On the rare occasions when a team threatens to trouble their 32-game unbeaten run, the journalists start calling, the images reappear – the yellow and green stripes, Loko's dreadlocks, Lama's flailing hand – and the fire is stoked all over again. 'We know that it'll be beaten at some point,' says Ouédec. 'Every year, we say to ourselves: "PSG will want to break it this year." But every year, they don't quite manage it. And you realise that, as it happens, what we did was pretty extraordinary.'

8

ITALIE

LEARNING TO WIN

'Our generation owes everything to Italian football and what we
learned from it.'

Didier Deschamps

'*Et ils sont où? Et ils sont où? Et ils sont où, les italiens?*'[54]

Hopping up and down on the spot in his all-white kit and black boots,
victoriously twirling a blue Italy jersey above his head, Lilian Thuram leads his
France teammates in a celebratory chorus in the Stade de France changing
room. His elated colleagues – a grinning David Trezeguet, sitting on the wooden
changing room bench; Emmanuel Petit, emerging from an embrace with
Zinédine Zidane; Frank Lebœuf, bouncing around in a pair of white briefs –
egg him on, clapping and stamping and singing along in unison, their voices
echoing off the walls. Boots, dirty socks, sports bags, towels and empty water
bottles litter the floor. France's coaching staff and a couple of grey-suited French
Football Federation officials look on with expressions of delight. The scene,
captured in the fly-on-the-wall Canal+ documentary *Les yeux dans les Bleus*
(Eyes on *Les Bleus*), unfolded minutes after France's players had left the pitch
following their penalty shoot-out victory over Italy in the quarter-finals of the
1998 World Cup. The result took France into the World Cup semi-finals for the
first time since 1986, but what made it doubly gratifying was the fact that it
came against a country where so many of their players plied their trade. Seven

54 'And where are they? And where are they? And where are they, the Italians?'

members of Aimé Jacquet's squad played for Italian clubs at the time of the tournament and four other players had prior experience of playing in Serie A.[55] Thuram, who played for Parma, had told his teammates that if France lost, his life would be unbearable. It made the game against Cesare Maldini's side – 120 minutes of taut, airless, goalless football in front of 77,000 rapt supporters – all the more fraught. It made victory all the more delicious.

Italy was where France's footballers went in the 1990s to learn how to win, to graft on to the athletic and technical qualities that they already possessed in abundance the *grinta* (grittiness) of dead-eyed champions. Italy's elimination by the French at the 1998 World Cup showed that the lessons learned in front of the tactics boards, on the training pitches and inside the seething stadiums of Serie A had been taken on board. As *Il Corriere dello Sport* was left to rue after the game: 'We have created monsters.'

Italy and Michel Platini were on a collision course long before he jetted in to join Juventus in 1982. Word of an exciting young French footballer with an Italian surname was quick to cross the border when he started to make a name for himself at Nancy and with his Piedmontese roots, he had long harboured ambitions of playing in Serie A. After announcing his decision to leave Nancy in early 1978, he signed a pre-contract agreement with Internazionale, but the club's confidence that the Italian Football Federation (FIGC) was poised to scrap an existing ban on foreign players proved misplaced and the move collapsed. Platini's performances against Italy with France only served to whet the appetites of the clubs who dreamed of signing him. He impressed in a 2–2 friendly draw in Naples in February 1978, twice beating Dino Zoff with trademark free-kicks (one of which was ruled out), and shone again when the

---

55 Lilian Thuram (Parma), Zinédine Zidane (Juventus), Marcel Desailly (Milan), Didier Deschamps (Juventus), Youri Djorkaeff (Internazionale), Vincent Candela (Roma) and Alain Boghossian (Sampdoria) were all on the books at Italian clubs. Laurent Blanc (Napoli), Patrick Vieira (Milan), Christian Karembeu (Sampdoria) and Christophe Dugarry (Milan) had all played in Italy previously.

teams crossed swords in February 1982, opening the scoring in a 2–0 win for *Les Bleus* with a skidding shot into the bottom-left corner. In between, he unknowingly got a glimpse of what lay in store for him when he lined up alongside his future Juve teammates Paolo Rossi, Marco Tardelli, Antonio Cabrini and Zbigniew Boniek in a June 1979 exhibition match in Buenos Aires between a FIFA World XI and world champions Argentina. Months later, the FIGC overturned its foreign player embargo and in the summer of 1982, Platini's love affair with *calcio* began.

His first goal in the black and white stripes was the perfect embodiment of his wit and audacity as a footballer. When a corner was cleared to him in the early stages of a Coppa Italia home game against Pescara, Platini controlled the ball on his chest and then, with the opposition defenders charging out to play offside, lobbed a pass over them to himself before running through to finish into the top-right corner. Despite that early flourish, his early months in Turin were difficult. Dogged by a groin injury that had plagued him for months, he struggled for form and was criticised by the Italian sports media for failing to create more goals for Rossi, now a national hero after returning from his two-year match-fixing ban to fire the *Azzurri* to World Cup glory in Spain. But gradually, things started to fall into place.

In late November, Platini marked his first appearance in the *Derby della Mole* against city rivals Torino by scoring the game's only goal. He was named man of the match in a 3–0 win over Fiorentina in February 1983, notched the equaliser in a 2–1 victory at title rivals Roma with a magnificent free-kick and then produced a virtuoso performance in the European Cup quarter-finals by scoring twice in a 3–1 win over defending champions Aston Villa. His display against Villa earned him the extremely rare score of 9/10 from the Italian sports press, with Turin-based *Tuttosport* declaring that he had played 'like an extra-terrestrial'. Giovanni Trapattoni's side finished runners-up behind Roma in Serie A and lost 1–0 to Hamburg in the European Cup final in Athens, Platini being successfully shackled by man marker Wolfgang Rolff. But he tasted success in the Coppa Italia, netting twice against Hellas Verona in the second leg of the final to earn the *bianconeri* a 3–2 aggregate win, and finished as top scorer in Serie A with 16 goals. Safely ensconced with his family in a secluded hillside mansion in Pino

Torinese, southeast of the city centre, and by now able to converse fluently in Italian, Platini felt that he was 'living in a waking dream'.

In moving to Italy, Platini discovered a football culture that was very different to the one he had left behind. 'Here, only the result counts,' he said. 'In France, we quibble about goalscoring chances or the domination of one team over the other. Here, there's no question of that. We bow before the result.' It made for tight, tense, low-scoring games, the rare sights of goal that he procured often the consequence of mistakes by opposition defences. But as much as Italian football proved a learning curve, he also opened his teammates' eyes with his determination to always remain on the front foot. 'He never wanted to sit back, he always wanted to attack,' says former Juve midfielder Massimo Bonini, who was nicknamed *I polmoni di Platini* (Platini's Lungs) due to the hard yards he put in on the Frenchman's behalf. 'Back then in Italy, when you lost possession you'd drop deep, regain your shape and try to win the ball back. Whereas he wanted to immediately attack. He was ahead of the game mentally as a footballer. These days when you lose possession, you don't drop off – you immediately go to close down the opposition. He was tactically ahead of his time.'

The fervour of the Juve fans took Platini by surprise, not least the moment when a star-struck supporter threw a baby into his arms ('like a rugby ball') for a post-match photograph. But he loved Italy and Italy loved him back, dubbing him *Le Roi* (The King) and hanging upon his every word. His second season yielded a first Serie A title, a second *Capocannoniere* (top scorer) award and his first piece of European silverware after Juve beat Porto 2–1 in the Cup Winners' Cup final. 'He had that natural talent that made everything easy,' says Bonini. 'Take his free-kicks: I played with him for five years and in all that time, I must have seen him practise them twice. He already had it within him. He put the ball wherever he wanted. Not only on free-kicks, but also during the game itself. He saw the game before everyone else, so he knew what to do by the time the ball arrived. He was our match-winner.'

In 1985, Platini completed a hat-trick of both Italian top scorer awards and Ballons d'Or, matching his hero Johan Cruyff's tally of wins in the latter and becoming the first player in history to take home *France Football*'s coveted golden orb for three years running. The 1984–85 season also brought what should have been the crowning moment of his club career when he scored the winner against Liverpool in the European Cup final to bring Juve their first success in the competition, but the match at the dilapidated Heysel stadium in Brussels had paled into insignificance long before kick-off as news began to filter through of a deadly rampage by English hooligans that would leave 39 people dead and over 600 injured. Strongly criticised both for celebrating his goal and reacting joyously at the final whistle, Platini has always insisted that he was unaware of the full scale of the tragedy until after the match.

He won his second *scudetto* in 1985–86 and helped his side to victory over Argentinos Juniors in the Intercontinental Cup final in Tokyo, albeit having been denied what would have been one of the finest goals of his career – flicking the ball over an opponent's head and volleying home left-footed – by an unfortunate offside flag. After retiring as a player in 1987, he embarked upon a short-lived coaching career, steering France to qualification for the 1992 European Championship finals with a perfect eight wins from eight games, only for *Les Bleus* to limp out in the group phase in Sweden. As a coach, he drew heavily on his experiences in Italy, priding himself on his tactical punctiliousness and explaining that he was 'closer to Trapattoni than [Michel] Hidalgo'. It would not be the last time that a Frenchman left Juventus with strong ideas about how to manage a football team.

The night before signing the contract with AC Milan that turned him into the world's most expensive footballer in July 1992, Jean-Pierre Papin and his wife, Florence, stayed at Villa d'Este, a stunning luxury hotel on the shores of Lake Como, as guests of club president Silvio Berlusconi. The following morning, a helicopter arrived to take the couple to Berlusconi's home, Villa San Martino, a vast, lavishly furnished neo-classical mansion in Arcore, northeast of Milan. There, Papin put pen to paper on a deal that tripled his salary and made him football's first £10 million player. The record did not stand for long – Juventus eclipsed it the very same summer when they signed Gianluca Vialli from Sampdoria for £12.5 million, only for Milan to then splurge £13 million on Torino winger Gianluigi Lentini

– but the direction of travel was clear. Having grown accustomed to the rough-edged charms of life at Marseille, Papin was going up in the world. 'What impressed me the most? Everything!' he says. 'Everything was so organised, it felt like arriving in another world. When you joined the squad, there were only stars, so that's pretty impressive. And then you realise that every time you encounter a different section of the club, it's organised, it's perfect. Above all, you realise that the institution is more important than any individual. It's AC Milan first and then, everyone who's part of it. When you arrive at Milanello [the Milan training centre], it had already been there for years. It's just what a player dreams of having, every day. You have your bedroom, the restaurant, the club, a gym, a weights room, a sauna . . . For a player, everything is perfect.'

Papin was the first Frenchman to play for Milan since Nestór Combin in 1971[56] and he opened the door for a succession of his compatriots to follow in his footsteps in the 1990s. They discovered a club where everything was done with a certain sense of discipline and decorum. Meals were always taken together, the same players at the same tables, and nobody was allowed to leave their seat until the captain had finished eating. Marcel Desailly, who joined from Marseille in 1993, recalled being mocked by Alessandro Costacurta one morning for having had the temerity to turn up at Milanello wearing white socks. Everywhere the players looked, they found little signs of a club that prided itself on presenting the very best appearance possible. 'The bus driver who wears the club suit – it might seem unimportant, but I'd never seen that anywhere else,' said Christophe Dugarry, who spent one season at Milan after arriving from Bordeaux in 1996.

At Milanello, a peaceful 16-hectare facility flanked by pine trees 30 miles northwest of Milan, the players each had their own private bedrooms. When they were not at the training centre, general manager Ariedo Braida made sure that their every need was attended to. 'I visited a few apartments, lavish places with four or five bedrooms, and I could pick whichever one I wanted. So I picked one,' Patrick Vieira wrote of his 1995 move to Milan from Cannes in his

---

56 Born in Argentina but capped by France at international level, Combin played up front for Milan between 1969 and 1971.

autobiography, *Vieira*. 'Two or three days later, I was taken shopping to select video equipment, a TV – everything I needed in fact. Within a week, the whole flat was completely kitted out. Cutlery, TV, beds, sheets, a cleaning lady booked in. Two or three days after that, a car was in the garage. If I had the slightest problem, I had a phone number I could dial to call someone 24/7. Ariedo Braida believed that if the club focused totally on our needs, we could be 100 per cent focused on the pitch.'

That attentiveness, unfortunately, did not only extend to kindly club employees, for France's transalpine football transplants also had to contend with Italy's obsessive sports media and excessively passionate supporters. Youri Djorkaeff, who joined Inter from Paris Saint-Germain in 1996, felt the judgements of the country's various sports newspapers were 'extremely severe' and learned to carefully weigh his words whenever he found a microphone or a Dictaphone beneath his nose. Zidane said that Italian journalists made their French counterparts look like 'choirboys'. Playing for major Italian clubs also exposed players to a level of fan scrutiny beyond comparison with almost anything found in France. Even Didier Deschamps, who had spent five years in the pressure-cooker environment of Marseille, struggled with the attention that he received on the streets of Turin following his 1994 switch to Juventus. 'They showed no restraint, no respect towards me,' he said. 'It was as if I belonged to them completely. I was disconcerted, my wife too. Even in Marseille, where football is a veritable religion, I'd never known that.'

Olivier Dacourt has experienced the fervour of two football-mad Italian cities following spells at Roma and Inter in the 2000s. He won back-to-back Serie A titles with Inter and played alongside the likes of Francesco Totti, Luís Figo and Zlatan Ibrahimović, but his encounters with the country's football-crazed *tifosi* left a mark. 'The players in Italy are rock stars,' he says. 'You go into a restaurant and everyone looks at you. You don't pay for anything. Things you didn't order turn up at your table. People want a picture everywhere you go. But you can't walk down the street. I didn't get to know Rome until the end of my career because I couldn't walk around among everyone else. I had to disguise myself: glasses, a moustache . . .' He wore a fake moustache? 'Yes! A moustache, even a beard, to go out. Otherwise you can't do anything, you can't go out for a drink. I never go to matches because of that. I'm afraid of crowds, I don't go to concerts. That started in Italy. It was crazy there.'

———

Zidane has never forgotten his first encounter with Juventus fitness coach Gian Piero Ventrone. After joining Juve from Bordeaux in the summer of 1996, Zidane met up with his new teammates for the first time at their picturesque pre-season training camp in the (very French-sounding) town of Châtillon in the Italian Alps. Nicknamed *Il Marine*, Ventrone was renowned for pushing his players to the limits of their physical endurance and he worked Zidane so hard – on the pitch, in the gym and on the athletics track of the local stadium – that the Frenchman often ended up vomiting. As unpleasant as it was, Zidane felt the benefits in the long run. 'Even today I still tell myself I would never have succeeded in my career if I hadn't gone to Italy,' he said after retiring. 'I stepped up a level there, in terms of the rigour and the physicality.' Deschamps knew all about Ventrone's gruelling regimes, having arrived two years earlier. 'Pre-season there lasted for a month and a half,' he said. 'It was two and a half hours in the morning, two and a half hours in the afternoon. The old guys knew it was going to be tough, but they didn't cut corners on laps of the pitch. If you had to do 15 reps in the gym, they did the 15. Not 13 or 14.' A common trope within French football discourse is that young players from France tend to shy away from gruelling physical work and struggle to submit to the authority of their coaches. At Juventus, not buckling down was simply not an option.[57]

Deschamps proved an important source of support for Zidane during what was to be a challenging first few months in Turin for him. Juve had spent big on the 24-year-old midfielder with the most famous bald patch in football, shelling out 7.5 billion lire (about £3.4 million), and his underwhelming performances during France's run to the semi-finals at Euro 96 had not filled their supporters with optimism. The constant comparisons with Platini did not help either. It was

———

57 Deschamps and Zidane played for Juventus at a time when the club was suspected of doping its players. During a 2004 trial in Turin, Zidane admitted he had taken creatine and received intravenous vitamin injections, but both players denied having taken illegal substances. The two officials on trial, club doctor Riccardo Agricola and chief executive Antonio Giraudo, were eventually acquitted.

not until late October and his first goal in Juve's colours, crashed home from distance with his left foot in a 2–0 home win over Inter, that Zidane began to feel that he had room to breathe.

In terms of tactical understanding, Serie A in the early to mid 1990s was something akin to the football equivalent of Harvard. When Thuram joined Parma from Monaco in 1996, Carlo Ancelotti put him in the stands and encouraged him to study the movement of the team's defenders, their management of the distances between each other and the location of the defensive line on the pitch in relation to the position of the ball. Exposure to Italy's meticulous tactical culture gave him the sensation that he was 'becoming more intelligent', which he found made playing football 'easier'. At Milan, Fabio Capello successfully converted Desailly into a holding midfielder and taught Papin how to play with his back to goal. Even Vieira, who made only five appearances for Milan before leaving for Arsenal, felt that he progressed under Capello's orders, being given special dispensation during training matches to follow Desailly and Demetrio Albertini around the pitch in order to learn from their positioning.

Reynald Pedros joined Thuram at Parma in 1997 and having spent his formative years being schooled in the *jeu à la nantaise* by Raynald Denoueix and Jean-Claude Suaudeau, it made for a dramatic gear change. 'We worked a lot on the tactical side of the game: formations, patterns of play and all that,' he says. 'Everything was very segmented. I got the impression that there was no room for fun or anything like that. It was very regimented – Italian coaches are known for that. But actually, it's strange, because I quite enjoyed it, learning more about the tactical side of the game. I had never experienced anything like it before.' Not that it was all one-way traffic either – the French players occasionally taught their coaches a thing or two as well. Ancelotti said that coaching Zidane at Juventus 'radically changed my conception of football', prompting him to abandon his preferred 4-4-2 system for a 3-4-1-2 formation designed purely to get the best out of the man in the number 21 jersey.

By the time Zidane left Juve in 2001, he was the best player in the world. He had won two Serie A titles, been named Italy's Foreign Footballer of the Year twice and been awarded the Ballon d'Or in 1998 after inspiring France to World Cup glory, the one black mark being the defeats suffered by the *bianconeri* against

Borussia Dortmund and Real Madrid in the Champions League finals of 1997 and 1998. He credited Marcello Lippi, his coach at the Stadio Delle Alpi from 1996 to 1999, with giving him the mentality of an elite-level footballer. 'He was like a light switch for me,' Zidane said. 'He switched me on and I understood what it meant to work for something that mattered. Before I arrived in Italy, football was a job, sure, but most of all it was about enjoying myself. After I arrived in Turin, the desire to win things took over.' Deschamps, who left Juve in 1999 with three *scudetti* and a Champions League winner's medal from 1996 to his name, was no less effusive in his assessment of what playing in Italy had given him. 'Our generation owes everything to Italian football and what we learned from it,' he said.

Lippi observed that as a player, Deschamps was 'already a coach'; the midfielder would occasionally surprise him during games by enacting the exact tactical adjustments that Lippi had just been about to ask him to make. As he embarked upon his own coaching career, Deschamps might have taken inspiration from the visionary Suaudeau, who had launched his career at Nantes, but when he entered the dug-out in 2001, taking up the reins at Monaco within weeks of hanging up his boots at Valencia, it was the Italian traditions that he sought to perpetuate. Deschamps has always been a pragmatist as opposed to a dogmatist, founding his coaching philosophy upon discipline, defensive solidity, creative freedom for attacking players and a robust team ethic. 'Lippi told me one day that there was no universal method for coaching, but that you have to take account of the environment that you're in. He's right, I think,' Deschamps told *So Foot* in June 2017. 'From a technical point of view, he's the coach who inspired me the most.' When Deschamps took charge at Monaco, one of his first moves was to appoint Lippi's former assistant Narciso Pezzotti and ex-Juve fitness coach Antonio Pintus to work alongside him. Later on, Zidane brought Pintus on to his own staff at Real Madrid when he became head coach at the Bernabéu in 2016. He, likewise, took his cue from Lippi, prioritising firm foundations over flair and togetherness over tactical ingenuity.

It brought Zidane three Champions League titles in a row. It brought Deschamps World Cup glory with France for a second time. Midfield architects of France's 1998 World Cup triumph become the two pre-eminent French coaches of the 21st century, Deschamps and Zidane have served up success by following an unmistakeably Italian recipe.

9

GESTE TECHNIQUE

LA ROULETTE À LA ZIDANE

'Stand there,' Zinédine Zidane tells the man behind the camera with a hint of a smile, indicating a patch of grass to his left. 'I'll show you.'

It is a sunny morning in Madrid and Zidane is standing on a football pitch filming a sequence for a forthcoming DVD. Wearing a grey, V-neck Adidas training shirt tucked into black shorts, black socks pulled up to the knees and his trademark Predator boots, he shows documentary maker Stéphane Meunier how to pull off his signature move. 'I've got the ball and I'm running with it and at some point, I push it too far towards you,' he says, nudging the ball in front of him with the outside of his right foot as he advances in Meunier's direction. 'You think you're going to take the ball. But if I'm certain that *I'm* going to get the ball, I do it.' At which point, Zidane pivots extravagantly on top of the ball with the studs of his right boot before spinning anti-clockwise to his left and dragging the ball with him using the studs of his left boot. 'I start with my right foot on top of the ball like that, bring it back on to my left foot and turn at the same time as I bring it with me,' he explains. 'You learn it when you're little, when you're playing in the neighbourhood with your mates. It's more about having fun because it's difficult to pull off a trick like that on a football pitch. It can be effective, but if you mess it up, you look a bit ridiculous.'

More than any other footballer, Zidane was characterised by the quality of his ball control and more than any of his other flicks and tricks, the quality of his ball control was characterised by *la roulette*, that spinning top of a skill move that left hundreds of opponents helplessly glued to the spot and launched a thousand YouTube compilations. It was a technique honed on Place Tartane, the long concrete plaza that served as a playing field for Zidane and his boyhood friends in the tough Marseille district of La Castellane, five miles north of the city centre, where they grew up. 'With my mates, we were always trying to invent a new trick,' he said. 'Whoever had discovered something had to show it to all the others. And we repeated it until everyone did it well. It was up to whoever did it best. I was like the others: I took a ball and I invented stuff. That's what street football is.'[58] Zidane may not have invented *la roulette* – Diego Maradona and Michael Laudrup, among others, would have had something to say about that – but he made it his own.

Zidane's mastery of *la roulette* meant that he could adapt it to the circumstances of the situation, such as the proximity of his opponent or the greasiness of the pitch: sometimes using the inside of his foot rather than the sole, flipping the ball from right foot to left foot as if between pinball flippers; sometimes dragging the ball towards himself with his right instep and then cannoning it in his intended direction of travel with his left heel. Occasionally, *la roulette* served to catapult Zidane past a defender in the final third of the pitch, but more often than not, it was simply a means of conserving possession in the middle of the park. Some *roulettes* found new life with the advent of video-sharing websites – the two he pulled off in rapid succession to confound a pair of opponents in his bouffant-haired Cannes days; a particularly slick version in a match against Atalanta with Juventus – but there is not one singularly great *roulette* that led to a defining goal or crucial assist. The closest he came was in a league match at Real Valladolid in February 2004 when, after gathering a lay-off from his Real Madrid teammate Ronaldo, he pirouetted past defender Alberto Marcos on the edge of the box and then rounded goalkeeper Albano Bizzarri, only to hoist his shot over the crossbar. As Zidane lay on his front on the wet turf, his right hand covering his face in disappointment, the Estadio José Zorrilla spontaneously broke into applause. Ronaldo said it would have been 'the greatest goal in the history of the game'.

---

58 Might *la roulette* have also carried traces of Zidane's childhood passion for judo? The young Zidane was a talented judoka, practising the sport until the age of 11 and obtaining his blue belt. Judo was all about anticipating an opponent's movements and then using their momentum against them – just as Zidane did when he lured a player into attempting a tackle, only to spin away from them with the ball.

Naturally, Zidane threw a *roulette* into the mix during arguably the finest individual performance of his career: the 90-minute masterpiece against Brazil in the quarter-finals of the 2006 World Cup in which his assist for Thierry Henry sent France into the last four. Having announced his retirement prior to the tournament, Zidane knew that every game could be his last. He also went into the match in Frankfurt carrying an injury, his right thigh having to be heavily strapped after he tweaked a muscle while scoring the last goal of France's 3–1 defeat of Spain in the previous round. But in his all-white change strip and golden boots, he dominated the game from first to last with a stately stream of sidesteps, stepovers and sombrero flicks. When Gilberto Silva lumbered towards him midway through the second half, a characteristically adroit *roulette* took the Brazil midfielder out of the game, drawing a delighted '*Olé!*' from the crowd. This was a collection of Brazilian players celebrated for the expressive vibrancy of their football – the team of Nike's *Joga Bonito* advertising campaign, of Ronaldo, Ronaldinho, Kaká, Adriano and Robinho – but at the age of 34 and with the sand timer of his career down to its very last grains, Zidane ran rings around them all. Pelé described him as a 'magician' and a 'master'. Former Brazil midfielder turned influential newspaper columnist Tostão called it 'one of the greatest displays I have ever seen from a player'. In the eyes of Marseille's regional newspaper *La Provence*, France's number 10 had shown himself to be 'more Brazilian than the Brazilians'.

Zidane used to bridle at suggestions that his technical superiority occasionally strayed into the realm of showing off, once asserting that he was 'a competitor, not a dancer'. But at the same time, showing off was an integral part of the street football culture that had spawned him in the first place. On Place Tartane, it was not simply about winning; it was about subjugating, demoralising, *crushing* your opponent, pulling off the kind of devastating dribble or humiliating nutmeg that would be talked about for weeks. As he waltzed around the Waldstadion pitch, Zidane was not merely beating Brazil; he was asserting the primacy of his football over theirs.

10

AUXERRE

ONE SMALL VILLAGE STILL RESISTS

Being shown around Auxerre by Guy Roux is like being shown around the Vatican City by the Pope.

Arriving by train at Auxerre's Gare Saint-Gervais on a hot June afternoon in 2022, I emerge into the ticket hall to find Roux surrounded by people, all eager to grab a word with the man whose legendary stewardship of the city's football club put Auxerre on the map. Everyone in Auxerre knows who he is and everyone recognises what he has done for the place. As we drive across town, a driver who has been honking his horn and angrily gesticulating about Roux's lane positioning laughs and raises a hand in apology once he has pulled alongside us and seen who it is. Walking through the city centre later on, Roux draws a smile or a wave from almost every person we pass. A young woman sitting outside a pizzeria with a group of friends calls out to tell him that she has just had the 'Pizza Guy Roux'. 'That's good,' the avuncular octogenarian replies with a grin. 'I get a cut from each sale!' (He seems to be joking, but Roux proved so adept at convincing local businesses to support the AJ Auxerre[59] cause during his time at the helm that it is impossible to be entirely sure.)

Football is at the forefront of people's minds once again in these parts as Auxerre have just secured promotion to Ligue 1 after an absence of 10 years. That this small Burgundy town of 35,000 inhabitants, 100 miles southeast of Paris,

59 The club's full name is Association de la Jeunesse Auxerroise (Auxerre Youth Association).

101

has any connection with football in the first place is down almost solely to Roux, who took over AJA at the age of just 22 in 1961 and led them from the amateur regional leagues to the very summit of the French game, while simultaneously launching the careers of players such as Éric Cantona, Basile Boli, Philippe Mexès and Djibril Cissé. Religiously set out in a counter-attacking 4-3-3 formation with man-to-man marking, Auxerre were French champions in 1996, reached the Champions League quarter-finals in 1997 and won the Coupe de France four times before Roux eventually relinquished the reins in 2005 after a remarkable 44-year tenure.[60]

Standing on the touchline in his tracksuit and trademark beanie hat, Roux was seen as football's answer to comic book hero Astérix; a crafty and resourceful *paysan* (country bumpkin) who dared to take on the heavyweights from the big cities. A notorious disciplinarian, Roux ruled over his players with a paternal authority that was by turns affectionate and impossibly strict. While he routinely shoots down accusations of parsimoniousness (asserting that he was 'thrifty rather than stingy'), a stroll around Auxerre's Stade de l'Abbé-Deschamps serves to reveal the pride that he still takes in his penny-pinching. The water used to hydrate the pitch comes from the nearby River Yonne, he explains, meaning that the club does not have to pay for it. 'And do you see that roof over there?' he asks, indicating the green corrugated roof of a tractor shed behind the stadium. 'That was the roof of the old main stand.' As the miserly puppet that incarnated him on satirical television show *Les Guignols de l'info* used to say: '*Faut pas gâcher!*'[61]

Roux is 84 now, his eyes even more crinkly than during his Auxerre pomp, his walking pace slow and steady, but he is full of stories. After a glass of Chablis, the local wine that he loves to promote, we sit down outside an Italian restaurant near the Hôtel de Ville and he tells me about a coaching career the likes of which we will never see again.

---

60 Roux briefly left the club to undertake national service between September 1962 and December 1963 and had a short-lived spell as sporting director during the 2000–01 season.
61 'Waste not, want not!' *Les Guignols de l'info* (The News Puppets) was the French equivalent of *Spitting Image*.

What are your earliest memories of football?

'It was 1943 or 1944 and I was five or six years old. The Germans were occupying my village[62] and the commanding officer was in the village château. But football matches still took place and the whole village would go to the stadium because it was the only distraction and the only way to meet up without falling under suspicion. There would be German soldiers around the pitch and that left an impression on me. There was a young 18-year-old lad who would come to play. He was in the Resistance and he would come on his bike, already wearing his football boots. He would play and then he would leave without getting changed, setting off into the forest with his boots on. I used to hold the water pump when he was washing himself before leaving. If you're six years old and a footballer takes an interest in you, even if it's a village footballer from Appoigny, you remember it your whole life. Afterwards, we became friends. But he died and about 10 years later, I bumped into his niece in the village and she told me that she had a treasure for me. It was his football boots.'

You began coaching at a very young age. How did you know at the age of 21 or 22 that that was what you wanted to do?

'Because I had always been the boss. At the village school, they had an avant-garde method of teaching in which the teacher created these groups. There were four groups in the class and I was the boss of mine. We had a corner in the classroom where we had green beans to grow and guinea pigs to look after. We had to feed them and give them water. I always had the best-looking guinea pig! In my group, someone was delegated to feed them every week. We also had a stove in the classroom to keep us warm and every group had to bring a log in each morning. Everyone in the village had wood-fired heating, either a fireplace or a wood-burning stove. In my group, I kept a list of names and everyone had to take turns at bringing in a log. In the other groups, there weren't any bosses and they would argue. "I brought it twice!" "There weren't any!" I didn't have any problems – everyone took it in turns. It wasn't football, but I was made for that.'

---

62 Roux was born in Colmar in Alsace in October 1938, but moved to the village of Appoigny, near Auxerre, with his family after his father, Marcel, was taken prisoner during World War II.

When you started out as a coach, where did your ideas about football come from? There wasn't much football on TV, so how did you develop your ideas about being a coach?

'As a player, I'd trained with professionals at Limoges FC. The coach was [Pierre] Flamion, a former France international from Reims.[63] I was the captain of the reserve team and we had our own coach as well. So I'd acquired a certain amount of experience and I'd read all the [coaching] books. I had my methods – I'd been developing ideas in my mind for quite a while. In the summer of 1960, I did a month-long placement at Crystal Palace. The manager there was Arthur Rowe, who was quite famous and worked on TV.[64] I took notes about everything. Every evening, I'd write things down. A year later, I started at Auxerre. My methods were the accumulation of everything I'd learned in terms of physical preparation and technical preparation. And the technical development of a squad of players, because when I started out, the players were still playing in boots with steel toecaps and nailed-in studs. They'd toe-poke the goal-kicks. I pinched things from anywhere I could. There was a genius fitness coach called Paul Frantz, a PE teacher who was the fitness coach for the national team for a while and who coached Strasbourg.[65] He wrote two booklets about fitness training that corresponded to what I had been searching for. They put into order something that for me had been disordered. I took a lot from Paul Frantz. Then if you think about how the mentality of French football developed, it really took off thanks to Georges Boulogne, a teacher who became National Technical Director and created all the [coaching] diplomas.[66] To become a professional coach, I did two

---

63 Flamion played on the left wing for Reims in the late 1940s and was capped 17 times by France between 1948 and 1953 before becoming a coach.
64 Rowe is chiefly remembered for his spell as Tottenham Hotspur manager (1949–55), during which he introduced a dynamic style of play based on one-touch passing known as 'push-and-run'.
65 Frantz was renowned for using isometric training exercises that developed muscle strength and endurance. As a coaching educator at the French Football Federation, he taught Roux, Aimé Jacquet and Roger Lemerre and also influenced Arsène Wenger.
66 Considered the father of modern French coaching, Boulogne became France's first National Technical Director in 1970 and introduced a pioneering programme of national coaching education.

weeks of evening classes, I spent some time at the CREPS in Dijon[67] and then I did three coaching courses in Paris with Boulogne. I also did some coaching during my military service in Germany, where I learned a lot.'

You were well known for your focus on discipline. Why was discipline so important?

'I don't know where I got it from, but I used to write in the changing room: "training + rest = form". I spent my whole life trying to perfect my training methods. But if the players weren't getting enough rest away from the pitch, I couldn't get the rest they needed on their behalf. It's a kind of "invisible training". And you can convince the players to do the necessary invisible training in two ways: firstly, persuasion, and secondly, policing. I did both. And I admit that I organised things that were worthy of the police. For example, in the early '60s, my players were amateurs and they only had one thing on their minds: going out dancing. There weren't any discos back then. People would erect a round canvas tent in a village, with an orchestra: saxophone, accordion, drums. You paid to go in and you would dance until 2 a.m. or 3 a.m. The best orchestra was called Alma 05 and I would look in the newspaper to see where it was playing. I'd drive past the players' houses at eight o'clock in the evening and read the kilometre gauges in their cars. I'd have my notebook. "OK, 3,742km." Then I'd come past again at eight in the morning, while they were still asleep. Plus 54km? When Alma 05 were playing in Saint-Florentin, it was 27km away, so there and back made 54km. So they must have been there. They played almost voluntarily in those days – the club found them jobs, but they were really unpaid – so I could only punish them by scolding them. Sometimes, when it annoyed me that lots of them were going out, I'd go and fetch them. Later on, it modernised when the professionals had cars. Djibril [Cissé] had a Ferrari at one point. I didn't allow him to take it out around the town. I told him: "The guy who applauded you for scoring on Sunday, who was sitting behind the goal, he paid 30 francs for his

---

67 *Centre de ressources, d'expertise et de performance sportives* (Centre for Resources, Expertise and Sporting Performance). The CREPS are publicly funded educational institutions for sports coaches. There are 15 in mainland France and two in the country's overseas territories.

ticket, which was 5 per cent of his salary. He would have to work for 100 years to be able to afford that Ferrari." I couldn't stop him having a Ferrari, but I didn't like him showing it off. He sold it in the end. The players would go to Paris and I knew which nightclubs they were going to.'

How?

'Sometimes I just got lucky. One day I was filming an advert for a mobile phone company in Paris. We finished filming at 2 a.m. at Place Vendôme and the crew took me to a nightclub on the Champs-Élysées. I sat down and someone told me I was sitting in Djibril's seat! [laughs] My tactic for finding out if they were going to Paris was that the motorway toll booths back then would give you tickets as you went through and came back. I arranged for the woman who gave out the tickets to write down the registration plate numbers – the time they left and the time they came back – and give them to me the next morning. It was all organised. Later on they started joining the motorway further along, at Joigny, but I had someone checking there too! The nightclub bouncers near Auxerre would tip me off as well. I got some of them to provide security at matches – I'd give them free entry and a free meal – and in return, they'd keep me informed about which players were going out. But the players had an arrangement with the DJs – when I turned up to check on them, the DJs would play a certain song to warn them that I was coming!'

I wanted to ask you about the Auxerre youth academy. The club reached the Coupe de France final in 1979, while still in Division 2, and the president, Jean-Claude Hamel, said that you could either use the funds from the cup run to buy the Nancy winger Olivier Rouyer or you could build an academy. You decided to build an academy and the first players to graduate from it included Éric Cantona, Basile Boli, Pascal Vahirua and William Prunier.[68] How can you explain that immediate success?

'There were three youth academies in France: Sochaux, Nantes and Lens. We were the fourth. Those three clubs had already taken the best players, who made

---

68 All four players went on to play for France at senior level, winning a combined 113 caps.

up the France Under-21s team. But there were still some left and there were no other academies to go to. So we took them. Daniel Rolland [Auxerre's academy director] would drive around looking for players and our approach was very simple: the club and the parents. Cantona is a typical example. One of my scouts went to watch a trial match in Aix-en-Provence. He waited until I'd finished training at 11:30 and called me to tell me he had found a phenomenon. A phenomenon! Cantona. Other clubs were interested, but I didn't worry about them. They didn't exist. You put yourself in a tunnel and at the other end of the tunnel is a light with Cantona in it! He would come to us. You find out his club, which was Les Caillols in Marseille. You find out the addresses of the parents and the grandparents and you go to see them. You tell them that you are Auxerre and that you're in the second division, but that you look after your young players. You go and see the player, but you don't tell him anything. I went down there in my car on a Sunday because we played on the Saturday. I was at Les Caillols by noon. I went to see the director who was there and told him why I was there. He said I wasn't the first and I told him I hoped to be the last! I took a little welcome gift – three new footballs. He appreciated it and told me nobody else had done that. That was what I wanted, to show him that we weren't like everyone else. Firstly, I went to see his grandfather because his parents were out at work. I went to see his grandfather, who had a lot of influence; he was a stonemason, head of the family, Italian, Sardinian. I introduced myself and told him why I had come. He said that all the clubs had come but they hadn't been to see him. We got to know each other; we had a coffee. After that, Cantona came for a trial. He played against [Auxerre right-back] Lucien Denis and almost nutmegged him, which made him angry! The last day of the trial, he held his own with the pros despite only being 14. Daniel Rolland told me that he'd asked for an AJA shirt, so I had a shirt, tracksuit, socks and shorts prepared in a package that I gave to him. He'd asked for the same thing at Nice and they sent him to the club shop!'

Tell me about Cantona.

'If you list the qualities you need to be exceptional, he ticked a lot of boxes: right foot, left foot, in the air . . . He was a very difficult pupil though, in terms of discipline. He would do stupid things, lots of stupid things. It was impressive! Daniel Rolland couldn't cope and I was the Court of Appeal. I was the final judge, but he still played in my team. I remember once, we went to Le Havre – torrential rain, wind straight off the sea. They had removed a stand due to renovation work. The wind was with us, Vahirua scored on the counter-attack: 1–0. Second half, he was the centre-forward, the number nine, and he was on the penalty spot – *our* penalty spot. And there, for the whole half, he either headed the ball clear or he chested it down and dribbled; he'd gain five metres, 40 metres. It was incredible. What [Diego] Maradona did against the English [dribbling through the England defence to score at the 1986 World Cup], Cantona did it 10 times in the French championship: picking the ball up on the edge of our area, beating three or four players and scoring with a little chip or something. When Sir Alex Ferguson bought him from Leeds [in November 1992], he came to see me. He arrived at 11 a.m. with his brother, Martin. He didn't have an interpreter and nor did I. I picked him up at the airfield, 7km away, and we went straight to Chablis and picked up a wine that he liked. We talked from 11 a.m. to 5 p.m. And we became friends. He went home with some Chablis and sent me some whisky in return. I told him everything [about Cantona]. And I think he understood it all.'

In the 1995–96 season, Auxerre won the Double of league and Coupe de France. At the winter break, you trailed Paris Saint-Germain by 10 points. How did you manage to bridge the gap?
'I knew as early as '92 that I was going to have a great team, provided there were no accidents or changes in the presidency. With all the young players we had coming through, I warned Hamel that we were going to get offers and I told him: "Reject them or I'm leaving. I know that we've got the team of our dreams." They played in our reserve team and the standard score was five goals per game. Our opponents knew it. We beat Nantes in the Coupe Gambardella [Youth Cup] final in 1986 and they had Didier Deschamps and Marcel Desailly. It finished 0–0 and [Lionel] Charbonnier kept us in it. He saved a penalty and we won in a shoot-out. I knew after that. And in 1995–96 I had Laurent Blanc, although he got injured at the start of the season and didn't return until after

The Saint-Étienne squad, nicknamed *Les Verts*, pose with head coach Robert Herbin before the European Cup final against Bayern Munich at Hampden Park, Glasgow on 12 May 1976.

AFP

Saint-Étienne goalkeeper Ivan Ćurković during the 1976 European Cup final in Glasgow.

James Bobby

Bordeaux president Claude Bez enjoys a characteristically indulgent meal.

Alain de Martignac

Patrick Battiston is carried away after a violent collision with opposition goalkeeper Harald 'Toni' Schumacher during the World Cup semi-final between France and West Germany in Seville on 8 July 1982. Michel Platini and Maxime Bossis are by his side.

AFP

Michel Platini with coach Michel Hidalgo after France's 2-0 victory over Spain in the European Championship final at the Parc des Princes on 27 June 1984.

David Cannon/Allsport

Alain Giresse finds himself outnumbered during Bordeaux's European Cup semi-final against Juventus in April 1985.

Michel Barrault

English footballers Glenn Hoddle (left) and Mark Hateley (right) of Monaco pictured with Rangers striker Trevor Francis at Stade Louis II in November 1987.

David Cannon/Allsport

A young Marseille ball boy looks up at Chris Waddle before a match between Marseille and Nice in December 1989.

Mark Leech/Offside

Jean-Pierre Papin wheels away after equalising with an acrobatic volley during France's 3-3 draw with Belgium in a friendly at the Parc des Princes in March 1992.

Marseille's players celebrate their 1-0 victory over AC Milan in the 1993 UEFA Champions League final in Munich.

Marseille president Bernard Tapie responds to questions during the VA-OM match-fixing affair.

The Nantes team photo prior to a 1-0 win over Paris Saint-Germain in Division 1 in August 1994.

Ross Kinnaird/Allsport

Éric Cantona coolly dispatches a penalty during Manchester United's 3-2 victory over Manchester City in an April 1996 derby match at Maine Road.

Juventus fitness coach Gian Piero Ventrone puts Didier Deschamps and Zinédine Zidane through an intense work-out during the 1996–97 season.

Christian Liewig/Corbis

Mark Leech/Offside

Emmanuel Petit celebrates after scoring the third goal for France during their 3-0 win over Brazil in the World Cup final on 12 July 1998.

Aimé Jacquet is hoisted aloft by his players after France's triumph in the 1998 World Cup final.

Bob Thomas

Pool Deville/Duclos/Gamma-Rapho

Jubilant supporters gather on the Champs-Élysées in Paris to celebrate France's 1998 World Cup victory. The words '*Merci Zizou*' ('Thank you Zizou') are projected onto the Arc de Triomphe in recognition of Zinédine Zidane's decisive brace.

Wearing the white of Real Madrid, Zinédine Zidane spins away from Málaga midfielder Juanito with a *roulette* turn during a Spanish league match in February 2004.

Javier Soriano/AFP

Clive Mason

Arsenal manager Arsène Wenger watches his side take on Leicester City in a Premiership match at Highbury in May 2004.

Auxerre coach Guy Roux looks on during a UEFA Cup match against Ajax in Amsterdam in February 2005.

Eddy Lemaistre/Corbis

Fred Dufour/AFP

Lyon's Brazilian midfielder Juninho lines up a free-kick during a Champions League match against Barcelona in February 2009.

France's players leave the pitch and return to the team bus before a scheduled training session during the 2010 World Cup in South Africa. The squad refused to train in protest at the decision to send striker Nicolas Anelka home.

Franck Fife/AFP

David Price/Arsenal FC

Loaned back to Arsenal by New York Red Bulls, Thierry Henry scores a trademark winner against Leeds United during an FA Cup third-round match in January 2012.

Franck Ribéry of Bayern Munich celebrates with the trophy after setting up Arjen Robben's winning goal against Borussia Dortmund in the 2013 Champions League final at Wembley.

Alex Grimm

Kheira Hamraoui, Amandine Henry and Camille Abily show their disappointment after France's penalty shootout defeat by Germany in the quarter-finals of the 2015 Women's World Cup in Montreal.

Barcelona supporters celebrate their side's 6-1 win over PSG at Camp Nou in March 2017, which completes a remarkable 6-5 aggregate victory in the Champions League last 16.

Kylian Mbappé sprints away from Javier Mascherano during the 2018 World Cup last 16 match between France and Argentina in the Russian city of Kazan. Mbappé's top speed was clocked at 38km/h during this game.

Karim Benzema receives the Ballon d'Or trophy from Zinédine Zidane during a ceremony in Paris in October 2022.

Aurélien Meunier

Captain Wendie Renard and outgoing Lyon president Jean-Michel Aulas prepare to lift the trophy after OL Féminin's 2–1 win over PSG in the 2023 Coupe de France final in Orléans.

Anthony Dibon

PSG's Kylian Mbappé, Lionel Messi and Neymar Jr walk onto the pitch for the Ligue 1 trophy presentation ceremony following a home match against Clermont in June 2023.

Aurélien Meunier – PSG

Christmas.[69] We were 10 points off the top [at Christmas]. By February, it was seven or eight. I didn't think we could be champions, but I was thinking about European qualification. That's when this mage turned up!'

A mage?

'This guy turns up and he tells me he's a "sports mage" who can move the ball with his eyes. He said he'd helped the Limoges basketball team become champions of France and he could do the same for Auxerre. Obviously, I didn't believe a word. He told me we could do a trial. I had to pay for a second-class train ticket for him from Bordeaux to Paris, a two-star hotel near Montparnasse and a ticket to watch Paris Saint-Germain. They had two matches that week – one against Martigues, who were bottom, and Lille, who were almost bottom. The guy told me: "You're going to make up five points. You'll get six points and they'll only get one." I got my six points because I had a good team. PSG drew 0–0 with Martigues. The second match, Paris were drawing 0–0 against Lille when the Lille right-back [Patrick Collot] went up, mishit his cross and it went between Bernard Lama's elbow and the near post. It finished 1–0 and we'd gained our five points. The guy called me the following morning and asked me if I'd seen it. He asked me if we were going to draw up a contract, if I wanted to be champions. I said I wasn't keen to write anything down, so he said not to worry, that he was a medium and that he trusted me. So we negotiated and we agreed a deal. I went to see Hamel and [vice-president Gérard] Bourgoin and they told me I was mad. We won the cup [beating Nîmes 2–1 in the final] and needed to get the same result as Paris Saint-Germain or better on the penultimate day of the season. We went to Guingamp and got a draw and they did too, at Bordeaux I think, and we were champions. The guy called me and told me he'd come round in the morning and to prepare the cash. I put two envelopes in a crate of Chablis, which I kept in my cellar. My wife didn't know; no one knew. We came back late from Guingamp because we'd been celebrating the victory. We landed, did three victory laps of the airfield, then went to a nightclub and I went to bed at 5:30 a.m. The phone rang at 7 a.m. and it was him. I took the crate and went outside.

---

69 Blanc joined Auxerre from Saint-Étienne in 1995.

He didn't even open it. He put it on the bonnet. I remember the sun was coming up, it was seven o'clock. I said: "Do you want to count it?" He said: "No, it's all there." The following season, we drew Ajax, Glasgow Rangers and Grasshopper Zürich in the European Cup. He called me and said we would get to the quarter-finals. I said I wasn't going to pay the same price as last year and he agreed to make it cheaper. We finished top of our group. Then one day we stopped winning and it all stopped, but we didn't fall out over it. We did two full years.'

What did he look like?
'Like you. Like me. A suit, a car similar to mine – a [Peugeot] 305, nothing fancy. He was an estate agent. I knew who he was. He was from Bordeaux, he came to matches.'

Do you really think that he was in some way responsible for you winning the Double?
'Well. I asked some psychology professors and several of them said the same thing. They said that he didn't change anything in the team because the players knew nothing about it. But he changed something with *me* and because I had such a big influence over my guys, by puffing me up, he'd puffed up the team. And that's what the Guy Roux method was: inventing silly little things. It was like the thing with the yellow flowers [one of Roux's superstitions was that he always had to find a yellow flower on the morning of a game]. I would always look for yellow flowers, even in winter. And then there was the place where I parked for home games [Roux always had to park in the same space]. If there was already a car there, I would have it taken away and park there myself. It was the winning space.'

Of all the teams you coached at Auxerre, which one gave you the greatest pleasure?
'The '79 team. Which I think of as the [Serge] Mesonès team.[70] That team was a real living thing. And they were all on the left [in political terms]. We had political discussions together!'

---

70 Straggly-haired attacking midfielder Serge Mesonès captained the Auxerre team that reached the 1979 Coupe de France final while still playing in Division 2, losing 4–1 to Nantes after extra time. Auxerre were promoted to Division 1 a year later.

Which opponents posed you the biggest problems?

'The good ones! Obviously, the Germans, Borussia Dortmund. And the coach, what was his name? Ottmar Hitzfeld. There's a story! We played his Borussia Dortmund team in the UEFA Cup semi-finals [in April 1993] and the day before, I sent [assistant coach Dominique] Cuperly to spy on their training session. I told him to stay there until they'd all left. [Hitzfeld] went to the 18-yard line and, with a fork, dug a hole, put something in it and covered it up again. Cuperly phoned me straight away. I told him to go and look and he called me back and told me it was a little Virgin Mary statuette. I told him to take it, put it in an envelope and put it in a drawer. We lost anyway. I was sent by TF1 to Cantona's last European Cup game against Dortmund [in April 1997]. I took the envelope in my pocket. I was with a guy from TF1 for the pre-match build-up at the side of the pitch. I saw [Hitzfeld], waved at him and he came over. I asked if he spoke French and he said of course. I told him that the gardener had seen him bury something, had recovered it and I thought it would make him happy to have it back. I told him that honesty was the most important thing for us! I gave him the envelope and he opened it. The colour drained from his face.'

You were in contention to become France coach after the World Cup in 1998, but in the end, Roger Lemerre was chosen. Is that still a regret for you?

'No. Because I had thought about it a lot. The first time [in 1994], it was me that said no because I had my team and I was confident that we could be champions so I didn't get mixed up in all that. My main argument against it was that there were six or eight matches per year [with the national team] and the rest of the time . . . What do you do for the other 350 days? Secondly, if you're any good, you do it for four years, but what do you do after that? You wouldn't know how to be a club coach any more. The second time wasn't the same. It was '98. All the clubs wanted me to vanish from the league so they could gain a place in the table. And they were the ones singing in *L'Équipe*: "It has to be him, etc." I more or less agreed because I turned 60 in 1998 and I thought it was time. I would do two or four years, maybe more. But then the [Auxerre] president told me I had a contract that they had always respected with me and that I should respect it with them.

I wasn't happy, but I decided to leave it. I was annoyed though. I didn't do it on purpose, but I was gloomy all year and that was when we almost went down.'[71]

If you look back over your whole career as a coach, what are you most proud of?
'My resistance. My endurance.'

What role does football play in your life currently?
'It's part of my routine. And my work, because I'm a pundit. They're long days. We're on air at eight o'clock if the France team are playing at nine. There's a debate from eight to nine, we're on again at half-time and then there's a debrief after. So I really have to know what's happening. That's the job and I don't allow myself not to be up to date. But I don't throw myself into *L'Équipe* at the moment. Today, I read the headlines and I chose what I was going to read. Apart from that, I watch cycling. If I wasn't here with you, I would undoubtedly be watching a cycling race on TV. And not just the Tour [de France]. I watch the Dauphiné, everything. I know all the riders. I used to go bike racing myself.'

Which teams do you enjoy watching?
'In France, I like watching PSG, Rennes, Strasbourg, because I was born in Colmar and because they've been playing well. In Europe, I really like the finesse of Real Madrid. The coach they have [Carlo Ancelotti] gets so much out of his players. The little Brazilian winger, Vinícius Júnior, is pure pleasure. I enjoyed watching the German league during the pandemic, particularly Bayern Munich.'

I read somewhere that you're a fan of Jürgen Klopp's Liverpool?
'Yes. A big fan. When they're at full strength and in full flight, they're so quick. If you play possession for possession's sake, when you come up against a team who keep the ball for half the time that you do but who know how to play with three touches, you'll be done for.'

---

71 Auxerre finished 14th in Division 1 in the 1998–99 season, which was the first time they had finished outside the top 10 since 1982.

Roux is approached by several passers-by over the course of our conversation – some of whom he knows, many of whom he does not; some just wanting selfies, one requesting assistance with some kind of rental dispute – and he is unfailingly polite and chatty with them all. Belying his reputation for stinginess, he leaves the table at the end of our meal and goes inside to settle the bill before I have an opportunity to protest. As nearby bars begin pumping out loud pop music in preparation for that night's Fête de la Musique, France's annual day of musical celebration, we walk back to his car and return to the railway station, Roux pointing out sights of historical interest as he navigates the town's narrow medieval streets.

Local nostalgia for the Roux era is only exacerbated a year later when Auxerre, now under Chinese ownership, drop back into Ligue 2 after a single season among the elite. Things were much less fraught when Roux was in charge: during his 44 years at the helm, Auxerre were not relegated once.

11

ANGLETERRE

THE SOUND AND THE FURY

'Guys flying into each other and not saying a word. Paul Ince,
I swear I chopped him in half. He doesn't say a *word*. In France
they'd have been crying.'

Olivier Dacourt

Snow pellets are hammering down on to the pavement and pinging off the
bonnets of the cars that line the quiet suburban street, a short drive from
Newcastle city centre, that Allan Saint-Maximin calls home. The thermometer
shows 2°C, the 'feels like' temperature is -3°C and the weather forecast on BBC
Radio Newcastle warns of more snow to come. The Côte d'Azur, where Saint-
Maximin lived prior to his 2019 transfer from Nice to Newcastle United, feels a
long way away. But although the twinkle-toed winger admits that it took him a
little while to adapt to the local climate after he swapped the French Riviera for
England's northeast, when he talks about Newcastle – the club and the city – and
his relationship with the local people, his words are full of warmth.

Comfortably dressed in a white hoodie and yellow tracksuit bottoms, he is in
a relaxed mood, playfully scooping up his two young daughters, Lyana and
Ninhia, as he sits at a table in the corner of his living room in the modest
apartment, located in an anonymous late-Victorian terrace, that he shares with
his partner and three children. Casting his mind back to his Newcastle debut
(which coincidentally took place in a friendly against his formative club, Saint-
Étienne), he recalls being struck by the affection he received from the moment
he set foot on the St James' Park grass. 'The fans gave me love from my first very

touch of the ball here,' he says. 'And I will always be grateful to them for that. I have a very special relationship with Newcastle. I've never had such a relationship at all the clubs I've been to.'

Saint-Maximin quickly threw himself into Newcastle life, visiting the city's West End food bank a few weeks after signing and delighting supporters with playful interactions on social media. Multiple displays of generosity – from donating care packages to local NHS workers to treating young fans to a toy shop shopping spree – only took him deeper into the hearts of the community. On the pitch, his crowd-pleasing displays on Newcastle's left flank immediately made him a terrace favourite (although not every member of the Toon Army went as far as the travelling fan who reacted to Saint-Maximin's extra-time winner at Oxford United in the FA Cup in February 2020 by unzipping his trousers and 'doing the helicopter' with his penis).

Saint-Maximin was the latest in a long line of French footballers drawn to England by the allure of its relentless, attack-minded football, its historic sporting culture and its raucous, teeming stadiums. He was, more specifically, walking a path previously trodden by a particular type of French footballer: the mercurial attacking star, the misunderstood maverick, the talented but temperamental showman. Starting with Éric Cantona in 1992, the Premier League has proven fertile terrain for a succession of French forwards seeking to rehabilitate tarnished reputations or simply hoping to unlock untapped potential. At Newcastle alone, David Ginola, Laurent Robert, Hatem Ben Arfa and Saint-Maximin all arrived from France carrying various forms of baggage and all departed having secured cult hero status, even if only momentarily, among the Geordie faithful.

Saint-Maximin's extraordinary ability was apparent from childhood, word of his virtuoso dribbling spreading rapidly through the community of scouts who monitored the amateur youth leagues in the southern Paris suburbs where he cut his footballing teeth. His early years in the professional game – Saint-Étienne, Monaco, Hannover (loan), Bastia (loan), Nice – were characterised by sporadic flashes of brilliance, but there was always a feeling that he was not fully exploiting his gifts. Moving to Newcastle brought him the adoration and, in his eyes, the acceptance that he had always craved and via stand-out performances against the likes of Liverpool, Manchester City and Manchester United, he showed that, on his day, he could mix it with the very best. 'For me, my qualities are more recognised in England than in France,' he says. 'In France, and I never understood why, my way of playing seemed to disturb people or annoy people, because they don't have the same way of seeing football. Whereas in England, when I dribble, they immediately understood that there's a point to it. The fans saw that I was there to punch holes and to create space for my teammates and they also saw that it worked. I feel the expectation when I receive the ball and I love it. But my style of play has evolved too, which is why I don't even blame the French [for their criticism]. I'm nothing like the player I was in France. I'm much stronger and more complete than before. I felt like I was starting to stagnate in the French championship. I was getting complacent and I needed to be competing against the best players. Here you're up against Liverpool, Manchester City, Manchester United, Arsenal, Chelsea . . . I needed to face that and it's made me a better player.'

I met Saint-Maximin in March 2023, two weeks after Newcastle's 2–0 loss to Manchester United in the League Cup final and two months before Eddie Howe's side qualified for the Champions League for the first time in 20 years. Saint-Maximin had left for Saudi Arabia by the time the Champions League hymn reverberated around St James' Park, but like so many French players before him, his time in England left a mark. 'Newcastle is home now,' he wrote in a heartfelt Instagram post announcing his departure. 'Once a Geordie, always a Geordie.'

'We have a substitution for Manchester United,' says the stadium announcer. 'Will you welcome number 12, Éric Cantona!'

Down on the touchline, wearing a short-sleeved number 12 jersey, a gum-chewing Éric Cantona trots on to the sodden pitch in place of Ryan Giggs, drawing a roar from the crowd. Manchester United are 1–0 up against Manchester City at half-time on a rainy December afternoon at Old Trafford and a debut that, unbeknown to anyone, will simultaneously revitalise United and revolutionise English football is under way. There are glimpses both of Cantona's talent – delicate touches, a perfectly flighted cross that Mark Hughes heads over the bar – and his temperament, as he angrily dismisses Steve McMahon's offer of a conciliatory handshake after being clattered from behind and remonstrates with Hughes for not playing him through in stoppage time. United win 2–1 and chants of 'Ooh, aah Cantona!' are already booming around the ground.

The circumstances of Cantona's 1992 move to Old Trafford have long been part of Premier League folklore: the call from Leeds United managing director Bill Fotherby to Martin Edwards, the Manchester United chairman, enquiring about the availability of left-back Denis Irwin; United manager Alex Ferguson sliding Edwards a note telling him to ask about Cantona; the bargain £1 million transfer fee, officially announced as £1.2 million in a fragile bid to assuage the Leeds fans' ire; a shy, tracksuit-clad Cantona being paraded on the Old Trafford pitch, holding up a red United jersey, smiling for the cameras and changing the English game forever.

He had only joined Leeds the previous February, after an unsuccessful trial at Sheffield Wednesday, having finally run out of road in France after one outburst too many.[72] A storm seeking a port, Cantona immediately found English football to his liking – the ball arrived more quickly, the football was 'much more physical but a lot less vicious', the fans were affectionate but respectful – and he was an instant hit, scoring three goals in 15 appearances (nine of which came from the bench) as Howard Wilkinson's team claimed the last championship crown of the pre-Premier League era. Ferguson's interest in the Frenchman was piqued after his centre-backs Steve Bruce and Gary Pallister recounted the difficulty they had had containing him while relaxing in the changing-room bath after a 2–0 win over Leeds in September 1992. 'The gaffer came in and started chatting to me and Brucey about him, asking what we thought about him, what type of player he was,' Pallister says. 'I think we were quite positive. He was 6'2", strong, had a bit of guile about him. When he came to us, there were a lot of big personalities in that dressing room, but he was like: "Yeah, here I am. I'm not afraid of this. This is where I want to be. This is my stage." And it became apparent quite quickly that he had the ability to go with that.'

---

72 France coach Michel Platini mandated his Anglophone assistant Gérard Houllier to help find Cantona a club in England in December 1991. After being suspended for four games for throwing the ball at the referee while playing for Nîmes against Saint-Étienne, he had responded by announcing his retirement.

United had not won the league since 1967 – the days of George Best, Bobby Charlton and Denis Law. They had led the way for much of the previous season, only to falter at the last, losing three of their final four games. But the team's attacking configuration was perfectly set up for Cantona – battle-hardened strike partner Hughes laying the ball off to him, jet-heeled wingers Giggs, Lee Sharpe and Andrei Kanchelskis already flying down the flanks in anticipation of a pass – and with his swagger, his audacious creativity and his dead-eyed finishing, he took them to the next level. After opening his United account at Chelsea, Cantona scored in four consecutive league games over the festive period and provided an early demonstration of his genius with an exquisite outside-of-the-foot pass to tee up Irwin for the second goal in a 4–1 home win over Tottenham Hotspur (commentator John Motson purring: 'This man is playing a game of his own!'). He did not defend very much, if at all, but it was part of the deal. 'We didn't mind doing that little bit extra so that Éric could be there and ready when we were in possession,' explains Pallister. United ended their 26-year wait for championship glory in 1993 and then went one better in 1994, successfully defending the title and beating Chelsea 4–0 in the FA Cup final at a rain-soaked Wembley (Cantona outfoxing Dmitri Kharine with two carbon-copy penalties) to complete the Double.

Advised by Gérard Houllier and Guy Roux, both of whom had worked with Cantona in France, that United's new goalscorer would need to be handled with care, Ferguson made a point of checking in with him in informal daily chats. He allowed him to observe his own warm-up routine and turned a blind eye when the Frenchman occasionally stepped out of line. Trusted by his manager and inspired by the grandeur of his surroundings, Cantona responded by breathing belief into every corner of the club. He strutted around Old Trafford 'as if he fucking owned the place', to quote Roy Keane, and United's fans loved him, loved the moments of magic he produced, loved the way he played with his chest out and his collar up, loved every disdainful gesture of frustration, every lofty pronouncement about the pitch being his canvas. Transposed to England, French football's troubled prince became 'King Eric'.

Away from the spotlight, Cantona lived a quiet, determinedly ordinary existence. After initially lodging in Manchester West Novotel at Worsley Brow, he moved into a semi-detached three-bedroom house in the suburban village of Boothstown with his then wife, Isabelle, and son, Raphaël. For all the enigmatic public proclamations about art and poetry and philosophy, his teammates found that he loved nothing better than a good session at one of the South Manchester pubs that the squad used to frequent. 'He became one of the boys pretty rapidly,' says Sharpe. 'Loved the beer, loved the chat, loved being one of the lads. Once Éric had shown what a superstar he was, we knew he'd get a lot of attention, so we'd always sit him in the furthest part of the group so people couldn't get close to him. I think he liked that safety net around him. But he also liked just sitting there chewing the fat over a few beers with the boys.'

For all the adulation, Cantona remained a hothead. The three red cards he received in the 1993–94 season made it clear to his opponents that he had a short temper and at Selhurst Park in January 1995, his fuse blew in jaw-dropping fashion. After being sent off for kicking out at Crystal Palace's Richard Shaw, Cantona was being escorted down the touchline by United kitman Norman Davies when he responded to a volley of abuse from a 20-year-old supporter called Matthew Simmons by launching a kung-fu kick and a volley of punches at him. The British press were outraged, the Football Association banned him for eight months and it took a desperate cloak-and-dagger dash to Paris by Ferguson the following summer to convince him not to leave the club. Ever the showman, Cantona used a press conference that followed his successful appeal against a two-week prison sentence for assault over the incident to utter his immortal line: 'When the seagulls follow the trawler, it is because they think sardines will be thrown into the sea.' In his absence, United narrowly missed out on another Double, finishing second behind Blackburn Rovers in the league and losing 1–0 to Everton in the FA Cup final.

Cantona's comeback match against Liverpool in October 1995 was pure footballing box office and he lived up to his billing, teeing up Nicky Butt for an early opener in the autumn sunshine and then rescuing a 2–2 draw with a characteristically unerring second-half penalty. Returning to spearhead a fresh-faced team in which youth-team graduates Butt, Gary and Phil Neville, Paul Scholes and David Beckham were all being given their heads, Cantona propelled United to the title with a decisive run of goalscoring form in the spring and then settled the FA Cup final against Liverpool with a late, awkward, technically impeccable strike to deliver a second Double in three years. After claiming a fourth league title with United as captain in the 1996–97 season (a campaign that featured his famous chipped goal and imperial celebration against Sunderland), he abruptly called time on his football career at the age of 30. Although he failed to reproduce his domestic performances in European competition, Cantona bowed out having provided the impetus for United's dominance of the Premier League in the Ferguson era, sprinkling Old Trafford with stardust and inspiring the next generation of players with his professionalism and perfectionism on the training pitch. Ferguson called him 'the perfect player, in the perfect club, at the perfect moment'. England would never look at French footballers in the same way again.

Cantona's ban over his Selhurst Park meltdown left the stage clear for another extravagantly gifted Frenchman to set English hearts aflutter. David Ginola joined Kevin Keegan's upwardly mobile Newcastle in a £2.5 million switch from Paris Saint-Germain in the summer of 1995 and with his model's cheekbones, luxurious brown hair and dashing wing play (not to mention his penchant for a post-match ciggie), he satisfied every British preconception of what a French footballer should look like. Ginola had become a pariah in France over his unwitting role in the national team's failure to qualify for the 1994 World Cup,[73] but had blocked out the boos and jeers to win the Division 1 title with PSG the same season, for which his peers elected him France's Player of the Year. He seized the limelight immediately in England, opening his Newcastle account with a powerful effort in his third appearance away at Sheffield Wednesday and being voted the Premier League's Player of the Month. Quick, strong and bewitchingly two-footed, Ginola became an integral member of Keegan's 'Entertainers', the buccaneering Newcastle team that streaked 12 points clear at the top of the table in January 1996, only to be reeled in by a Cantona-inspired Manchester United. Ginola took Keegan's

---

73 Ginola's overhit cross in a November 1993 qualifying match at the Parc des Princes led to Bulgaria scoring a 90th-minute winner that took them to the World Cup at France's expense.

departure midway through the following season as a betrayal ('I felt like I'd been stabbed in the back,' he later said) and after falling foul of incoming manager Kenny Dalglish, he left for Tottenham, where in 1999 he won the League Cup and was named Player of the Year by both the Football Writers' Association and the Professional Footballers' Association.

England had traditionally struggled to accommodate free-spirited footballers – Rodney Marsh, Tony Currie, Alan Hudson, Glenn Hoddle, Paul Gascoigne – but as the English game became more cosmopolitan following the launch of the Premier League (a process expedited by the Bosman ruling of 1995), it found that it was more willing to make room for such players when they came from overseas. Cantona and Ginola put French footballers in the vanguard of that evolution and although both attracted criticism – the former for his disciplinary record, the latter facing accusations of diving – they were indulged and celebrated in a manner that must have drawn envious looks from the homegrown mavericks who had preceded them; nonconformist players were clearly less problematic when their curlicued edges did not have to be wedged into the rigidly square grooves of the England team. Likewise, British fans found it easier to ostentatiously worship foreign (and specifically French) footballers than players who had grown up around the corner. Manchester United fans called Cantona 'God'; Newcastle supporters threw themselves at Ginola's feet. It was a new kind of idolatry – effusive, emotional and knowingly overblown, the football equivalent of a holidaymaker's declaration of love to a foreign barmaid – and it helped to turn Cantona and Ginola into household names.

The French footballers who crossed the Channel in the 1990s encountered the Premier League in the early throes of the transformation that would turn it into the world's biggest national championship. Television money had started to pour in, there was an American-style razzmatazz to Sky's coverage and squads were becoming more diverse, but facilities remained basic, pitches were often poor and the players' diets had not evolved in decades. Olivier Dacourt joined Everton from Strasbourg in 1998 and was taken aback when he saw what was slopped on to his plate in the canteen at the club's Bellefield training base. '*Beans!*' he blurts out (in English) over lunch at a busy Parisian café. 'Potatoes, baked beans, things like that. The food was difficult for me at the start. I had to re-learn how to eat!' French players relished not having to spend the night before games at a hotel, which was common practice in France, but English changing rooms were full of surprises. 'The approach to matches in France was very different,' recalls Gilles Grimandi, who signed for Arsenal in 1997. 'No one spoke in the dressing room, no music, everyone's waiting, you feel the pressure. You turn up there [in England] and Ian Wright's dancing on the table in his undies. If you did that in France you'd be banned from the club! But then you go into the tunnel and the faces change. And on the pitch, Wright was exceptional.'

Once across the touchline, French players discovered a style of football that was quicker, more physical and more direct than anything they had experienced before. For some, it came as a rude awakening. Marcel Desailly, who joined Chelsea from AC Milan in 1998, confessed that he made for a 'sorry sight' in his early days at Stamford Bridge as he struggled to get to grips with the pace and intensity of the English game, which he likened to 'trench warfare'. His France teammate Robert Pirès left Marseille for Arsenal in 2000 and watched on in horror from the sidelines after being named on the bench for his new team's opening league fixture at the Stadium of Light. 'I'll always remember my first match, at Sunderland,' Pirès says. 'It was 2000, I'd just become a European champion with France, I'd got the wind in my sails. The day of the game, Arsène Wenger calls me over and says: "I've decided to put you on the bench. I want you to sit on the bench and see what it's like in England." "OK, sure, no problem." After 20 minutes, I said: "This isn't going to be for me. This isn't a football that I know." Twenty minutes, I swear. Pat Vieira had already been on the receiving end of two tackles and *oh la la la la*! I've never said this, but I even regretted having signed for Arsenal. I wasn't ready for the physical combat. It took me six or seven months to adapt.' The welcome he got from the terraces was no less robust. 'The supporters were very close to the pitch, so I heard all the insults,' Pirès says. What kind of thing did rival fans say, I wonder. 'You really want me to tell you?' he asks. 'Most of the time it was [and here, he breaks into very deliberate English]: "*You are a French cunt*." Ha ha ha! I didn't know if that word was important, but I heard it quite a lot!'

Fighting for a foothold amid the unrelenting hustle and bustle of the English top flight, many French players struggled to establish where the line was in disciplinary terms, picking up more yellow cards than they had been accustomed to despite feeling that they were merely giving as good as they got. But for the players who already had a physical side to their game, the Premier League proved a perfect fit. 'In England, there's a recognition for the work you do, whatever position you play in,' said former Arsenal midfielder Patrick Vieira. 'You don't have that in other countries, where it's rare to have a defender or a defensive midfielder who is as fêted and loved as a striker.'

Dacourt got a taste of English-style midfield combat when his Strasbourg side came up against Paul Ince's Liverpool in the UEFA Cup in October 1997 and it convinced him that the Premier League was where he needed to be. 'I liked Paul Ince a lot, but he wanted only one thing and that was to kill,' grins Dacourt, who also went on to play for Leeds. 'Well, I put some tackles in . . . I cut my eyebrow, I had blood in my mouth. But I loved that match! Guys flying into each other and not saying a word. Paul Ince, I swear I chopped him in half. He doesn't say a *word*. In France they'd have been crying. What was good was that as soon as you started playing and you showed that you could look after yourself, no one would touch you.'

From a tactical perspective, French players helped to bring greater sophistication to the English game. Cantona's success with Manchester United ushered in a new trend for foreign players in the withdrawn striker role (Dennis Bergkamp at Arsenal, Gianfranco Zola at Chelsea and Juninho at Middlesbrough being the most notable examples). Wingers like Ginola and Pirès, who were predominantly right-footed but played on the left, prefigured the rise in wide players being deployed on the opposite flank to their stronger foot. Claude Makélélé proved so effective at the base of midfield in the 4-3-3 system introduced at Chelsea by José Mourinho that it became known as 'the Makélélé role'.

French players showed their British teammates how to stretch properly, how to eat better, how to hone technique. In return, they acquired qualities that would help to take the French national team into a new dimension. While analysis of France's success at the 1998 World Cup has tended to focus on the influence of the players who played in Italy, Emmanuel Petit – who joined Arsenal a year before the tournament – feels that the experience acquired by the squad's 'English' contingent played an important role as well. 'A lot of us also played in England, and in England it was an open style of football, much less focused on tactics than the Italian *catenaccio*, where you score a goal, then shut up shop,' he says. 'We had players who had that culture, starting with Didier Deschamps. But he was surrounded by players who loved to play spectacular football and who could bring that *folie* (madness) that we needed in certain games. Imagine if we'd only had players with the Italian mentality. I'm not sure we would have won the World Cup.'

England's stadiums – boisterous and full, nestled in the hearts of their local communities, their stands set tight against the edges of the pitch – delighted the French players that discovered them. There was a thrilling fervour to the baying English crowds, a visceral quality not often found in France, which stiffened the sinews and heightened the senses. But there was also respect: for tradition, for the game, for players simply putting in an honest shift. 'To play here is an extraordinary privilege,' said Thierry Henry. 'Even when you miss something, when you lose the ball, people don't boo, people clap. And that's what I love: people are aware that you've given everything you had in your guts.' There is also widespread reverence, among the Frenchmen who have played in England, for the way the English game honours its past, be it the statues erected outside stadiums in honour of former players or the dignified solemnity of the annual Remembrance Day commemorations. It is all, as the French love to say, *so British*.

And then there were the songs. French football fans tend not to go in for chants dedicated to specific players, but in the English game it is part of the landscape. Manchester United supporters worked Cantona's name into a variety of melodies, many of which still reverberate around Old Trafford today. At Newcastle, they sang Ginola's praises to the tune of 'Lola' by The Kinks. Chelsea fans celebrated one of their French centre-backs by singing: 'He's here, he's there, he's every-fucking-where, Frank Lebœuf! Frank Lebœuf!' Same tune, different theme for the chant with which Arsenal's fans serenaded Petit: 'He's blond, he's quick, his name's a porno flick, Emmanuel! Emmanuel!' The songs were irreverent and silly, their creators unlikely to wind up on any Ivor Novello shortlists, but for the French players in whose honour they were sung, they represented something powerful. 'It's a bit like the Holy Grail for a player to have a song invented for him by his own fans,' says Petit. 'It means that there's a love attached to it, that they really appreciate what you do, both as a player and as an individual. The ultimate goal for a player is to win a place in people's hearts. So for me, having a song is the ultimate show of appreciation. And we still don't have it in France.' Yet if English fans were noisier than their French counterparts inside the stadium, they were quieter away from the ground. 'What touches me the most with these British supporters is that, when we lose a match, they wait for us beside our cars smiling, to tell us that it doesn't matter,' said Lebœuf. 'Some even walk away crying. When I see such reactions for the first time, I can't believe my eyes. It's really moving to meet people who are so passionate about their team. And a huge contrast with French fans, who, even though you shouldn't generalise, are more likely to call you a "fucker" or smash up your car!'

English food, inevitably, took some getting used to. As did the weather. Ginola had initially hoped to join Johan Cruyff's Barcelona when he left PSG and after arriving in Newcastle, he was soon pining for the cultural distractions that he had left behind in the French capital. 'Newcastle is not Paris,' he wrote in his autobiography *Le Magnifique*. 'In Paris, there are so many things to occupy your time after training. There are all the museums, shops and parks, whereas in Newcastle it used to be a case of: "What am I going to do now?" We used to take a drive and perhaps go to the seaside, but it was not the same.' Like so many French visitors before them, well versed in the pleasures of a few quiet glasses of wine over dinner, France's footballing expats were shocked by British attitudes towards alcohol consumption – or what Desailly described as 'the systematic pursuit of drunkenness'. There was consternation, too, over the stark contrast between the respect shown for the private lives of public figures in France and the insatiable appetite for tawdry gossip of Britain's tabloid press.

But there was nevertheless much to appreciate about living in Britain. Arsenal's players relished the anonymity of big city life in London, establishing an informal clubhouse at a bistro called Base on Hampstead High Street.

Grimandi became familiar with his local bus routes, zigzagging across north London on the 139 and the 189. Pirès regularly made a beeline for Selfridge's on Oxford Street. Vieira got into the habit of reading the Sunday papers. Lebœuf got into the habit of *writing* the papers (or at least, a fortnightly column in *The Times*). Ginola advertised L'Oréal shampoo, was invited to open the Notting Hill Carnival and performed on *Stars in their Eyes* as French crooner Sacha Distel. Petit made a cameo appearance (as himself) in *The Bill*. Henry's Renault Clio car adverts, with their confident Gallic suggestiveness and playfully enigmatic 'Va-va-voom' catchphrase, further embedded France's footballers within the cultural fabric of their adopted home country.

For the black and mixed-race players who came to London, the feeling of freedom was doubly resonant. 'Here, contrary to Milan, I don't have the feeling that I'm a rare specimen, primarily accepted because I kick a ball around,' Desailly wrote in his autobiography. 'In restaurants, pubs, nightclubs, I see other black people who aren't just other football players or basketball players. Nobody, in the English capital, is surprised to see a black person driving a nice car. Nobody is surprised either to see black people presenting the TV news or appearing in an advert.' In Desailly's eyes, the contrast between attitudes towards race in France and Britain was embodied by a surprising figure: British celebrity chef Ainsley Harriott. 'Would we accept, in our country, a big cooking programme presented by a chef "of colour"?' Desailly asked. 'I doubt it. Here, that chef exists – and he's a star!'

An unwelcome airport encounter in March 1999 brought home to Gérard Houllier the distance he would need to travel if he was to succeed in restoring Liverpool to former glories. Confronted by a two-week gap in the team's schedule, he decided to take his squad to Le Touquet in northern France for a training camp. On arrival at Manchester Airport, the Liverpool delegation bumped into a group of Manchester United fans who were en route to Milan for the second leg of their team's Champions League quarter-final against Internazionale. Their mockery was not slow in coming. United's 1–1 draw at San Siro kept them on course for a historic Treble of Premier League, FA Cup and Champions League trophies. On the same night, Liverpool lost 2–1 in a friendly against French fourth-tier side Boulogne-sur-Mer. They were gloomy days for Liverpool fans, memories of the glory years of the 1970s and 80s fading a little further with every season. But only two years later, they would be celebrating a trophy triple of their own.

A former English teacher and avowed Anglophile, Houllier made his name as an amateur coach in his native northern France before leading Paris Saint-Germain to the club's first league title in 1986. He then spent 10 years attached to the French Football Federation's National Technical Directorate, working as assistant to national coach Michel Platini, presiding over France's catastrophic failure to qualify for the 1994 World Cup as head coach and then assisting Aimé Jacquet during the host nation's triumph at the 1998 tournament. He was on the verge of taking charge at Sheffield Wednesday in the summer of 1998, but when Liverpool chief executive Peter Robinson intervened at the 11th hour, Houllier did not take much convincing to change course. He already had a strong connection to the city, having lived there for a year between 1969 and 1970, teaching part-time at Alsop High School and working on his master's thesis, 'Growing Up in a Deprived Area', which documented the lives of children living in Toxteth. He was appointed by Liverpool in July 1998, initially as joint-manager alongside Roy Evans and then, from November 1998 onwards, in sole charge.

Liverpool had finished third in the Premier League in the 1997–98 season and boasted England internationals such as Robbie Fowler, Steve McManaman and boy wonder Michael Owen, but Houllier was dismayed by the lack of professionalism he encountered. He immediately banned the use of mobile phones at the club's Melwood training base, got to grips with the squad's drinking culture (having been 'flabbergasted' by the sight of players throwing up in training after a night on the tiles) and made an early power play by sanctioning the departure of strong-willed captain (and self-styled 'Guv'nor') Ince. Houllier gave his players meticulously detailed feedback on their performances, gleaned from his own video analysis of the team's matches, and brought new intensity to a training regime that fidelity to the club's Boot Room traditions[74] had turned stale. 'Liverpool had probably been doing the same training sessions for 20 or 30 years because, you know, if it ain't broke, don't fix it. But it was getting to the stage where it *was* "broke" and Liverpool needed to change,' says Jamie Carragher, who had broken into the first-team squad the season before Houllier's arrival. 'The eye-opener was the standards he demanded in training: everyone had to be 100 per cent. The British view was: "As long as we play well on Saturday, that's all that matters." But Gérard Houllier knew that how you trained impacted your performance.'

Schooled in developing young talent from his time as coach of France's Under-18s, where he had worked with players including Henry, David Trezeguet and Nicolas Anelka, Houllier paid special attention to Carragher and his fellow academy graduate Steven Gerrard. Houllier taught Gerrard about the importance of off-pitch preparation, arranged for him to receive treatment for recurrent back problems from France team osteopath Philippe Boixel and fielded him in different positions – wide midfield, right-back – in a bid to 'widen his range'. Gerrard later said that Houllier had been 'as good as a father to me'.

The Frenchman's early signings all hit the mark. Sami Hyypiä, Stéphane Henchoz and Dietmar Hamann gave Liverpool the meanest defence in the Premier League, while veteran Scottish midfielder Gary McAllister brought guile to midfield and professionalism to the changing room. The team reached a memorable peak in the 2000–01 season when they defeated Birmingham City on penalties in the League Cup final, came from behind to beat Arsenal 2–1 in the FA Cup final courtesy of a late Owen brace and then, having eliminated Roma, Porto and Barcelona along the way, edged Alavés 5–4 in extra time of an extraordinary UEFA Cup final in Dortmund to claim a first European honour in 17 years. Houllier, who died in 2020, was renowned for his creative oratory and his team talk before the UEFA Cup final focused on the trophy itself: its distinctive vase shape, the eight stylised footballers ringing its base, its 15kg weight, which made it the heaviest of all UEFA's silverware. Subsequent successes

---

74 Used as an informal meeting place where the club's coaches could exchange ideas, the Anfield boot room was credited with shaping the methodologies of Liverpool managers Bill Shankly, Bob Paisley, Joe Fagan, Kenny Dalglish and Roy Evans.

in the Charity Shield and UEFA Super Cup allowed his players to develop their trophy expertise even further.

Fate struck a cruel blow in October 2001 when Houllier suffered a heart attack at half-time of a league game against Leeds, which kept him on the sidelines for five months. Blighted by his poor recruitment, Liverpool failed to build on the promise of their historic 2000–01 campaign and he departed in 2004, but within a year, they had become European champions under Rafael Benítez. 'He was a massive part of that,' says Carragher, who went on to make 737 appearances for the club. 'A lot of the players on the pitch [in the 2005 Champions League final], he brought to the club. Then you think of the role he played in my development and Steven Gerrard's development, the way we looked after ourselves, compared to the way we were when he first came in. He made huge changes – more than people on the outside realise. He put Liverpool back on the map.'

From Old Trafford to Anfield, via St James' Park, Stamford Bridge and Goodison Park, very few Premier League stadiums have not been lit up at one time or another by a footballer from the other side of the Channel. But there is one English club in particular where French football succeeded in burrowing its way right into the very foundations.

12

ARSENAL

A VERY ENGLISH FRENCHMAN

'I had a shock, an emotional shock. I realise: "Now I know why football was created here, in this country." I said to myself: "If I ever get an opportunity to work here, I want to take it."'

Arsène Wenger

It has been 15 years since Robert Pirès last set foot on the pitch at Highbury, but he remembers his old match-day routine as clearly as if it was yesterday.

'The bus would arrive on Avenell Road,' he tells me over lunch at an upmarket Paris hotel. 'We'd get off, nice and relaxed. Always the same routine: I'd be at the back of the bus and I'd be one of the last to get off. We'd climb the little steps, which are still there, and then turn right towards the changing room. You went past the visitors' changing room first, because ours was at the end of the corridor. Into the changing room and the first place on the right was mine, next to Dennis Bergkamp. We always had the same places and everything would be laid out ready. The music would be on full blast – Martin Keown would be doing a moonwalk to Michael Jackson or something. You'd feel the atmosphere, growing and growing, you'd hear the chants. And at Highbury, we felt unbeatable.'

If English stadiums represented the ultimate in football authenticity for the Premier League's first wave of French expatriates, then Highbury, with its marble halls, its magnificent Art Deco facade and its characterful 1930s stylings, was on another level altogether. 'You could smell the history,' says Gilles Grimandi, who played there between 1997 and 2002. Rémi Garde and Patrick Vieira signed for Arsenal on the same day in August 1996 and were immediately made aware that

130

in this particular corner of north London, decorum was all important. 'We took a taxi to Highbury to sign our contracts,' remembers Garde. 'We were due to sign them in [Arsenal chairman] Peter Hill-Wood's office and when we got out of the taxi, someone said: "You can't go in like that, not dressed like that. You need ties!" So we went to the club shop and bought new ties – I had to tie Pat's for him because he was only 20 and didn't know how to do it. That's what changed when you entered Highbury, with the bust [of former manager Herbert Chapman] in the lobby, then going up that majestic staircase . . . You felt the soul of the place, the sense of tradition and power. It struck me.'

This very English stadium would provide the setting for the rise to glory of a very French football team, coached by a visionary French manager, Arsène Wenger, and built around a collection of supremely talented French players – Pirès, Vieira, Emmanuel Petit, Thierry Henry, Sylvain Wiltord – who would lay waste to the Premier League with a level of style and panache that the English game had rarely seen. The club's departure from Highbury in 2006 broke the spell and broke Wenger's heart, but for a few golden years around the turn of the millennium, the entire footballing world was enraptured by an English team with a distinctly Gallic soul.

—————

England and English football were already reaching out to Wenger during his childhood. As a boy growing up in the 1950s in the Alsatian village of Duttlenheim, 10 miles southwest of Strasbourg, he was captivated by black-and-white broadcasts of the FA Cup final, which stuck in his mind as 'the definitive image of football'. Convinced that a command of English would serve him well in later life, he spent three weeks learning the language in Cambridge one summer when he was 29 and dutifully continued to read in English when he returned to France. In the early 1980s, a trip to Anfield with Gérard Houllier to watch a game between Liverpool and Manchester United brought decisive confirmation of the English game's allure. 'While I was watching, I thought: "It's so different here,"' Wenger told *FourFourTwo* magazine in 2020. 'I had a shock, an emotional shock. I realise: "Now I know why football was created here, in this country." I said to myself: "If I ever get an opportunity to work here, I want to take it.'"

By the time he was appointed by Arsenal in 1996 as the successor to Bruce Rioch, Wenger was in possession of a fully formed football philosophy. During his time as a player at Mulhouse, he had played under Paul Frantz, whose pioneering approach to isometrics (resistance exercises designed to build muscle strength) and nutrition had a profound influence on him. At Strasbourg, where he combined a peripheral role in the first team with youth coaching responsibilities, he got a first taste of working with young players. His first head coach role, at Nancy, introduced him to the art of managing a squad on a tight budget and enabled him to put his ideas about holistic player management (encompassing nutrition, sleep, physical preparation and psychological well-being) into practice. Monaco exposed him to the demands of an elite-level club, brought him into contact with British players for the first time, in the form of Glenn Hoddle and Mark Hateley, and yielded the first trophies of his coaching career.[75] The 18 months he spent in Japan with Nagoya Grampus Eight allowed him to discover a new culture, gave the wounds from his battles with Bernard Tapie's scandal-scarred Marseille team time to heal and, critically, helped him to develop the calmness that immediately set him apart amid the blood and thunder of the English top flight. 'Japan changed Arsène,' says Damien Comolli, who worked under Wenger as a youth coach at Monaco and Nagoya and then followed him to Arsenal as a scout. 'Japan changed his management style from black to white, from A to Z. And from a man-management perspective, he took to Arsenal a lot more of the Japanese Arsène than the French Arsène. I remember, we'd signed [Nwankwo] Kanu from Inter [in 1999]. A few weeks later I was at London Colney [the Arsenal training centre] and he was not doing any stretching. Arsène said: "You have to stretch." He was not stretching. And I'm looking at Arsène, I'm looking at Kanu. I'm looking at Arsène, I'm looking at Kanu. I'm thinking: "He's going to kill him." He didn't say anything. And after training, I said: "Arsène, the Arsène of Monaco would have destroyed Kanu." He said: "Pfff, for

75 Wenger won the French league title with Monaco in 1987–88 and the Coupe de France in 1990–91.

what?" And that change happened in Japan. He became a different person and a different manager in Japan.' Wenger's Nagoya stint also marked the beginning of his collaboration with Bosnian coach Boro Primorac, who worked as his assistant throughout his time at Arsenal, as well as his habit of wearing a suit on matchdays.

Wenger had first met David Dein, the Arsenal vice-chairman, in January 1989. Passing through London, Wenger decided to take in a game at Highbury between Arsenal and Tottenham Hotspur and got chatting to Dein, who invited his new acquaintance to join him and his wife, Barbara, for dinner at a friend's house (the evening ending with a game of charades in which Wenger acted out *A Midsummer Night's Dream*). The pair kept in touch over the years that followed – communicating by fax during Wenger's time in Japan – and Dein, who speaks fluent French, became convinced that with names so similar, Arsène and Arsenal had to be destined for one another. The move nearly happened in 1995 after George Graham was sacked as Arsenal manager for receiving an illegal payment from an agent, only for the club's directors, concerned as to whether a foreign manager would be able to handle some of the big personalities in the changing room, to get cold feet.[76] But a year later, and despite well-known figures such as Johan Cruyff and Terry Venables being touted as frontrunners for the post, they did turn to Wenger, who was presented to the media on the Highbury turf on an overcast Sunday afternoon in September 1996. Moving to England gave Wenger a stake in the game that had fired his imagination as a child. Arsenal, a club of traditions and propriety, corresponded to his personal sense of elegance and class. And being appointed as an English-style manager, as opposed to a French-style coach, meant that he would have an opportunity to refashion an entire club in his own image. Which, over the 22 years that followed, is precisely what he did.

---

76 At the time, Slovakian Jozef Venglos̆ (Aston Villa, 1990–91) and Argentinian Ossie Ardiles (Tottenham, 1993–94) were the only managers born outside the United Kingdom and the Republic of Ireland to have taken charge of an English top-flight club.

Garde joined Arsenal from Strasbourg while Wenger was seeing out the final weeks of his contract at Nagoya. Then aged 30, he was a reliable centre-back or defensive midfielder, but he had two additional roles: first, to act as a chaperone to the young Vieira, who spoke no English and had arrived from Italy having failed to break into the first team at AC Milan; second, to keep Wenger informed, as he made his final preparations to move to London, with regard to the lie of the land at the club. The first few days were an eye-opener: prior to one of Garde's first training sessions at the London Colney training base that Arsenal shared with University College London, club captain Tony Adams gathered his teammates together and announced that he was an alcoholic.

Arsenal's squad was crammed full of experienced English players the wrong side of 30 and when a tall, thin, bespectacled foreigner who looked – in right-back Lee Dixon's memorable phrase – 'like a geography teacher' walked in and immediately turned their routines upside-down, there was inevitable scepticism. Out went the chips, pies, chocolate, Jelly Babies and fizzy drinks, in came the broccoli, mangetout, pulses, pasta and chicken breast. French nutritionist Dr Yann Rougier introduced dietary supplements (creatine, caffeine tablets) and vitamins (chiefly B6 and B12), taken either as tablets or injections, to give the players an extra edge. France national team osteopath Philippe Boixel attended to their aches and pains. Training was transformed – dynamic stretching, plyometric drills,[77] shadow play against teams of mannequins – with everything minutely timed to maintain the players' focus.

The new regime was less of a gear change for Garde and Vieira, as well as Dennis Bergkamp (a pre-Wenger signing from Internazionale), who had encountered a similar approach during his time in Italy. Their ready adherence to Wenger's methods helped to set an example. 'It was extremely natural for me,' says Garde. 'And for Patrick too, I imagine. In France, stretching was very common. I'd had less exposure to the nutrition and the vitamins, but I was aware of it so when Arsène arrived, it didn't pose problems for me. I saw that it was very difficult for some of the English players because it was a Frenchman, a foreigner,

---

77 Designed to increase muscle power, plyometric exercises typically involve players making short, explosive movements using hurdles, cones, poles, hoops and agility ladders.

who was coming to their country and telling them that what they had been doing for a century was going to be changed and things would be done very differently. But Arsène provided explanations and what helped was that they had pretty quick results. When Patrick joined the team, he brought something important from a footballing perspective. And he did the stretches, he trained as we were being asked to, so he embodied the new things and they saw that it worked. That helped the transition to take place.' It helped, too, that the squad's senior players felt the benefit. 'Eating all the new food, taking all the tablets, doing all the new training stuff, I felt fitter, sharper, faster than I'd ever been,' said striker Ian Wright.

Wenger's first match at the helm, a 2–0 win at Blackburn Rovers on 12 October, 1996, established a template for what was to follow. His pre-match team talk at Ewood Park was brief and at half-time, with Arsenal holding on to a slender 1–0 lead, he surprised the players by allowing several long minutes to elapse before calmly delivering his instructions. Over the weeks and months that followed, Arsenal's players came to realise that the central tenet of the new manager's approach was trust. The changes he had made behind the scenes meant that they had been given everything they needed. When they found themselves in a spot of bother on the pitch, he trusted them to figure out a solution.

Wenger's authority was enhanced by his early successes in the transfer market. He had first met Vieira on a trip to Milan to visit George Weah, his former Monaco protégé, in January 1996 and when he learned, the following summer, that his young countryman's proposed move to Ajax had stalled, he pounced. Whereas Éric Cantona and David Ginola had taught British football fans that French footballers were flamboyant, enigmatic types, the long-limbed, tough-tackling Vieira showed that they could get their hands dirty too. He was joined a year later by the pony-tailed Petit, who had played at centre-back under Wenger at Monaco before being moved into midfield by Jean-Luc Ettori. The pair formed a devastatingly well-balanced partnership – Petit the organiser, Vieira the attacking launchpad – which became the fulcrum of Wenger's first great Arsenal team. 'We complemented each other in so many ways,' says Petit. 'He loved to break the lines with the ball at his feet, whereas I liked to break the lines with passes; he was right-footed, I was left-footed; he was black, I was white! We were two sides of the same coin.'

Nicolas Anelka, a nimble 17-year-old striker signed from Paris Saint-Germain in February 1997, provided further evidence of Wenger's ability to unearth gems seemingly from nowhere, while Dutch speedster Marc Overmars, brought in from Ajax, gave Arsenal lethal thrust on the left flank. The 1995 Bosman ruling had opened the floodgates for overseas talent to join the Premier League and Wenger was the first manager to fully exploit the competition's new cosmopolitan potential, ingeniously splicing continental flair on to the formidable defensive unit that had been assembled by Graham. After a third-place finish in 1997, Arsenal swept all before them in Wenger's first full season, firing the first salvo in an era-defining rivalry with Manchester United by beating Alex Ferguson's side to the league title and then sinking Newcastle United 2–0 in the FA Cup final to complete only the sixth Double in England's post-war history. The unthinkable had come to pass: a Frenchman had taught the English how to play football.

An even more exciting future began to take shape in August 1999 when Henry arrived in an £11 million move from Juventus. Handed his senior debut aged 17 at Monaco by Wenger (who left the club three weeks later), Henry tasted Division 1 glory at Stade Louis II in 1997 and won the World Cup with France in 1998, but he had lost his way after a January 1999 move to Juve, where he was played out of position at left wing-back. Although he had spent much of his career playing on the wing, Wenger was convinced that his destiny lay at centre-forward and despite Henry's scepticism ('But Boss, I don't score goals,' is how he is said to have responded when the idea was first mooted), he duly emerged as one of the finest marksmen the English game had ever seen, a majestic, irresistibly smooth thoroughbred of a striker who topped the Premier League scoring charts four times and became Arsenal's all-time leading scorer with 228 goals. Arsenal signed Henry using some of the £23 million fee they had received for Anelka from Real Madrid. The rest went on the construction of a new 143-acre training centre at London Colney, carefully overseen by Wenger, which gave the club one of the best such facilities in Europe.

United responded to Arsenal's 1998 Double by winning the Treble in 1999 and romped to victory in the title race in the two seasons that followed, but all the while, Wenger's next Arsenal team was being patiently slotted together. Henry's France teammates Wiltord and Pirès arrived in the summer of 2000, fresh from making decisive contributions in the European Championship final against Italy. The members of the old back four were phased out, but not before passing on their expertise (Wenger being notoriously inattentive when it came to defensive coaching himself) to the men who would succeed them: academy graduate Ashley Cole, former Spurs centre-back Sol Campbell and converted midfielders Lauren and Kolo Touré.

Arsenal claimed a second Double in 2002 and successfully defended the FA Cup in 2003. Brazilian World Cup winner Gilberto Silva arrived to partner Vieira in midfield, Germany's Jens Lehmann replaced David Seaman between the posts. With each new signing, with each new success, Wenger's vision crystallised, his team's football now a breath-taking symphony of rapid passing exchanges and rapier-like attacking raids; Bergkamp the orchestrator, Henry, Pirès and goalscoring Swedish midfielder Freddie Ljungberg the finishers, the whole thing played out on an immaculate Highbury pitch that resembled a carpet. 'At Highbury, we knew we'd hurt our opponents,' says Pirès. 'The atmosphere between us and the fans was exceptional. We had such confidence in ourselves and we never doubted ourselves. Sometimes we were behind at half-time, but in the second half we knew there'd be magic. It was the magic of Highbury.' The 2003–04 season yielded Wenger's crowning glory as Arsenal became 'The Invincibles', completing the extraordinary feat of winning the league without losing a single game. Sporting immortality, for manager and players alike, was secure.

After another FA Cup triumph in 2005, on penalties against United, Arsenal set out in pursuit of the one trophy that had eluded them, only to come up agonisingly short in the 2006 Champions League final at the Stade de France, losing 2–1 to Barcelona. Wenger never watched the match again. Arsenal had beaten Wigan Athletic 4–2 in their final game at Highbury 10 days earlier to pip Spurs to a Champions League place, Henry bringing down the curtain on 93 years of history with a match-winning hat-trick. Leaving the famous old ground was an almighty wrench for Arsenal's fans, but as they prepared to move into the club's gleaming new 60,000-seater home at Ashburton Grove, 500 yards away to the west, they could not have known quite how much they were leaving behind.

When Bacary Sagna discovered that Arsenal were interested in signing him from Auxerre in the summer of 2007, he did not have to mull things over for very long. 'For me, it was a no-brainer,' he tells me in a video call from Paris. 'I was delighted that I was going to Arsenal because it was the club that all French footballers dreamed of playing for. It was an iconic club and one of the teams that played the best football in Europe. Plus the facilities were magnificent. The training ground was perfect and the quality of the pitches was insane.'

Outwardly, Arsenal were every inch the modern super-club, but the £390 million move to the Emirates Stadium saddled the club with a financial burden that left Wenger fighting with one arm tied behind his back. To make matters worse, just as Arsenal were making the move that was designed to lock in their economic sustainability for decades to come, the goalposts shifted. Chelsea had been taken over by Russian oligarch Roman Abramovich in 2003 and in 2008, at the peak of the global financial crisis, Manchester City came under the control of Abu Dhabi's Sheikh Mansour. Coupled with the impact of the stadium move, the competition's increased firepower – dubbed 'financial doping' by Wenger – made it harder for Arsenal to hold on to the players they had and harder to attract the ones they wanted. As 'The Invincibles' slipped away one by one, Wenger replaced them with some of the brightest young talent in Europe, but whereas Arsenal had previously sold players after several years of loyal service, now they were snatched away the second they reached footballing maturity. 'It was as if we were being cut down before the harvest,' he later lamented. Between 2011 and 2012, club captain Cesc Fàbregas, Samir Nasri, Gaël Clichy, Robin van Persie and Alex Song all left and went on to win trophies elsewhere. Sagna followed suit in 2014, joining Nasri and Clichy at City. Collective conviction – the notion that if everyone pulled in the same direction, a team could become more than the sum of its parts[78] – had always been integral to Wenger's stewardship, but with each high-profile departure, each barren season, that communal belief was eroded. Grimandi returned to Arsenal in a recruitment role in 2004 and saw first-hand what the club's loss of status meant. 'To start with, when I arrived, you had the Sagnas, the [Abou] Diabys, the Nasris,' he says. 'We'd done a lot of work on our recruitment in France and when you went in for a player, that was it. There wasn't even any discussion. But then other clubs copied us. You'd go in for a guy, there'd be other clubs involved and it wasn't as easy. We almost got [Kylian] Mbappé. Three years earlier, with the aura we had, we'd have got him. Same with [Eden] Hazard. We almost got [Franck] Ribéry as well. One or two players can change the future of a club. Instead we were left with players who wanted to use Arsenal as a stepping stone.'

Shorn of the charismatic, mature players who had brought the club glory in the first part of Wenger's tenure, Arsenal became English football's nearly men: always there, always competing, occasionally mounting a title challenge or reaching a final, but almost always falling short. Arsenal were fragile, went the refrain; Arsenal were weak, Arsenal could be bullied. They lost 8–2 at Old Trafford, 5–1 at Anfield, 6–0 at Stamford Bridge in Wenger's 1,000th game in charge. Bayern Munich trounced them 10–2 on aggregate in the Champions League. José Mourinho called Wenger a 'specialist in failure' and it was cruel but it stung. The FA Cup provided solace: Arsenal won it three times in four years between 2014 and 2017, taking Wenger's tally of victories in the competition that had held him spellbound as a boy to a record seven. Mindful of the economic constraints with which the club had had to contend, he argued that qualifying for the Champions League, which Arsenal succeeded in doing for a remarkable 19 consecutive seasons, was as valuable as a trophy. But as much as he wanted to win, Wenger seemed equally committed to the idea of defending a particular, dwindling, fundamentally very English vision of how a football club should be run, with an all-powerful manager at the top. 'Director of football? I don't know

---

78 In September 2008, a written briefing that had been given to Arsenal's players prior to a 3–1 win at Bolton Wanderers was discovered by journalists at the team hotel in Manchester. Among other things, it emphasised the importance of 'having an unshakeable belief that we can achieve our target' and 'believing in the strength of the team'.

what it means,' he said in May 2017 when it was suggested that Arsenal might consider appointing someone with strategic oversight to work above him. 'Is it someone who stands on the road and directs the players left and right? I'm manager of Arsenal and as long as I am manager, I will decide what happens on the technical front.' Eventually, the top-four finishes dried up too. With the fanbase bitterly divided between 'Wenger In' and 'Wenger Out' factions and the criticism he faced increasingly venomous, he finally called it a day, walking away from the stadium he had built for the last time after a 5–0 win over Burnley in May 2018.

Wenger turned Arsenal into one of the world's biggest football clubs, but never managed to replicate the winning formula he had found at Highbury. He has admitted that when in London, where he still owns a house, he will occasionally get into his car and drive past the old stadium, which has since been converted into luxury flats. 'Highbury was my soul,' he said in a 2021 Amazon documentary. 'The Emirates, my suffering.' English football's great moderniser always kept one foot in the past.

13

LES BLEUS

CHAMPIONS DU MONDE!

'I think that after watching that, we can die happy! Well, as late as possible, but we can!'

TF1 commentator Thierry Roland

'History only remembers the winners. In 40 years' time, no one will care how the French national team played in 1998. All they'll remember is that we were the winners.'

Emmanuel Petit

There were a few minutes remaining in the 1998 World Cup final and Emmanuel Petit needed to say something to Frank Lebœuf. 'I remember, our defence cleared the ball and the crowd made a huge noise,' says Petit, perched all in denim on the edge of a blue crescent-shaped sofa in his Parisian apartment, a pack of Marlboro cigarettes and an espresso in a small glass cup sitting on a low, glass-topped coffee table in front of him. 'The French people in the stands were already celebrating, it was: "Fucking hell, we're going to win the World Cup! We already have one hand on the trophy!" I looked over to Frank and said: "Franky!" He heard me call him, but he looked over and said: "What?" We were about 10 metres apart and he was going: "What?" And I said: "My dream is coming true!" And he said: "I can't hear a thing you're saying!"'

As a young child growing up in his native Normandy, Petit dreamed one night that France had played Brazil in the World Cup final and beaten them 2–0. It was a dream that he had mentioned to his teammates, a silly story that he occasionally shared with journalists. And now, years later, he was on the pitch at the Stade de France, a blue shirt on his back, Lebœuf alongside him in central defence, and France were beating Brazil 2–0 in the World Cup final. It was exactly as his dream had foretold – until he spoiled things. After a Brazilian corner came to nothing in the second minute of stoppage time, France substitute Christophe Dugarry carried the ball out of defence and into midfield, Patrick Vieira peeling away to his left as he did so. Brazil were beaten, every last semblance of resistance having seeped out of their weary limbs, and as Dugarry played the ball wide to Vieira, Petit spotted his chance. 'I had a quick glance at what was around me and I thought: "Fucking hell, none of the Brazilians are getting back,"' he says. 'So I ran forwards. I saw Pat receive the ball and it reminded me of Arsenal, so I thought why not? I ran in behind. Everyone knows what happened next. And I thought to myself: "Shit, in my dream it was 2–0 and now I've made it 3–0!" But I was quite happy about ruining my premonition.' Petit's strike – hit low across Cláudio Taffarel into the bottom-right corner – was the 1,000th goal scored by the French men's national team. It sealed the biggest, most desperately longed for victory in the history of French sport.

Seconds later, Moroccan referee Said Belqola blew the final whistle and the Stade de France pitch became a tableau of ecstasy: Lebœuf collapsing to the ground face first, Dugarry bursting into tears in an embrace with his room-mate Zinédine Zidane, Fabien Barthez sinking to his knees in his penalty area and burying his weeping face in his goalkeeper gloves. '*Et c'est fini!*' Thierry Roland told the 20.6 million viewers watching spellbound on TF1, the emotion strangling his voice. 'France are the world champions! Can you believe that? France are the world champions by beating Brazil 3–0 – two goals from Zidane, one goal from Petit. I think that after watching that, we can die happy! Well, as late as possible, but we can!'

Maintaining the quiet dignity that had characterised his approach to the tournament from the start, France coach Aimé Jacquet, clad in a white Adidas polo shirt with navy-blue trim and blue tracksuit bottoms, walked calmly along the touchline and shared an embrace with his beaten counterpart, Mário Zagallo. In the stands, supporters rejoiced, *Tricolores* twirled, tears flowed. Youri Djorkaeff momentarily broke away from the French celebrations to console his crestfallen

Internazionale teammate Ronaldo, whose mysterious fit in his hotel room hours earlier had sent the tournament into a frenzy. As they awaited the presentation ceremony, France's players danced, sang, hugged, stared into the stands in wonder and wiped disbelieving tears from disbelieving eyes, giddy cries of '*Champions du monde!*' emanating from every embrace and huddle. When skipper Didier Deschamps passed Michel Platini after climbing the steps to the VIP box, the former France number 10, present in his capacity as joint-president of the organising committee, locked him in an embrace. Mindful of how quickly things had flashed by when he had captained *Les Bleus* to European Championship glory 14 years previously, Platini, a blue France jersey visible beneath his dark suit jacket, told Deschamps: 'Take your time.' After Deschamps had received his winner's medal from outgoing FIFA president João Havelange and allowed his teammates to file past him, Jacquet helped him to climb on to the blue presentation parapet. Beaming French President Jacques Chirac, a blue and red scarf draped around his neck, handed the famous golden trophy up to Deschamps and he kissed it, twice, before thrusting it into the air above his head, the other players' hands flying up in unison alongside him, an enormous roar rolling around the ground. The competition that France had delivered to the world 68 years previously had found its way into French hands at long last.

In central Paris, in scenes not witnessed since the liberation, over a million people streamed on to the Champs-Élysées for a party that would last all night. It was the same in every corner of the country. France had won. France *could* win. Once considered 'the world champions of friendly matches', so long convinced of their own inferiority compared to the leading football nations, France had taken on the best and beaten them all. Nobody in the country aged under 60 had ever seen anything like it.

But victory had not come easy. The national team had needed to be rebuilt, piece by piece, after the failure to qualify for the previous two World Cups and the staff and players had had to put themselves through the wringer to make it across the finish line. They had not all emerged unscathed.

When Jacquet was appointed France coach in December 1993, Christmas was a week away and *Les Bleus* were not getting any presents from anyone. They had needed only a single point from their final two World Cup qualifying matches to book a place at the following year's tournament in the United States and yet incredibly, inconceivably, they had contrived to fall short, losing 3–2 at home to Israel and then 2–1 at home to Bulgaria. Images from the fatal November defeat by Bulgaria at the Parc des Princes were seared upon the national consciousness: David Ginola's notorious overhit cross in the final minute of normal time; Emil Kostadinov's dramatic winner, seconds later, thumped high past Bernard Lama like a dagger in the night; TF1 momentarily flashing up the wrong scoreline – France 2–1 Bulgaria – because surely this could not really be happening; Gérard Houllier's look of silent horror on the touchline; Deschamps' face crumpling with emotion as he walked off the pitch in tears.[79] France had already been announced as hosts of the 1998 World Cup; they would stage it having not graced the tournament for 12 years. After the shame of the VA-OM match-fixing affair, it brought a sorry year to a wretched conclusion.

Initially handed the reins on a provisional basis, Jacquet began his tenure with an awkward trip to Naples to face Italy in a February 1994 friendly, but came away with a 1–0 win after Djorkaeff marked his full debut by dinking in his first international goal. France won each of their next three games too, against Chile, Australia and Japan, and when they found themselves 2–0 down against the Czech Republic in an August friendly at Parc Lescure, a 22-year-old midfielder wearing the number 14 shirt rose from the bench to get them out of trouble. Making his senior international debut as a 63rd-minute substitute for Corentin Martins, Bordeaux playmaker Zidane halved the arrears with a swerving left-foot effort from range five minutes from time and then equalised with an emphatic

---

79 Ginola had publicly complained about his lack of playing time prior to the Bulgaria match and during a press conference the day after the game, Houllier accused him of having committed 'a crime against the team' by doing so. The remark was not, as Ginola suggested in his autobiography, a reference to his overhit cross from a late free-kick that allowed Bulgaria to counter-attack. Nor did Houllier say that Ginola had 'sent an Exocet missile through the heart of French football', as has commonly been reported. The pair remained at loggerheads for years – Ginola unsuccessfully suing Houllier for slander and defamation in 2012 – although Houllier later recognised that his criticisms had been 'a huge mistake'.

near-post header from a corner. Interviewed by a TF1 reporter as he left the pitch after the 2–2 draw, France's heavily perspiring saviour could only shyly mumble: 'I have no words. *C'est fabuleux.*' In the changing room, France captain Éric Cantona sought him out to present him with the Czechs' match pennant as a souvenir. But what could have been the start of a spectacular association between two children of Marseille who played the game with rare grace was actually more of an ending. Cantona and Zidane would only spend a further 19 minutes on the pitch together in their country's colours.

For all the promise that his players had shown in their first friendly outings, Jacquet initially struggled to find the right formula in France's Euro 96 qualifying campaign. His side drew four of their first five matches 0–0 and their solitary win came against Azerbaijan. He intended to make Cantona the figurehead of his team, but the eight-month ban that the Manchester United striker received for attacking a Crystal Palace supporter at Selhurst Park in January 1995 forced a rethink that would prove pivotal. Cantona or no Cantona, France seemed to misfire regardless of how many attacking players Jacquet crammed into his starting XI, so for the visit of Slovakia to Nantes in April 1995 he changed tack, bulking up his midfield with Deschamps, Marcel Desailly and Paris Saint-Germain's Vincent Guérin and handing Zidane his full international debut in the number 10 role behind Ginola and Patrice Loko. France won 4–0 and Zidane ran the show.

After a 1–1 draw at home to Poland (Djorkaeff rescuing a crucial point with a late free-kick) and a 10–0 demolition of Azerbaijan, France travelled to Romania for a game that served as a vital staging post on the road to World Cup glory. Quarter-finalists at the 1994 tournament, the Romanians boasted the talents of Gheorghe Hagi, Dan Petrescu and Ilie Dumitrescu and had gone five years without losing a competitive home game. But in front of a hostile crowd, France produced a brilliant, battling performance and prevailed 3–1 through goals from Christian Karembeu, Djorkaeff and Zidane. 'That match in Romania was the first step on the road to the World Cup title in '98,' says Éric Di Meco, who captained the team in Bucharest. 'Because Barthez is in goal, "Zizou" is on the pitch and he's the boss, there's Youri, there's Didier, there's Marcel, you've got Christian Karembeu in midfield, you've got "Duga" [Christophe Dugarry] up front. You already had the spine.' A 2–0 home win over Israel – no wobbles this time – secured qualification. Where Michel Hidalgo had tried to wedge as many playmakers into his starting XI as possible, Jacquet was organising his entire team in the service of just one: Zidane.

The victory in the Romanian capital occurred 10 days after Cantona's heavily anticipated United comeback against Liverpool, but although he was once again available for selection, Jacquet's thinking had by now evolved. The muscular three-man midfield had proved its worth and in Zidane and second striker Djorkaeff, he felt that he had found the team's 'technical leaders'. It left only one position vacant, at centre-forward, but when Jacquet travelled to Manchester in January 1996 to ask Cantona to play there, he did not get the answer that he had been counting on. 'Éric refused,' says team manager Henri Émile, who sat in on the meeting. 'He said: "No, I want to play in midfield [i.e. at number 10], I don't want to play up front." Aimé reformulated the question a few times, but each time he said no. He found it hard to accept that the conductor's baton that he had held had been taken by Zidane and Djorkaeff.' In spite of Cantona's sparkling performances for United, Jacquet decided that the squad would do without him. Likewise for Ginola, who had hogged the headlines in his first few months at Newcastle United before fading from view, and Jean-Pierre Papin, who was coming to the end of an injury-plagued two-year spell at Bayern Munich. 'In order to help [Zidane and Djorkaeff] flourish, I progressively sidelined the older players, Papin, Ginola and Cantona,' said Jacquet. 'A terrible and exciting decision. I was sure of myself. I had faith in them.' The exclusion of two Marseille old boys (Papin and Cantona) and one former PSG player (Ginola) had the added benefit of soothing long-standing changing-room tensions between players connected to the two clubs, which had blighted the Houllier era.

Jacquet had his shape, his midfield set-up and his attacking configuration and in the Euro 96 group phase in England, he found his defence. Adding the all-action Karembeu to the midfield three allowed Desailly to drop back into central defence alongside the elegant Laurent Blanc, while in the full-back positions, Monaco's Lilian Thuram (a centre-back who Jacquet preferred to play at right-back) and Bordeaux's buccaneering left-back Bixente Lizarazu were putting Jocelyn Angloma and Di Meco under serious pressure. In France's final group game, a 3–1 win over old foes Bulgaria at St James' Park that sent *Les Bleus* through to the last eight, Thuram, Blanc, Desailly and Lizarazu started together for the first time. They would start 28 games together over the next four years and would not lose a single one.

In the short term, France immediately became a very difficult team to score against. Unfortunately for Jacquet, penetrating opposition defences abruptly became equally problematic. France finished the tournament with four consecutive hours of goal-free football, beating the Netherlands on penalties after a 0–0 draw in the quarter-finals, but losing on spot-kicks to the Czech Republic after another goalless stalemate in the last four.

After the tournament, Jacquet withdrew to his chalet in the Alpine town of Thônes, where, 'pencil in hand', he evaluated his squad's performances in England with a view towards the World Cup. He had identified a core group of 12 to 13 players, he had found his first-choice back four and despite his side's continued attacking shortcomings, he remained convinced that the Zidane-Djorkaeff axis represented the team's future. He brought Roger Lemerre, gregarious former coach of the French military team,[80] on to his back-room staff to work as lead fitness coach and began plotting what would be required for France to reach the start line in 1998 in the best shape possible. Yet while the coach was certain that things were moving in the right direction, not everybody in the country shared his conviction.

———

Before opening its doors to the world in the summer of 1998, France did a bit of refurbishing. A brand-new, 80,698-seater national stadium, the Stade de France, alighted like a spaceship upon Saint-Denis in the northern Paris suburbs at a cost of €364 million. The other nine host stadiums – in Lens, Nantes, Lyon, Saint-Étienne, Bordeaux, Toulouse, Montpellier, Marseille and the Parc des Princes in Paris – all underwent renovation work, with associated infrastructure projects raising the overall cost of staging the tournament to around €1.43 billion. But if

---

80 Lemerre coached the France military team from 1986 to 1996 at the Joinville battalion in Fontainebleau, southeast of Paris. Military service in France was compulsory throughout that period, prior to being abolished in 2001, and Lemerre coached several future France internationals including Zidane, Djorkaeff, Thuram, Barthez, Vincent Candela and Alain Boghossian.

the World Cup was an opportunity to show off France's gleaming stadiums and revamped public transport systems, it would also serve as a showcase for the country's pioneering work as a developer of young footballers.

Olympic humiliation proved the spur for sweeping reforms within French sport that enabled France to emerge as a world leader in the domain of producing football talent. At the 1960 Summer Games in Rome, France won only five medals – none of which were gold – and finished in 25th place in the medals table, which represented the country's worst ever showing at a Modern Olympics. In response, President Charles de Gaulle commissioned his Minister of Youth and Sport, celebrated mountaineer Maurice Herzog, to devise a roadmap for the country's sporting future. One of Herzog's recommendations was the creation of a network of technical advisors for each of the major sporting disciplines, known as Directeurs Technique Nationaux (DTN) or National Technical Directors, whose role was to create strategic frameworks for their respective sports and establish comprehensive centralised training programmes for their coaches. Georges Boulogne, a former player who was part of the French Football Federation's technical committee, became France's first footballing DTN in 1970. Two years later, he set up the Institut National de Football (INF) in Vichy, central France, which served as an academy for the most promising footballers in the country aged 15–18. In 1973, Boulogne succeeded in pushing through the French Professional Charter, which obliged all professional clubs in France to establish youth academies (known as *centres de formation*). Bureaucracy has always been a central plank of French life. In football terms, at least, it has been weaponised to great success.

Seeking more room in which to work, the FFF relocated the INF to a larger site at Clairefontaine-en-Yvelines, 30 miles southwest of Paris, in 1988. Surrounded by dense, tranquil forest, Clairefontaine would become the centrepiece of a web of youth training centres spread across France and its overseas territories, as well as doubling up as the headquarters for the FFF's various representative teams. But when Houllier took over as DTN in 1988, his conversations with then national coach Platini made him realise that there was still progress to be made. Platini confided in Houllier that he was worried French footballers were technically inferior. The average French player, Platini said, was solid physically and tactically and possessed the requisite levels of discipline, but lacked the technical refinement needed to make it to the very top. Houllier's response was radical: rather than working with players aged 15–18, Clairefontaine would enrol them at the age of 12, allowing the coaches more time to develop their technical abilities at ages when they would be most receptive – in a developmental sense – to being coached. The drills they were put through had an unrelenting focus on technical skills: control, pass, move, control, pass, move; day after day after day, year after year after year, until they could do it all without thinking. Clairefontaine, which took in the best young players from the Paris region, became what was known as a *centre de préformation* or 'pre-training centre' and the other academies in the network, which sprung up over the years that followed, operated in the same way.[81] It gave French football a head start on the rest of the world.

'We'd been working with the big kids, so now we had to think about working with the little ones, which was different,' says Claude Dusseau, who was director of the INF from 1984 to 2004. 'We realised that young French players didn't have good technique and that we weren't doing enough work on technique at that age. Depending on their age, you have different obligations in terms of the orientation of their work. If you just make them run for an hour-long training session, you've got it all wrong. If you don't make them work on their technique, they'll be able to run, but you won't be able to put together a decent team. They had big [technical] shortcomings.'

Candidates hopeful of a place at Clairefontaine were whittled down via a series of trials to groups of 23 per year group. They lived at Clairefontaine during the week, attending a school in nearby Rambouillet during the day and training every evening, before returning to their families – and their local junior teams – at weekends. The first significant sign that the new approach was paying dividends came in 1996 when a France Under-18s side coached by Houllier and containing Clairefontaine graduates Thierry Henry, Nicolas Anelka and William Gallas won the European Championship. Part of the INF's remit was to transmit its ideas to

81 There were 16 such academies – known in France as *pôles espoirs* (centres of excellence) – for male players and eight for female players at the beginning of 2024.

French professional clubs, so the new emphasis on *préformation* and technique-focused coaching soon became the norm nationwide. 'We worked with the professional clubs, who were initially a bit sceptical, to give them a totally different orientation that was in line with what they should be doing with players at that age,' Dusseau says. 'They were used to doing more physical work with the players. We arrived on our high horses and said: "No, you have to focus on technique." But we were right!'

Henry's inclusion in France's 1998 World Cup squad planted Clairefontaine's flag in the national team for the first time, while the other young players in Jacquet's band – Vieira, Robert Pirès, David Trezeguet – showed the fruits of the youth coaching reforms in the country as a whole. As the footballing world came to learn over the decades that followed, there would be plenty more where they came from.

———

Jacquet was determined to leave no stone unturned in his preparations for the World Cup. In the spring of 1997, over a year before the tournament began, he arranged a get-together at Clairefontaine for 37 players liable to be selected for the big event. Under the supervision of team doctor Jean-Marcel Ferret, they provided urine samples, underwent blood tests, had X-rays taken and submitted themselves to dental examinations, with some even undergoing dental surgery to head off problems that might otherwise have arisen further down the line. Jacquet organised a week-long getaway at altitude in the Alpine ski resort of Tignes over Christmas in December 1997, which the players attended – some more than a little reluctantly – with their partners and children, the idea being that while the altitude primed their bodies, the social interaction between teammates and their families would bring the squad closer together.[82] Jacquet used the occasion to hold a meeting with his senior players – Deschamps, Blanc, Desailly, Thuram, Djorkaeff and Zidane – at which he explained how France

82 The players based in England, constrained by the Premier League's intense festive fixture schedule, were excused.

would approach the World Cup from a tactical perspective. A further training camp at Tignes followed shortly before the tournament in mid-May 1998.

The whole of French football was on a World Cup footing. Monaco coach Jean Tigana had previously agreed to play Thuram at right-back to help him familiarise himself with the position and in the season preceding the tournament, he carefully managed the playing time of Henry and Trezeguet, his two young strikers, so that they would report for the World Cup in peak condition. Jacquet regularly visited Deschamps at his home in Turin to discuss France's preparations and find out about the mood among the players. He also made time to visit Lizarazu in Munich, where the Bayern left-back was struggling to overcome a groin injury. In an episode that brought to mind the dispute that had polluted France's preparations for the 1978 World Cup,[83] Jacquet assuaged his players' frustrations over a sponsorship agreement that obliged them to wear Adidas boots when on international duty by promising them that they would be free to wear whichever brand's boots they wished to once the 1998 tournament was over. When the World Cup squad arrived back at Clairefontaine to begin their final preparations after a training camp in Morocco at the end of May 1998, Lemerre led them through gruelling physical exercises designed to equip them with a level of fitness that would carry them all the way to the final. With France's opening game against South Africa in Marseille looming, everything seemed to be in place. Everything, that is, but the football.

As hosts, France went two years without playing a single competitive match before the World Cup and their displays in the 18 friendly games they played were not particularly encouraging. In Le Tournoi, a friendly tournament hosted by France in the summer of 1997 that also featured England, Italy and Brazil, *Les Bleus* failed to win a game. Jacquet's men were jeered off after a 2–1 win over South Africa in Lens in October 1997 and fans expressed their impatience again during another 2–1 victory over Scotland in Saint-Étienne a month later. France beat Spain in the inaugural match at a wintry Stade de France in January 1998, Zidane firing in the only goal, but won only two of their last six pre-tournament friendly matches.

83 See page 5.

Where Jacquet saw a team that was being deliberately rotated in order to keep the players on their toes, *L'Équipe* perceived only uncertainty, sluggish football and stasis. And its criticism was brutal. *L'Équipe*, which is the country's only national sports daily, had described France's football as 'destitute' at Euro 96, despite the team's run to the semis, and *Les Bleus*' stuttering friendly performances did nothing to alter that opinion. When Jacquet named a provisional 28-man squad for the World Cup, rather than immediately revealing his final 22, *L'Équipe* reacted with the mocking front-page headline: 'So we play with 13?' In an accompanying editorial, managing editor Jérôme Bureau accused Jacquet of incoherence and declared that he was 'decidedly not the right man for the job'. After France laboured to a 1–0 friendly win over Finland in Helsinki in their final warm-up game, the paper wrote that trying to win the World Cup would be like 'trying to climb Everest in espadrilles'. The paper's public criticism, which was accompanied by mocking cartoons, hurt Jacquet deeply. 'There could be no suggestion of forgiveness,' he wrote in his autobiography, *Ma vie pour une étoile* (My Life for a Star). 'Because it's without doubt the most distressing and most hateful element of this sinister attitude: they targeted the man, they attacked the man, because they couldn't fault his work.'

His response was to erect what he described as an 'iron curtain' around the squad's base at Clairefontaine, limiting the amount of information that came in from outside and urging his players not to let any details about the squad's preparations leak out. Though he tried to put a brave face on things, it was clear to his players that he was suffering. 'It hurt him,' says Pirès, who was 24 at the time of the tournament and on the verge of leaving Metz for Marseille. 'Because he was being attacked gratuitously. The tournament hadn't even started and the French press were saying that we were playing badly, that we weren't going to win, that he'd made the wrong choices with his squad. Yes, our football was laboured, but like lots of national teams. We were getting no positive vibes from the outside world. When he brought us all together, he said: "Nobody believes in us, but no problem. I believe in you."'

In spite of the criticism, Jacquet's faith in his players remained unshakeable – as Dusseau, the former INF director, recalls. 'The forest around Clairefontaine was idyllic and we used to go jogging together,' he says. 'We'd talk about this and that. Then one day, during the preparations for the tournament, he stopped me,

put his hands on my shoulders and said: "We're going to be world champions."
Just like that. And then we went off running again.'

———

The mistral, the cold, northwesterly wind that sweeps across Provence, was blowing
hard as France's players arrived at the Stade Vélodrome for their World Cup opener
against South Africa on 12 June, 1998, but they were not blown off course. Derided
for his goal-shy displays prior to the tournament, Dugarry headed in France's
36th-minute opener from Zidane's inswinging corner and celebrated by sticking
his tongue out in the direction of the press box (his instinctive reaction had been
to raise both middle fingers, but he thought better of it). A Pierre Issa own goal and
a late solo effort from Henry completed a 3–0 success. *Les Bleus* made equally light
work of Saudi Arabia at the Stade de France, Henry's brace and strikes from
Trezeguet and Lizarazu securing a 4–0 win that sent the hosts into the knockout
phase with a game to spare, but the match was marred by the 71st-minute dismissal
of Zidane. Jacquet had specifically warned his players not to react to provocation
before the game, but when Saudi captain Fuad Anwar slid in to challenge France's
number 10, he reacted by raking his studs down the midfielder's side. It was the
first red card shown to a French player at a World Cup and it earned Zidane a
two-match ban, ruling him out until the quarter-finals. Jacquet shuffled his pack
for the final Group C game against Denmark in Lyon, but his charges prevailed
2–1 courtesy of a Djorkaeff penalty and a drilled effort from Petit.

The first heart-in-mouth moments arrived with France's last 16 fixture against
Paraguay at Stade Félix-Bollaert in Lens. On an afternoon of hot sunshine and
stifling tension, Paraguay goalkeeper José Luis Chilavert repelled everything that
the blue shirts threw at him until the marauding Blanc popped up in extra time
to score the first golden goal in World Cup history from Trezeguet's intelligent
knock-down. The only French person in the ground not celebrating was the
goalscorer's mother, Yvonne, who had sought refuge from her nerves in the toilets.

Every game from that point on would be played at the Stade de France,
which for Jacquet's players came with the added benefit of no longer having to
leave a Clairefontaine base that was feeling more like home with each passing

day. Within the peaceful confines of the 19th-century Château de Montjoye, the players wiled away their free time playing cards, pool and table tennis or going for walks and bike rides in the surrounding woodland. Dugarry, Zidane and the shaven-headed Vincent Candela, Lizarazu's deputy at left-back, were the squad's resident *chambreurs* or 'piss-takers', habitually assembling – like any self-respecting group of piss-takers – on the back row of the team bus. Candela was responsible for turning the Gloria Gaynor hit 'I Will Survive' into the squad's unofficial tournament anthem, after the players spontaneously started goading Alain Boghossian by singing its tune when he found himself stuck in the middle of a *toro* (the French name for the *rondo* possession exercise, taken from the Spanish word for 'bull') in training one day.[84] In the evenings, the players all sat around the same large, oval-shaped table – always in the same seats – for a buffet dinner and a glass of wine, Thuram routinely tucking into a gigantic self-prepared salad. A busy, chatty, natural changing-room animal, Deschamps did the rounds, kept abreast of everyone's issues and maintained a steady stream of gentle mockery flowing in every direction. After all the tension of the build-up, Clairefontaine came to feel, in Dugarry's words, like 'a kind of sanctuary'.

The quarter-final against Italy carried special significance for the seven members of the squad who played their football in Serie A. Wearing their all-white change strip and with Zidane back from suspension, France had the better of the game, but it took penalties to separate the sides after a nervy 0–0 draw. Luigi Di Biagio was Italy's fall guy, scudding their final spot-kick against the bar. Five days later, *Les Bleus* returned to the Stade de France for the semi-final against Croatia and produced their worst first-half display of the tournament, prompting a despairing rebuke from Jacquet at half-time. Inattentive positioning from Thuram allowed Davor Šuker to put Croatia ahead within seconds of kick-off in the second half, but the defender atoned in entirely improbable fashion, equalising from Djorkaeff's through ball and then curling a magnificent 70th-minute winner into the bottom-left corner with his weaker left foot. They would be the only goals of his 142-cap international career.

---

84 The France players specifically sang the 'la la la' part of the song that features in Dutch pop group Hermes House Band's 1994 cover version.

'When you win matches like that in difficult circumstances, you realise that luck is on your side,' says Pirès. 'Lilian Thuram never even scored in training.'

The one disappointment was the red card shown to Blanc for catching Slaven Bilić's chin with his hand as they jostled for position at a France free-kick, ruling him out of the final; an injustice that moved Jacquet to tears in a post-match TV interview. But there were also reservations about the lack of atmosphere within the Stade de France, which the players blamed on the high number of corporate ticketholders. 'When we came out on to the pitch on Wednesday [to face Croatia], there was almost a whole stand of black suits,' said Deschamps. 'You'd have thought you were at a funeral.'

Strategically isolated from the world at Clairefontaine, the only glimpses France's players got of the fervour that was gripping the country was on their bus journeys to and from the stadium, which brought fans flocking to the roadsides to show their support. Yet in spite of the players' grumbles, football fever was belatedly taking hold. After the win over Croatia, some 300,000 people spilled on to the Champs-Élysées in celebration and the scenes were mirrored across the country. TV viewing figures were on the rise (along with sales of *L'Équipe*) and replicas of the France jersey – which recalled the shirt worn by the 1984 team, with its one red and three white horizontal bands – became increasingly conspicuous. It helped, too, that the Tour de France, to which French eyes are usually drawn every July, was overshadowed by the Festina doping scandal.[85] Standing one match from glory, Jacquet's team were the only show in town. But they were still waiting for their leading man to turn up.

––––

Zidane had featured prominently against both Italy and Croatia, creating chances for his teammates and shooting at goal with a frequency that occasionally bordered on the unhelpful, but his one decisive contribution to the tournament remained the goal

---

85 French police discovered a huge cache of doping material in a support car belonging to the Festina team shortly before the race began, sparking an investigation that would result in nine riders admitting to using the banned blood-booster EPO and 10 team officials receiving suspended prison sentences.

that he had teed up for Dugarry in France's opening fixture. It had been a similar story two years previously at Euro 96, where, freshly ushered into the limelight as the man who had usurped Cantona, he had failed either to score or create a single goal. In England, Zidane had been diminished by a painful buttock injury sustained when he crashed a BMW car loaned to him by one of Bordeaux's sponsors prior to the tournament and was struck by the gear stick. Two years on, he only had himself to blame for his reckless dismissal against Saudi Arabia and with only the final now remaining, a second major tournament was in danger of passing him by.

Zidane represented a continuation of the tradition of the great French number 10, following in the footsteps of Raymond Kopa and Michel Platini. But whereas they had been dashing goalscorers, he was a prowling playmaker who decorated games at the same time as he dominated them. A player of sublime, sinewy elegance, Zidane combined the delicate poise of a ballerina with the strutting stagecraft of a matador, slowing the game to his own languid tempo before reducing opposition defences to ruins with a sudden flash of genius. There was something unique, even iconoclastic, about the very manner in which he controlled the ball. For generations, French schoolchildren had been taught to control the ball with their instep, but Zidane preferred to use the outside of his foot, deliberately imparting spin upon the ball and thereby expanding the palette of effects that he could apply to it with his subsequent touches. His was a football of backspin and sidespin, of bluff and misdirection, of shimmies and stepovers, twists and twirls, nudges and nutmegs; the gossamer touch to control a 50-yard pass, the gentle brush of the ball with the studs that left an opponent languishing. It was football of the housing estate, of the concrete of Place Tartane, of endless afternoons of playing, provoking, experimenting and inventing amid a forest of shins and swiping feet. 'Everything that I learned with the ball, I learned there,' he said. The hours on Place Tartane equipped Zidane with a technical repertoire unlike anything French football had ever seen. As Cannes youth scout Jean Varraud excitedly told his employers after spotting a 14-year-old Zidane playing in a trial match in Aix-en-Provence: 'I've found a boy who has hands where his feet should be.'

Zidane's parents, Smaïl and Malika, both hailed from the mountainous Kabylie region in northern Algeria. After meeting in Marseille in 1962, when Smaïl had been preparing to return to Algeria after nine years working on building sites in the suburbs north of Paris, they settled in La Castellane and had five children. Zinédine, known as 'Yazid' to his family and close friends, was the youngest. He was obsessed with football from an early age – his elder brother, Majdid, recalled him hugging a ball against himself 'like a security blanket' as he slept. A shy, sensitive child, he would lie awake in bed fretting when his father worked night shifts as a security guard at the local Casino supermarket. Zidane said that when he left home to join the Cannes youth academy at the age of 15, initially living with a host family in the nearby village of Pégomas, he cried himself to sleep every night.

Bypassing the youth team, Zidane was fast-tracked into the reserves following his arrival at Cannes and was promoted to the first-team squad by head coach Jean Fernandez a year later. He made his professional debut a month before his 17th birthday, coming on as a 78th-minute substitute in a 1–1 draw away to a Nantes team containing Deschamps and Desailly in May 1989. Luis Fernandez joined Cannes from Racing Club de Paris the same summer and watched the young Zidane's development at close quarters. 'I remember him arriving in the team,' he says. 'You saw his ability, his qualities. You saw how attentive he was too. I enjoyed playing with him, because this boy had all the creative qualities – the technical mastery, the ball control, the passing – and all with such ease. On the pitch, he was perfect. He was remarkable. It was all so easy for him.'

Zidane broke into the first XI during the 1990–91 season and scored his first goal in senior football against Nantes in February 1991, coaxing a pass into his path with the outside of his right foot and then calmly lobbing the goalkeeper. His 1992 move to Bordeaux, after Cannes were relegated, elevated him to national prominence. It was at Bordeaux that he became 'Zizou' (a nickname invented by his coach and fellow Marseille native Rolland Courbis), that he acquired a reputation as a dead-ball expert and that he established an understanding with his future France teammates Lizarazu and Dugarry. The trio's performances during Bordeaux's 1995–96 UEFA Cup run brought all three international renown. Zidane scored his most famous goal in a Bordeaux shirt at Real Betis in the third round – a dipping left-foot lob from 40 yards out – and created two goals for Dugarry as *Les Girondins* overturned a 2–0 deficit against AC Milan in the quarter-finals with a storming 3–0 win at a riotous Parc Lescure.

Taking his place among the 32,500 spectators that evening was Juventus coach Marcello Lippi, who would become Zidane's boss a few months later. Bordeaux lost 5–1 on aggregate to Bayern in the final, Zidane missing the first leg through suspension, but he left for Turin as the newly anointed French Player of the Year.

For all his many technical attributes, one thing that Zidane was not renowned for was his heading. When he first arrived at Cannes, his coaches were surprised to see the tall, wiry teenager deliberately ducking out of headers in training. It was not an aspect of the game that particularly appealed to him. 'In the neighbourhoods, we don't give a fuck about headers,' he said. 'You play with your feet.' But thanks to some observant preparation work by Jacquet, he would achieve something with his head more enduring than anything he had ever done with his feet.

After waking up at five o'clock in the morning on the day before the World Cup final, Jacquet decided to re-watch footage of Brazil's quarter-final win over Denmark and noticed that Zagallo's players had a tendency to switch off when defending free-kicks and corners. 'At set-pieces, they're pretty careless,' he told his players during their pre-match briefing at Clairefontaine. 'If you're a bit crafty, you can move them around and cause them problems.' In the 27th minute of the game, France won a corner on their right flank after Roberto Carlos inadvertently chested the ball over the byline as he prepared to volley it downfield. Petit curled the ball towards the near post and Zidane outjumped Leonardo to plant a firm downward header past Taffarel. When France won another corner on the other side in first-half stoppage time, Zidane was walking over to take it, as per the team's plan for set-pieces, only for Djorkaeff to shoo him away. Like Petit minutes earlier, Djorkaeff targeted the near post, albeit with a flatter trajectory. Darting in from the edge of the box, Zidane shrugged off Brazil captain Dunga and stooped to steer another header inside the near post, the ball passing between Carlos' legs on its way in. After the violence of his dismissal against the Saudis, the frustration of his suspension and the fruitless toil of his performances in the knockout rounds, he had won the World Cup for his side in the space of 19 minutes. As France's gleeful supporters caroused on the Champs-Élysées after the game, Zidane's face was projected on to the side of the Arc de Triomphe by his sponsor, Adidas, accompanied by the message: '*MERCI ZIZOU*'. Not only had he finally succeeded in putting his mark on the tournament, not only had he scored the goals that won France their first ever World Cup, but in so doing, he had turned himself into a cultural icon.

The players got to savour the fervour of the Champs-Élysées the following day when around 600,000 people flocked to the famous avenue to watch them parade the trophy on an open-top bus. As the fans massing in the July sunshine looked up at Zidane and his teammates, they saw their own identities reflected back at them: white, black and Berber, drawn not just from every nook and cranny of France and its former empire but from almost every corner of the world. Desailly was born in Ghana, Vieira in Senegal, Karembeu in New Caledonia; Thuram, Henry and Bernard Diomède had roots in the French Antilles, Lama in French Guiana; Trezeguet's parents were from Argentina, Zidane's from Algeria, Pirès' from Portugal and Spain; Djorkaeff and Boghossian both had Armenian heritage; Deschamps and Lizarazu hailed from the Basque country; striker Stéphane Guivarc'h was Breton. They were the *black-blanc-beur*[86] team, a 22-man rainbow nation, shining symbol of modern, multiracial, multicultural France. Looking out across the sea of faces, Thuram saw 'the real France, not the banal idea that people have about French people, but the true, heterogenous France'.

Subsequent events showed that it would take more than a brilliant football team to bridge France's deep-seated racial divides. A politically charged friendly match between France and Algeria at the Stade de France in October 2001 – the first game between the countries since the north African nation gained independence in 1962 – had to be abandoned due to a pitch invasion by Algeria supporters. The following year, far-right politician Jean-Marie Le Pen sent shivers up the spines of French moderates by reaching the second round of the country's presidential elections. In the autumn of 2005, towns and cities across France erupted in riots after two teenage boys fleeing police in the Paris suburbs were

---

86 *Beur* is a corruption of the word *arabe* and comes from the branch of French slang known as *verlan* (a corrupted form of *à l'envers*, meaning 'back-to-front'), in which the syllables of words are swapped around, with the last syllable typically moved to the front. It is used to refer to people born in France to parents from the Maghreb.

fatally electrocuted in an electricity substation. Football, it transpired, could not fix France's social problems after all. But then the players themselves had never presented themselves as saviours. They had simply wrought a moment of national communion that had, fleetingly, allowed a fractured country to feel whole.

In a more general sense, World Cup victory enabled France to look at itself in a new light. No longer the eternal gallant losers, no longer in thrall to *le complexe Poulidor*, this was *la France qui gagne*: the France that wins. The leading players instantly became superstars, invited to film premieres and glamorous parties, plastered across magazine front covers and assailed with interview requests and sponsorship opportunities. Zidane modelled for Christian Dior. Barthez dated supermodel Linda Evangelista. Petit recorded a single with a former Miss France. 'We were The Beatles,' said Lizarazu. Season ticket sales in France rose by 30 per cent over the summer of 1998 and the following year, average top-flight attendances surpassed 20,000 for the first time. A name was even coined for people who had mysteriously developed a burning interest in football at exactly the same time as France were closing in on World Cup glory: *Footix*, after the official tournament mascot.

The euphoria succeeded in dousing any criticism that might have otherwise come the team's way regarding the quality of their football. *Les Bleus* had not swaggered to victory playing Hidalgo's *football à la française*, the victories over Paraguay, Italy and Croatia owing more to grit and good fortune than fearlessness and flair, but when you have been waiting for success for so long, there is no great appetite for splitting hairs. 'There's not only one way to win,' says Petit. 'Personally, the duel between the romantics and pragmatists, I don't get involved in that. History only remembers the winners. In 40 years' time, no one will care how the French national team played in 1998. All they'll remember is that we were the winners.'

Jacquet immediately stepped down as France coach and took over from Houllier as DTN, staying on in the role until his retirement in 2006. France's victory represented the most emphatic vindication for the former Bordeaux coach, who abruptly found himself feted for the same humble, steadfast, provincial qualities that had previously earned him only mockery and derision. In the days that followed France's success, journalists from *L'Équipe* covering the Tour de

France were abused and their cars pelted with stones, while the FFF's offices were inundated with letters and faxes from supporters apologising for having doubted him. Although he steered clear of public triumphalism, Jacquet made it clear how hurt he had been by the personal attacks to which he was subjected. 'He was never vengeful about it,' says team manager Émile. 'But he never forgave them.'

Lemerre, Jacquet's assistant, took on the baton as head coach and led the team to their footballing apotheosis two years later at the European Championship in Belgium and the Netherlands. Bolstered in midfield by a fully mature Vieira, invigorated in attack by the additions of Anelka and Sylvain Wiltord and inspired by a Zidane at the very peak of his powers, *Les Bleus* saw off Denmark (3–0) and the Czech Republic (2–1) in the group phase before losing 3–2 to co-hosts the Netherlands in an entertaining dead rubber in Amsterdam. Fortune smiled on the French in the knockout rounds: Raúl skied a last-minute penalty that would have sent the quarter-final against Spain to extra time, while the semi-final against Portugal looked destined for penalties until a handball by Abel Xavier allowed Zidane to settle the tie from the spot. Galvanised, as they had been two years earlier, by the sense that fate was on their side, France pulled off the ultimate Italian-style victory against Italy in the final in Rotterdam. The *Azzurri* took the lead through Marco Delvecchio's 55th-minute volley and were within touching distance of the trophy, only for three substitutes to come to France's rescue in impossibly dramatic fashion. Wiltord equalised in the fourth minute of stoppage time and then, with two minutes to play in the first half of extra time, Pirès sashayed past Demetrio Albertini and Fabio Cannavaro on the left and cut the ball back for Trezeguet to slam a golden goal winner into the top-left corner with his left foot. It felt, Trezeguet later said, like 'achieving total beauty'.

As a football nation, France had to be dragged kicking and screaming into the 20th century: resisting professionalism for as long as possible, struggling to embrace the sport as a mass cultural phenomenon and, for decades, proving incapable of winning the most prestigious club and international prizes. But with its athletic, tactically astute, trophy-winning national team, drawn from right across the country's ethnic spectrum, its newly renovated stadiums and its world-leading youth development structures, French football arrived in the 21st century before anybody else.

14

GESTE TECHNIQUE

LA SPÉCIALE HENRY

Plat du pied, sécurité. As any budding French footballer will tell you, as any amateur coach will never tire of repeating, the most reliable way to strike the ball is with the inside of your foot. 'Inside of the foot, security,' goes the saying in France, one popularised over the years by the former Saint-Étienne captain turned television co-commentator Jean-Michel Larqué. For one French player more than any other, the inside of the foot proved to be the surest route to goal time and time again.

When Thierry Henry picked up the ball on the left flank and drove towards goal, you knew what was coming next. Using the outside of his right foot to carry the ball with him, he would draw the goalkeeper towards him and then open his shoulders and hips to steer a shot inside the right-hand post with his right instep. Henry would talk about 'freezing' the goalkeeper: waiting until the precise moment when he sensed that the keeper's feet were planted to quickly whip the ball past him. The legacy of the time he spent cutting in from the left wing at his formative club Monaco or in the France youth teams, it became his calling card, a trademark finish with which he became more synonymous than perhaps any other striker and any other type of shot.

In France, such a signature move is known as a player's *spéciale*, or 'speciality'. Whether a first-time finish or the *coup de grâce* at the conclusion of a one-man counter-attack, Henry's *spéciale* brought him some of the most important and fondly remembered goals of his career. The match-winning solo effort that sank Liverpool at Highbury in April 2004 and kept Arsenal on course to become 'Invincible'. The crucial equaliser past Iker Casillas that set Pep Guardiola's

Barcelona on their way to a historic 6–2 rout of Real Madrid at the Bernabéu in May 2009. The breakaway strike past Peter Schmeichel that made sure of victory for France over Denmark in their opening game at Euro 2000. A gorgeous, languid, 25-yard lob for New York Red Bulls against Toronto FC in September 2012. And the goal that meant the most to him: the one he scored, having returned to Arsenal as a mid-season loanee, to snatch victory over Leeds United in an FA Cup third-round tie at the Emirates Stadium in January 2012; the first goal, he said, that had ever given him the same massive emotional rush as a supporter.

After scoring in what was to become signature fashion for Monaco at Cannes in August 1996, at the beginning of his second full season of first-team football, Henry explained that he preferred playing on the left wing precisely because it made it easier to shoot for goal in such a manner. 'I'm right-footed and I really like playing on the left,' he said in a post-match interview on Canal+. 'I find it easy to carry the ball using the outside of my foot, rather than carrying it on the other side with the inside of my foot. I feel more comfortable there, where you can cut in and shoot.'

Henry's habit of side-footing the ball into the net seemed so easy and so natural that it was tempting to assume that he had been scoring goals like that his whole life. Old video footage of him playing football as a boy with his first clubs in the southern Paris suburbs – Les Ulis, US Palaiseau, Viry-Châtillon – shows him repeatedly streaking clear of opposition defences and then calmly slotting the ball past the goalkeeper with the inside of his right foot. But he has always insisted that his *spéciale* was something he had to work on, rather than something innate, pointing to the long hours he spent on the training pitch with fitness coach Claude Puel and reserve goalkeeper Stéphane Porato during his time at Monaco, learning how to strike the ball with just the right amount of curl for it to bend inside the right-hand post. 'He'd come on at the end of the game in his first year to play 20–25 minutes,' said Puel. 'He'd come on left wing, cut inside on to his right foot and then unleash rockets. From time to time, he'd get one or two on target, but most of the time they flew into the clouds. We did lots of exercises with mannequins: I'd give him a ball to control, he'd beat the mannequin and then he'd curl in a shot. He worked and worked and we then saw those movements in his matches. He was capable of putting the ball where he wanted and with the power he wanted.'

According to Henry, when he first started honing the technique with Puel at Monaco's La Turbie training ground, he would master only one shot in every 50. 'The amount of work behind it was just crazy,' he told The Athletic in 2020. 'Repetition creates habits. Once you have that habit, your body doesn't even think that you're doing it. You just do it, it becomes natural.' As much as he worked on it, Henry also possessed a subtle but helpful natural advantage: he was born duck-footed, meaning that his feet were slightly splayed. It obliged him to wear special shoes during childhood to straighten his feet, but it also meant that from his earliest age and without anybody having the merest inkling of the destiny that lay in store for him, his right foot was already predisposed to make flush contact with a football.

So how many goals did Henry score with his trademark finish? I decided to count them. For the purposes of the exercise, I defined his *spéciale* as an attempt made in open play using the inside of his right foot, from the left-hand side or the centre of the pitch, towards the right-hand side of the goal and with the goalkeeper still to beat. Half-volleys were included, full volleys were not. Provided the principal criteria were met, distance from the goal was not taken into consideration. Some goals appeared to fit the bill on first viewing, only for a replay to reveal that Henry had struck the ball with the top of his foot rather than his instep (a rasping drive into the bottom-right corner for France in a European Championship qualifier against Malta in March 2003 being one example). The final, not entirely scientific calculation revealed that Henry's characteristic finish brought him (drumroll please) . . . 98 of the 411 goals that he scored for club and country over the course of his senior career.[87] Or 24 per cent. Or roughly one goal in every four. Few footballing signatures have been signed with such a deadly flourish.

---

87 Nine of the 28 goals he scored for Monaco, none of the three he scored for Juventus, 51 of the 228 he scored for Arsenal, 11 of the 49 he scored for Barcelona, 15 of the 52 he scored for New York Red Bulls and 12 of the 51 he scored for France. This includes three goals where Henry hit the ball in trademark fashion but the shot took a deflection off a defender on its way into the net.

15

LYON

THE MAGNIFICENT SEVEN

'You'd go on to the pitch and you'd be like: "I *know*
I'm going to score today!"'

Sidney Govou

The tension is so great that it has brought Juninho Pernambucano to his knees.
Lyon's substitutes are on their feet behind him, arms around each other's shoulders
for support, but the Brazilian midfielder, clad in his all-white strip, no longer has
the strength to stand. As the final minutes tick by, he kneels on the wet turf in
front of the home dug-out and stares out across the pitch, hands dumbly placed
on his thighs, a haggard expression on his face. Lyon lead 3–1 against title rivals
Lens and will be confirmed as champions the second referee Gilles Veissière
blows for full-time, but while the ball remains in play, a sliver of doubt remains.
Beside him, Sonny Anderson theatrically waves his arms across his face, imploring
Veissière to end the torment. Both he and Juninho have been substituted as OL
look to wind down the clock. In the Stade de Gerland tribunes, the party has
already started. Red flares have been lit and a chant of '*On est champions!*' ('We
are champions!') is being belted out by every soul in the ground. The force of so
many people jumping up and down in unison causes the stadium roof to shake.
After five interminable minutes of stoppage time, the whistle finally sounds and
Gerland erupts, the players on the touchline joyfully gambolling on to the pitch
and forming a mass huddle with their teammates in front of an ecstatic Virage
Nord. Midfielder David Linarès is in tears and has to be helped to his feet by a

member of the coaching staff. Collared in front of the dug-out by Canal+ touchline reporter Laurent Paganelli, OL coach Jacques Santini is lost for words. 'There is nothing to say,' he says, gesturing mutely towards the pitch before melting away into the throng of photographers and cameramen surrounding him. Juninho grabs a huge red and blue Lyon flag and marches towards the centre circle as the fans begin to spill from the stands on to the pitch. It is Saturday 4 May, 2002, the rain is pouring from the evening sky and Olympique Lyonnais are champions of France for the very first time.

The first title had been a long time coming, but it had been coming. Lyon had finished third in the table in 1999 and third again in 2000. A year later, they ended the campaign like a train, winning their last seven games, only for Raynald Denoueix's Nantes to pip them to glory by winning their last eight. But the 2000–01 season had at least yielded a first piece of silverware in 28 years, with Swiss centre-back Patrick Müller's extra-time volley against Monaco at the Stade de France earning OL a dramatic and extravagantly celebrated 2–1 win in the final of the Coupe de la Ligue. The team's performances during the club's maiden Champions League campaign, which included a 1–1 draw against Arsenal at Highbury and a resounding 3–0 demolition of future champions Bayern Munich, only enhanced the impression that something was stirring in the Rhône Valley.

A squad of sturdy French pros complemented by the Brazilian brilliance of Juninho and Anderson, Lyon played second fiddle to Lens throughout the 2001–02 season and trailed the club from northern France by eight points in early February. When a 2–0 defeat at Lille in mid-March left Lens six points clear with a game in hand, young winger Sidney Govou threw in the towel, telling a post-match TV interviewer: 'It's dead.' But Lens tied up in the home straight, failing to win any of their next four games, and Lyon took advantage, snatching victory at fellow title challengers Auxerre thanks to a 92nd-minute breakaway goal from Govou and winning 1–0 at Bordeaux to set up a last-day showdown at Gerland. Desperate to get over the line and put the 'Poulidor' taunts[88] to bed, Lyon pulled out all the stops during the run-in. Club president Jean-Michel

---

88 Although France loves Raymond Poulidor, his name is still used to characterise teams or sportspeople who seem condemned never to finish higher than second place.

Aulas invited Daniel Constantini, coach of France's world champion handball team, to address the squad on their psychological preparations. At the suggestion of Brazilian centre-back Edmílson, on the eve of the decisive match against Lens, the players were shown supportive video messages from their partners and children. Mindful of Lyon's superior goal difference, Aulas had for weeks been encouraging his players to believe that as long as they were within three points of Lens going into the game between the sides on the season's final day, the title would be within their grasp.

As it transpired, Lens led by a single point, meaning that if Lyon won, they would be champions. On a day of leaden skies and jangling nerves, OL quickly took control courtesy of goals from Govou and Philippe Violeau in the first 14 minutes. Former Lyon defender Jacek Bąk's deflected reply for Lens injected an element of suspense into proceedings, but early in the second half, Juninho freed Pierre Laigle for a left-foot shot that cruelly flicked off Jean-Guy Wallemme and looped over visiting goalkeeper Guillaume Warmuz to restore the hosts' two-goal cushion. With the home support raucously urging them on to glory, Lyon finally reached their destination. 'The atmosphere at Gerland that day was insane,' recalls goalkeeper Grégory Coupet. 'The Lyon fans were renowned for being a bit quiet and subdued, but they were terrific that day, which meant a lot to us. Imagine being the first players to win the league for your club. For the players, it was incredible. Honestly, it was incredible. The scenes in the dressing room were unbelievable.'

Lyon's players and staff celebrated the title at a floating nightclub on the Rhône called Le Fish and then, in what was to become an annual tradition, with a post-season trip to Saint-Tropez. But no sooner had the tickertape settled than Aulas was appearing on Sunday morning TV show *Téléfoot* to challenge his players to win the title again the year after. The most dominant era in the history of the French top flight was only just beginning.

———

By his own admission, Aulas knew 'nothing' about the world of football prior to becoming Lyon president in June 1987. A local businessman, born and raised in the nearby village of L'Arbresle, he had made his fortune as the founder of Cegid – an IT company servicing the financial industry. At the time, OL had spent four seasons in Division 2 and were facing serious financial problems. Having already accepted an invitation from former Lyon president Roger Michaux to put money into the club, as part of a group of local investors called the Club des 100, Aulas abruptly found himself in the headlines when Marseille president Bernard Tapie – eager to raise the level of competitiveness in French football – told a journalist from regional newspaper *Le Progrès* that the young entrepreneur would make an ideal candidate to take over.[89] Bolstered by Tapie's patronage, Aulas presented an ambitious plan to the OL board and was duly elected president. Despite being only 38 and having stumbled into the role almost by accident, he immediately made it clear that he was aiming for the sky, setting OL the targets of promotion to Division 1 within two years and European qualification within five. Just to show how serious he was, when he failed to find a kit sponsor, he put '*LYON: VILLE EUROPÉENNE*' ('LYON: EUROPEAN CITY') on the front of the players' shirts. Never mind that OL were in the second division and had not played a game in Europe since 1975.

Advised by Bordeaux president Claude Bez (over a dinner of stewed eels at Le Haillan) to surround himself with people who knew the club, Aulas brought in former OL players Raymond Domenech and Bernard Lacombe to work as head coach and sporting director respectively in 1988. Over the years that followed, he would repeatedly turn to former players or promote from within when a key strategic position needed filling, giving Lyon a sense of identity and continuity rarely found in the French game. 'It brings this common thread,' says Rémi Garde, who became Lyon captain under Domenech and later worked for the club as assistant coach, academy director and head coach. 'Everyone loves the club and feels indebted to it. It's a place where there are rules that evolve over time and that builds strength. There's a kind of framework in which everyone has their place.'

---

89 Tapie had become acquainted with Aulas after inviting him to work with him on the Bouygues group's acquisition of public television channel TF1 in April 1987.

Coupet discovered the strength of Lyon's local ties when he joined the club from hated rivals Saint-Étienne in December 1996. He arrived in unusual circumstances to replace Pascal Olmeta, who had been sacked for punching teammate Jean-Luc Sassus after he found him chatting to his girlfriend in the Gerland tunnel after a match. Lyon's squad was full of players from the local area – Florent Laville, Florian Maurice, Alain Caveglia, Ludovic Giuly – and it quickly became apparent to Coupet that having arrived from the enemy ranks, he would have to work doubly hard to fit in. 'When I arrived, the fans graffitied the training ground and wrote: "Olmeta for president, [reserve goalkeeper Christophe] Breton in goal, we don't want a dirty *Vert*,"' Coupet recalls. 'That was the welcome message! I remember having the fans right behind the goal during a training match and whenever I let a goal in, they'd say: "That's a Lyon goal, you Saint-Étienne bastard." It was pretty strong. You couldn't wear green, that was for sure. And I had to change the number plate on my car – you couldn't have the 42 [the number of the Loire department, of which Saint-Étienne is the capital]. But you learn quickly.'

Domenech led Lyon to promotion in his first season in the dug-out and delivered European football a year earlier than scheduled courtesy of a fifth-place finish in 1991. Propelled by Aulas' investment and a bountiful youth system, Lyon gradually emerged as contenders. They finished second in the league under Jean Tigana in 1995, reached the Coupe de la Ligue final under Guy Stéphan in 1996 and enjoyed some famous nights in the UEFA Cup, eliminating Italian heavyweights Lazio and recording a prestigious 2–1 victory at San Siro over the Internazionale of Ronaldo, Youri Djorkaeff and Javier Zanetti. The key moment in Lyon's modern evolution occurred in the spring of 1999 when French film company Pathé ploughed 104 million francs into the club in return for a 34 per cent stake, enabling Aulas to complete the game-changing signing of Anderson from Barcelona. With his explosive pace, his razor-sharp finishing and his impeccable professionalism, the Brazilian striker took Lyon to a new level on and off the pitch, giving the team the vital star quality that turns challengers into champions. 'He generated a change of mindset within the club,' says Govou, the free-wheeling winger who broke into the Lyon first team a few months after Anderson's arrival. 'He showed us how far we were from the top level. He was a great, great player, but he educated us at the same time.' In addition to his footballing gifts, Anderson was also the player who would inspire an entire generation of footballers to play with the tops of their socks pulled up over their knees.

Over the years that followed, the samba rhythm became more and more insistent at Gerland. It was thanks to a collaboration between Lacombe – appointed sporting director in 2000 after a four-year stint as head coach – and former Lyon centre-back Marcelo Kiremitdjian, who began working for the club as a scout in his native Brazil as he wound down his playing career. Lacombe would travel to Brazil to watch players recommended to him by Marcelo and then fly them over to Lyon with their wives, where they would be walked around the Gerland pitch, wined and dined at local brasserie L'Argenson and introduced to Isabelle Dias, a local translator (and OL fan) who played a precious role in helping the new recruits to bed in. Centre-backs Edmílson, Claúdio Caçapa and Cris provided the Brazilian bedrock to Lyon's success in the 2000s. Anderson and (to a slightly lesser extent) Fred scored the goals. And Juninho[90] supplied the magic.

Lacombe only watched Juninho play once in the flesh, but convinced Lyon's decision-makers of his quality with the aid of a VHS cassette featuring grainy footage of a famous free-kick that he had scored against River Plate during Vasco da Gama's triumphant 1998 Copa Libertadores campaign. A stand-off with Vasco meant that he had not played for five months by the time he joined Lyon in June 2001 and Santini struggled to find a place for him in his preferred 4-4-2 formation, regularly aligning him on the right of midfield. Juninho lacked the pace to play wide, but he had everything else: strength, tenacity, a fierce will to win, a dream-like ability to play a killer pass and ball-striking technique of such purity that it turned him into the greatest dead-ball expert of the modern era.

For free-kicks around the box, Juninho hit the ball as powerfully with his instep as most players could with their laces and without having to sacrifice

---

90 Born Antônio Augusto Ribeiro Reis Júnior, he was nicknamed 'Juninho' – a common diminutive of 'Júnior' in Brazil – and became known as 'Juninho Pernambucano' (in reference to his home state of Pernambuco) to distinguish him from the former Middlesbrough midfielder Juninho Paulista.

anything in terms of accuracy. But his genius lay in having devised an entirely new way of striking the ball from distance. Urged by his former Vasco coach Antônio Lopes to make sure that his free-kicks from wide areas always plunged right in front of the goalkeeper, the Brazil international taught himself how to hit through and across the ball at the same time, striking it with the flat part of the foot at the base of his first three toes and with no follow-through. The technique 'stunned' the ball and sent it speeding towards goal with an unpredictable, wobbling trajectory that was every goalkeeper's worst nightmare. He beat Iker Casillas from 35 yards against Real Madrid, embarrassed Oliver Kahn from similar range against Bayern Munich and scored one free-kick against Ajaccio in March 2006 from a spot a few paces shy of the centre circle. Juninho used to practise free-kicks once or twice a week and when Lyon were due to play away, he would ask the coaching staff to provide him with the brand of balls that would be used by the host club so as to get a feel for them in advance. Andrea Pirlo, Cristiano Ronaldo and Gareth Bale were among the celebrated players who sought to imitate his technique. And they were not the only ones. 'We all tried in training, but people ended up with sprained knees!' laughs Govou. 'The way he struck the ball was weird. The suppleness in his ankle, his knee . . . The only player I've seen come close was maybe [former Lyon midfielder] Miralem Pjanić. But Juninho did it so consistently. You'd spend 10 minutes in training just watching him. It was amazing.' In the European football landscape of the mid-2000s, few things created a greater sense of anticipation than the sight of Juninho pacing out his run-up before an invitingly positioned set-piece. Of the 100 goals that he scored in Lyon's colours, 44 were from free-kicks. More than any other player, he came to symbolise the unprecedented period of success that brought OL seven league titles in a row.

Santini's departure in the summer of 2002 to take over from Roger Lemerre as France coach brought former Paris Saint-Germain midfielder Paul Le Guen into the OL dug-out. A typically taciturn Breton, Le Guen had only three years' experience as a head coach at Rennes behind him but would lead Lyon to three successive league titles (extending their run to four in a row). While the first two triumphs were built upon late-season surges, in the 2004–05 campaign Lyon left everyone in the starting blocks, losing only three games all season and finishing 12 points clear of nearest rivals Lille. It was Le Guen who introduced the 4-3-3 system that would become Lyon's trademark during this era, built around a formidable midfield trio of Juninho, unflappable Mali international Mahamadou Diarra and Ghanaian powerhouse Michael Essien. Exhorted by Le Guen to equip themselves with 'the superior desire to win', Lyon monstered their opponents both with their football and their physicality. The only thing they lacked, in the mid-decade hinterland between Anderson's 2003 departure and the emergence of Karim Benzema, was a world-class centre-forward.

In addition to their dominance on the pitch, Lyon's mastery of the transfer market during this period turned them into a global reference for smart player recruitment. They signed players relatively cheaply, often from smaller teams in France, sold them on at huge profit to the biggest clubs in Europe – Diarra to Real Madrid, Essien and Florent Malouda to Chelsea, Éric Abidal to Barcelona – and yet by lining up replacements in advance, managed to remain a force both at home and abroad. Aulas acquired a reputation as one of the most obdurate transfer negotiators in Europe, adopting a ruthlessly commercial approach to his dealings with other clubs and making sure to wring every last drop of value from his players before he would agree to let them go. 'Every international at Lyon is untransferable,' he once said. 'Until the offer surpasses by far the amount we had expected.' He became equally well known for the doggedness with which he defended the OL cause and the pressure he put on match officials, regularly speaking out in the media (and later on Twitter) to denounce injustices both real and imagined. 'When he talks, it doesn't resonate in the same way that it does when it's the president of Dijon,' said former Ligue 1 referee Tony Chapron. 'When you don't award a penalty to Lyon and Jean-Michel Aulas talks about it, the whole of France will know. With Dijon, it's at best the whole of Bourgogne.'

When Le Guen left – somewhat abruptly – in 2005, Aulas turned to Gérard Houllier, who had been away from the dug-out for a year after leaving Liverpool.

Aulas would occasionally bump into Houllier while on business with the many organisations his success with Lyon had enabled him to infiltrate – France's Ligue de Football Professionnel, the G-14 group (precursor to the European Club Association), FIFA – and saw in the 57-year-old former France coach a widely respected figure capable of taking the club to the next level in European competition. The players, initially, were sceptical, having heard on the football grapevine that the new coach was an uncompromising figure ('Anything but Houllier,' was Sylvain Wiltord's scathing response when a TV microphone was put in front of him during the squad's summer trip to Saint-Tropez). But Houllier quickly won them over. Recognising the strength of Lyon's sporting dynamic, he had the good sense to leave things largely as they were on the pitch, albeit while introducing a more patient approach to build-up play. Away from the pitch, he brought a new professional exactitude to Lyon's preparations, having a canteen constructed for the players at the club's Tola-Vologe training base, installing an air-conditioning system (which the players had been requesting for years) and limiting media access to the squad. He built close personal bonds with his players, taking a keen interest in their families and their lives away from the pitch. And his stirring team talks – minutely detailed, rehearsed aloud in front of his hotel room mirror and delivered with the panache of a natural orator – blew the players away. 'He was the best,' says Govou. 'I've rarely seen someone give team talks in that way. You really felt it. You'd go on to the pitch and you'd be like: "I *know* I'm going to score today!"'

Under Houllier, Lyon's grip on Ligue 1 tightened yet further. They finished 15 points above Bordeaux in 2006 – the players celebrating the title by dyeing their hair in Lyon red and blue for a riotous 4–0 derby win over Saint-Étienne – and 17 points clear of Marseille in 2007, having taken 50 points from a possible 57 over the season's first half. Commonly felt to be assured of victory before the season had even started, Lyon's players came to devise specific targets – points tallies, goal records, unbeaten runs – in an attempt to keep motivation levels high. But although OL continued to reign supreme at home, success in the Champions League eluded them. Their first experiences in the competition were chastening. Humbled 3–0 on aggregate by Slovenian champions Maribor in the third qualifying round in 1999, they reached the second group phase in the following campaign, but failed to make it beyond the first group stage in the two seasons that followed. The 2003–04 season brought a first foray into the knockout rounds, but despite topping their group above Bayern and Celtic, Lyon lost to José Mourinho's Porto in the quarter-finals, their disappointment sharpened by the fact that with Real Madrid, AC Milan and Arsenal all falling at the same hurdle, they would have been strong contenders for overall victory had they progressed.

By now, OL were becoming accustomed to the rarefied air of Europe's elite competition. Prior to home games, their directors would entertain visiting delegations at celebrated local chef Paul Bocuse's restaurant L'Auberge du Pont de Collonges, where a Michelin three-star menu showcased the very best of the city's internationally renowned cuisine. Aulas and his associates got used to rubbing shoulders with the most powerful people in the European game. Yet while the doors along the corridors of power were all open, it was a different matter on the pitch. The regal Lyon side of the mid-2000s fared no better in the Champions League than a succession of bitterly disappointing quarter-final exits. In the 2004–05 season, OL tore through their group and annihilated German champions Werder Bremen 10–2 on aggregate in the last 16, but lost on penalties to PSV Eindhoven in the next round after Brazilian striker Nilmar had been denied a penalty for a clear foul by PSV goalkeeper Heurelho Gomes with three minutes remaining in extra time of the second leg.

Echoing Tapie's move for Franz Beckenbauer after Marseille's contentious European Cup semi-final defeat by Benfica in 1990, it was in response to Lyon's elimination by PSV that Aulas opted to replace Le Guen with a man of status such as Houllier. Yet the former Liverpool manager fared no better. At the same stage of the competition a year later, Lyon were holding on to a 1–1 draw against Milan at San Siro that would have sent them into the semi-finals on away goals, only for Filippo Inzaghi and Andriy Shevchenko to strike twice in the dying minutes and break their hearts all over again. Diarra, who had headed in Lyon's goal, was so distraught that he walked off the pitch and on to the team bus without getting changed. 'The defeat against Milan hurt us the most,' says Coupet. 'Because that season, we had an incredible team.' OL made it no further than the last 16 in the next two seasons and although they would reach the semi-finals in 2010 and 2020, the team that would have stood the best chance of winning the tournament never even got to within sight of a final.

For all that their continental adventures occasionally took fans to the edges of their seats, Lyon never enjoyed the kind of nationwide adulation that had been afforded to Robert Herbin's Saint-Étienne or Tapie's Marseille, for which various explanations have been advanced. Lyon as a city was cold and bourgeois, it was said, not a football place. Aulas' ubiquity was grating. There was no run to a European final to attract the eyes of the entire nation. The recent successes of the national team meant that French football fans no longer felt as invested in the European exploits of the country's leading club side. And as much as French teams had occasionally dominated the championship in the past, nobody had ever taken charge as ruthlessly, as relentlessly and for quite simply as long as OL had. 'What was missing at OL was winning a title at European level,' says Garde. 'But if the squad at that time had taken that step and even just played in a Champions League final, I think we would have moved on to something similar to Saint-Étienne [in terms of popularity]. Maybe we weren't adored on a national level, but we were respected and we were liked.'

Armand Garrido has never forgotten the first time that he saw Karim Benzema play. Chiefly because it was a bit of a let-down. Benzema, who hailed from the Lyon suburb of Bron, was 15 and had been at OL since the age of nine. As coach of Lyon's Under-17s, Garrido was due to start working with Benzema the following season so he decided to have a look at him. Having walked over to Pitch 8 at La Plaine des Jeux, the municipally owned playing fields that abutted Lyon's old Tola-Vologe training centre, Garrido found himself watching a tall, slender, slightly uncertain teenage footballer who had clear potential but struggled to impose himself. Fortunately for both, that would soon change.

'I came away a bit disappointed,' says Garrido, who spent 30 years as a youth coach at OL. 'I'd seen a good player, who did some interesting things, but there was a lack of activity, a lack of combativity. But he was a hard-working boy and things clicked very quickly. If I said we were staying out to do extra work after training, he'd work like a madman. He was playing football 24/7, training intensively. His physique changed – he became an athlete. And he gained self-confidence. Suddenly you realise: "Fucking hell, we've got ourselves a pearl here." I remember, we went to play at Sochaux – he must have been about 16 and a half. He plays an incredible game and scores four goals. We go to the Montaigu Tournament [a prestigious youth football competition organised annually in the Vendée] and he finishes as top scorer and best player. He's called up by France Under-17s and he becomes European champion [in 2004].[91] And a few months later, he's playing with the pros.' Benzema made his first-team debut for Lyon a month after his 17th birthday in a 2–0 home win over Metz in January 2005, teeing up a late goal for Bryan Bergougnoux after nonchalantly flicking the ball over an opponent's head. Not that his teammates had not been warned about what was coming. During an initiation speech in front of the senior squad, he told them: 'Don't laugh too much, but I'm here to take your place.'

Hatem Ben Arfa had stolen a march on him, having made his own first-team bow the previous August. As the pair had progressed through the Lyon youth system, the expectation had long been that it would be Ben Arfa, nine months Benzema's senior, who would make the bigger splash in the professional game. 'If I'd had to predict who was going to win the Ballon d'Or, it would have been him,' says Garrido. Ben Arfa was already a star, having featured prominently in a 2002 Canal+ documentary series tracing the steps of young footballers coming through the ranks at Clairefontaine. Armed with an impossibly dextrous left foot, spellbinding close control and a devastating change of pace, the boy from the southern Paris suburbs made jaws drop every time he took to the pitch, and yet he caused his teammates as much frustration as his opponents. 'He started training with the first team

91 Along with his France Under-17 teammates Hatem Ben Arfa, Samir Nasri and Jérémy Ménez, Benzema formed part of a group of promising but wayward young players who became known as *La génération '87*.

when he was 16 and he'd do things that were crazy,' says Govou. 'His dribbling was peerless. And not flashy stuff, stepovers – it was all in the way he carried the ball. His ball skills were extraordinary. But Hatem is mad. He can be the sweetest guy, but he was very tough to handle. You'd be queuing in the canteen with your tray and Hatem would take a tray and push in front of you. If you explained it to him, you realised that he didn't understand. He would say: "OK, sorry, you're right." Deep down, he didn't know. I think it was a lack of education. Karim was the opposite. Very respectful, a bit crafty, never in trouble – he'd be at the side of things but never in the middle!' Benzema was destined for Champions League triumphs, Ballon d'Or glory and legendary status at Real Madrid; Ben Arfa for a career of fits and starts that never truly got going. Both were products of one of the most fruitful youth production lines in the history of the European game.

The architecture of Lyon's development pathway was set out by José Broissart, an uncompromising midfielder turned uncompromising youth coach who took charge of the club's academy after finishing his playing career at Gerland in the late 1970s. Together with recruiter Alain Thiry, another former OL player, Broissart was responsible for assembling the collection of talented, locally born youngsters who propelled Lyon up the top-flight standings in the 1990s. Aulas immediately appreciated the sporting, economic and symbolic value of a team packed with homegrown stars and made the youth system one of his top priorities. By the time his long tenure as president was drawing to a close in late 2022, he estimated that he had poured over €400 million into it. The success of OL's *centre de formation* meant that the Lyon squad maintained not just a strong French identity but a strong local identity throughout the club's 2000s heyday, from Govou, Laville and left-back Jérémie Bréchet in the first title-winning season to Govou, Benzema and right-back François Clerc in the last. And while the trophies dried up as the 2000s gave way to the 2010s, the academy's remarkable hit rate – Alexandre Lacazette, Anthony Lopes, Samuel Umtiti, Nabil Fekir, Corentin Tolisso, Anthony Martial, Houssem Aouar, Maxence Caqueret, Rayan Cherki, Malo Gusto, Bradley Barcola (to name but 11) – allowed Lyon to remain a major player in the French game and an example for youth development around the world.

Lyon's nickname, *Les Gones*, which means 'The Kids' in the local dialect, has always been particularly fitting.

On paper, the 2007–08 season represented a continuation of the sparkling dynamic that had been propelling the club since the beginning of the decade. Lyon won the trophy they always won – the league, for the seventh year running – and the trophy they never won – the Coupe de France, for the first time in 35 years; Govou's predatory extra-time strike against PSG at the Stade de France completing the club's first Double. Juninho was at the peak of his powers, Ben Arfa was now a first-team regular and Benzema was developing into one of the most exciting young strikers on the continent, finishing as Ligue 1's top scorer with 20 goals and netting 31 times in all competitions. But scratch the surface and all was not well.

Houllier had left the previous summer, worn down by a never-ending power struggle with Aulas and Lacombe, and the squad chafed against the confrontational approach of his successor, Alain Perrin, who took charge after leading Sochaux to victory in the Coupe de France. The (blink-and-miss-it) former Portsmouth manager thought nothing of calling out players for their shortcomings in front of the rest of the squad and it set many of them against him from the start. Aulas would later remark that the players had won the Double 'in quasi-autonomy'. Although it would finish with Lyon's colours adorning three trophies – Perrin's men also prevailing against Sochaux in the curtain-raising Trophée des Champions – the season was long and trying. Coupet and Cris sustained serious knee ligament injuries in August, sidelining both for months. There were tensions in the changing room between the older generation and those just breaking through. Lyon's football, meanwhile, had none of the swagger of previous campaigns, making the team over-reliant on isolated moments of magic from Juninho, Benzema and Ben Arfa. Whereas OL had become accustomed to leaving their rivals for dead, they won the league by only four points from Laurent Blanc's Bordeaux, who would succeed them as champions 12 months later. Coupet left for Atlético Madrid in 2008, Juninho bowed out in 2009 and Govou followed suit a year later. The golden age of the first great French club side of the 21st century had finally come to an end.

Aulas launched a new era by installing former Lille coach Claude Puel as an English-style general manager on a five-year contract and spending big on the likes of Lisandro López, Michel Bastos and Yoann Gourcuff in a bid to make a breakthrough in the Champions League, marking a sharp shift from the club's previous approach. It did not work. The headstrong Puel proved a divisive figure and was sacked in 2011 after three seasons without silverware, Lacombe branding his appointment 'the president's biggest mistake'. The beginning of the Qatar Sports Investments project at PSG that same summer immediately relegated Lyon to the second rank of clubs vying for glory in Ligue 1, although the trusty youth production line allowed them to finish best of the rest in 2015 and 2016.

While Lyon drifted on the pitch, Aulas remained as pioneering as ever behind the scenes. He had succeeded in getting the club listed on the French Bourse in February 2007,[92] which enabled him to pilot the construction of the spectacular, 59,186-capacity Groupama Stadium in Décines-Charpieu in the eastern Lyon suburbs. When it opened in January 2016, it made Lyon the first major French club to own their own ground. A brand-new training facility, housing the men's and women's senior teams, opened beside the stadium a few months later. But Aulas' drive to keep Lyon competitive would eventually come at the cost of his own involvement. He sold OL to American investor John Textor in December 2022 in a deal worth €886 million and although the agreement allowed for Aulas to stay on as president for a further three years, differences over strategy forced him out a few months later. Aulas bade farewell to the club in May 2023 during a 3–0 win over Reims in Lyon's final home game of the season. Standing at the front of the Virage Nord with the Bad Gones supporters' group, his shirt collar splayed open, a thin scarf in Lyon's colours loosely slung around his neck, the 74-year-old was moved to tears more than once when the crowd sang his name.

---

92 OL Groupe, the club's holding company, could only be floated on the stock exchange after Aulas and the presidents of several other leading Ligue 1 teams went to the European Commission and successfully challenged French laws that prevented sports clubs from being publicly listed.

Aulas, who was awarded France's *Légion d'honneur* in 2006, confided in his recent autobiography that he considered the Lyon men's team's lack of European honours 'a failure'. By every other metric, his 36-year tenure was a remarkable success. Under his enterprising stewardship, Lyon mushroomed from a middling, second-tier French club with an ageing stadium and a reputation that barely extended beyond France's borders to a confident, modern sporting institution with historically successful men's and women's teams, a bulging trophy cabinet and a global profile. Even PSG, for all their riches, have not yet come close to equalling Lyon's feat of seven consecutive league titles. And while Aulas regularly provoked the irritation of referees, journalists, other club presidents, rival coaches and opposition fans (not to mention people simply trying to enjoy a quiet evening on Twitter) for his combative, shamelessly one-eyed defence of all things OL, he broke with an unfortunate tradition in French football by achieving all of it without ending up in prison. *France Football* took just such factors into account in March 2021 when it named him France's greatest post-war football president. Against the backdrop of French football's occasionally murky modern history, success without swindling represented something of a novelty.

16

LES BLEUS

FROM THE GUTTER TO A SECOND STAR

'It's a scandal! They don't want to train.'

Former French Football Federation official Jean-Louis Valentin

'*Vive la France! Vive la République!*'

Paul Pogba

The first subtle indication that things were not going exactly according to plan was the fact that all the players were wearing trainers rather than football boots. As they descended the steps of the team bus in their blue training kit and set out across the pitch to sign autographs for the 200 local people who had come to watch them train in the late-afternoon sunshine, team captain Patrice Évra and coach Raymond Domenech disappeared behind the bus for a brief conversation. When the pair re-appeared, pacing slowly together across the pitch, their faces were taut and when fitness coach Robert Duverne joined the conversation, the temperature suddenly rose. Duverne wagged his finger sternly at Évra, who looked at him impassively, his hands thrust into the pockets of his long, Capri-style training shorts. Domenech stepped between them, Duverne continuing to rage. As Évra walked away to join his teammates on the far side of the pitch, Duverne stormed off furiously in the other direction, stopping only to angrily hurl away his stopwatch. After a brief discussion with the other players, Évra removed a sheet of white A4 paper that had been folded into quarters from his right shorts pocket and handed it to team press officer François Manardo. Then the players walked back across the pitch and climbed back on to the bus. For the 50-odd journalists watching on from the top of a hill overlooking the pitch, it was a difficult scene to decipher until a middle-aged man in a dark-blue anorak and light-blue jeans came storming up the hillside in a furious rage. Quickly surrounded by cameras and microphones, French Football Federation team director Jean-Louis Valentin vented his spleen. 'It's a scandal!' he said. 'They don't want to train.' He was, he said, resigning on the spot.

In consort with Domenech and various other officials, Valentin had tried to persuade the players to get off the bus and go ahead with their scheduled training session, but to no avail. They remained in their seats. Their intention had been to make an immediate return to the team hotel, but Domenech had nixed that plan by forbidding the bus driver from getting behind the wheel. So they pulled the blue curtains closed, they waited and they stewed. 'We waited a long time,' Sidney Govou tells me, arms folded, across the table of a café in Paris' 16th arrondissement as the staff clear up around us after lunch. 'There were discussions about it. "Titi" [Thierry Henry] said we should be careful. He said: "Be careful of how this will be perceived in France. They'll be all over you." Pat [Évra] said that if anyone wanted to get off and train, there was no problem. "We won't blame anyone. We've taken a collective decision, but if someone prefers to get off and train, they should get off and train."' Nobody did.

The piece of paper that Évra had handed to the team press officer was a typed statement prepared by the players, in consultation with their advisors, explaining the reasons for their actions. But neither they nor the FFF communications staff were prepared to read it to the press, so after a 40-minute stand-off, Domenech decided – remarkably – that he would do it himself. Standing in front of the horde of journalists, the players still sat on the bus behind him, the 52-year-old coach read: 'The players of the France team, without exception, wish to express their opposition to the decision taken by the French Football Federation to expel Nicolas Anelka [from the squad].' After reading the rest of the statement, he twirled on his heels and walked away to a waiting car. Finally, the bus pulled away. The 2010 World Cup in South Africa was nine days old and *Les Bleus* had hit rock bottom.

The squad, the staff and the federation itself had been sleepwalking towards disaster for some time, but the blue touch paper was truly lit in the home changing room of the Peter Mokaba Stadium in Polokwane at half-time of France's second group game against Mexico. Previously held to a goalless draw by Uruguay in their opening match in Cape Town, France were drawing 0–0 in a game they would eventually lose 2–0. In his half-time team talk, Domenech told lone striker Anelka to stop dropping deep in search of the ball and give the team an outlet by running in behind. There was a terse exchange of views and Anelka was replaced by André-Pierre Gignac.

Throughout the month of June, deodorant company Mennen ran a competition in *L'Équipe* in which people were invited to guess the front-page headline of the following day's edition. It is probably safe to assume that nobody correctly predicted the splash that the newspaper published two days later: '*VA TE FAIRE ENCULER, SALE FILS DE PUTE!*' ('GO AND FUCK YOURSELF, DIRTY SON OF A WHORE!') These, the paper said, were the words addressed to Domenech by Anelka during their changing-room contretemps in Polokwane.[93] Scandalised, like the whole of France, by the unprecedentedly explicit headline, the FFF ordered Anelka to apologise in front of the squad and when he refused, the decision was taken to send the Chelsea striker home. In a heated press conference, Évra hit out at the 'traitor' within the camp who had leaked the story to the press. Then the players hatched their plan: they would not train. It was intended to be a show of solidarity with a wronged teammate. Unfortunately for them, it was immediately categorised (this being France after all) as a 'strike'. 'People started talking about a strike, but it wasn't a strike,' says Govou. 'We just wanted to show the coach that we didn't agree with what had happened.' On the morning of the ill-starred training session, an episode of long-running TF1 show *Téléfoot*, broadcast live from the France team hotel in the Western Cape resort of Knysna, had been interrupted when Franck Ribéry wandered on to set unannounced in a pair of flip-flops and tearfully denied reports that he was bullying playmaker Yoann Gourcuff. It was testament to the

---

93 Several of the players who were present are adamant that the *L'Équipe* headline did not accurately reflect what Anelka said (there is a degree of unanimity about Anelka's use of the word '*enculer*' or '*enculé*', meaning 'fucker', much less so about the '*sale fils de pute*' bit). The journalists who broke the story, culled from multiple sources, have always stood by it.

momentous nature of what was to follow that within hours, the incident had been reduced to a footnote.

Figures from France's 1998 World Cup triumph were united in their outrage. 'The image of French football is catastrophic,' said Bixente Lizarazu. 'We're the laughing stock of the world!' lamented Aimé Jacquet. Lilian Thuram said that, as captain, Évra should never be allowed to play for his country again. The team's humiliation was complete when they lost their final group game 2–1 against South Africa in Bloemfontein, ending their already thin hopes of going through. Domenech compounded matters by refusing to shake hands with his opposite number Carlos Alberto Parreira at the final whistle (later explaining that it was because Parreira had criticised France over Thierry Henry's notorious handball in their qualifying play-off victory over the Republic of Ireland). *L'Équipe* called it 'the most resounding failure in the history of the France team'. In the French Parliament, Minister of Health and Sport Roselyne Bachelot condemned 'the disaster of a France team where immature bullies command frightened kids, with a helpless coach who has no authority and a federation in disarray'. As the FFF and the French government launched inquiries into what had happened, France's players flew home in disgrace to a nation where professional footballers were now Public Enemy No. 1.

A menacingly moustachioed full-back known as 'The Butcher' in his playing days, Domenech cut his teeth as a coach at Mulhouse and then Lyon, leading the latter to promotion to Division 1 in the early years of the Jean-Michel Aulas era, before beginning a long stint as France Under-21s coach. When Jacques Santini vacated his position as France senior coach in 2004 in order to join Tottenham Hotspur, Jacquet pushed hard – in his capacity as Directeur Technique National – for his replacement to be appointed from within the FFF. Domenech had been Jacquet's captain at Lyon and had also played under him at Bordeaux. France's reign as world champions had come to a juddering halt at the 2002 World Cup when a shock 1–0 defeat by Senegal in Seoul proved the precursor to a humiliating group-stage exit. They ceded their European crown two years later after losing to surprise future champions Greece in the quarter-finals at Euro 2004.

Domenech arrived pledging to enact a generational reset, but the team's bid to qualify for the 2006 World Cup was flatlining until Zinédine Zidane, Claude Makélélé and Thuram were persuaded to come out of international retirement in August 2005. Propelled by a rejuvenated Zidane, *Les Bleus* made it to the World Cup final in Berlin, only to lose on penalties to Italy after the returning hero brought his playing career to a sensationally violent conclusion by being sent off for headbutting Marco Materazzi in the chest in extra time after the Internazionale centre-back insulted his sister. Save for a few centimetres here and there, Domenech could have been a world champion coach, although the team's achievements were widely perceived as having had more to do with Zidane than with the man in the dug-out. Two years later, a France squad caught in a delicate transition between generations crashed out calamitously in the group phase at Euro 2008. Domenech's response was to propose to his TV journalist girlfriend, Estelle Denis, live on M6 after France's final game (she declined to respond while presenting the programme that followed). Although widely ridiculed, he remained under contract, retained Jacquet's backing and was allowed to stay on.

By the time France's qualifying campaign for the 2010 World Cup began, Henry was the only survivor from 1998 still on the scene and the future appeared to belong to a new generation of players that included Ribéry, Gourcuff, Karim Benzema, Samir Nasri and Hugo Lloris. But *Les Bleus* spluttered through qualifying, finishing second in their group behind Serbia, and only made it past Ireland in the play-offs after Henry's blatant handball in the build-up to William Gallas' extra-time winner in the second leg at the Stade de France escaped the attention of the match officials. Cue Irish fury, international outcry, demands for a replay, calls for Ireland to be reinstated at France's expense, 'Hand of Frog' headlines abroad and an avalanche of negative press at home. 'Things with the media exploded after Thierry Henry's handball,' says right-back Bacary Sagna. 'They never forgave us and we went into the World Cup in the worst possible conditions.' On top of the handball furore, Henry, now 32, was being slowly phased out at Barcelona. Despite having appointed him captain, Domenech resolved not to take him to South Africa, only to be talked round when the former Arsenal striker said that he would accept a place on the bench. It made him the first France player to appear at four World Cups, but the handball affair and the loss of the captaincy to Évra diminished his status within the squad.

Fans chanted '*Domenech démission!*' ('Domenech resign!') during a 2–0 friendly defeat by Spain at the Stade de France in March 2010 and two months later it was confirmed that Laurent Blanc would replace him after the World Cup. The Spain fixture served to expose France's complete lack of playing identity, which was not helped by the fact that none of the team's attacking players were happy about where they were being asked to play. Ribéry was playing on the right but wanted to play on the left in place of Henry, Florent Malouda was playing in central midfield but *also* wanted to play on the left and Anelka was playing up front but wanted to be given a free role. Gourcuff, doe-eyed star of the Bordeaux team that had ended Lyon's Ligue 1 hegemony under Blanc's stewardship, was touted as the successor to Zidane in the number 10 shirt, but his diffident personality prevented him from imposing himself and he irked his teammates by discussing the team's tactical shortcomings with the media. Reports of tensions between him and the squad's other leading players dogged the build-up to the World Cup. When Domenech was asked if the other players were annoyed by the media hype surrounding Gourcuff, he replied: 'Allow me not to answer that question.' He would later assert that Ribéry had felt 'jealousy tainted with hatred' towards Gourcuff. France gave a reasonably good account of themselves in their opening 0–0 draw with Uruguay, but from the moment of Anelka's substitution against Mexico, the squad fell apart.

Domenech's divisive personality did little to defuse the tension. He rubbed his players' club coaches up the wrong way by failing to communicate with them, created friction within the FFF by obsessing about secrecy and confounded journalists with his sarcastic answers in press conferences. Organisational failings, meanwhile, meant that whereas FFF delegations at previous major tournaments had included seasoned campaigners from the professional game such as Aulas and former Lens president Gervais Martel, whose experience helped to keep the France ship on an even keel, the officials who accompanied the squad to South Africa, drawn from French football's amateur ranks, had no such expertise. 'They spent all their time on safari or getting us to sign bucket hats,' Govou says. 'One day, one of them asked a player to sign a hat and said: "Put your name as well because I don't know who you are." These guys were supposed to work with you, to guide you. It was impossible. Nothing worked!' As the players prepared to leave the Pezula Nature Hotel and Spa after their elimination from the tournament, some of them noticed that FFF president Jean-Pierre Escalettes was furiously engaged in a game of pinball on an arcade machine in the lobby. As the officials fiddled, French football burned.

The moral compass of French footballers was already under the microscope before the 2010 World Cup after Ribéry and Benzema were accused of having slept with an under-age escort girl called Zahia Dehar. Both players were eventually acquitted[94] (albeit not until January 2014) in what became known as *L'affaire Zahia*, but it served as further grist for the mill for those who sought to portray footballers as the dregs of society. Reacting to Anelka's expulsion from the World Cup squad, outspoken philosopher Alain Finkielkraut described the players as 'a generation of trash' and 'a band of thugs, who know only one morality: that of the mafia'. The players complained that when the finger-pointing started, it was always the non-white and Muslim squad members who found themselves in the firing line. 'When France fail to win, people start talking straight away about the players' skin colour and religious beliefs,' Anelka said. 'When times get tough we find out what people really think. They said Franck Ribéry had hit Yoann Gourcuff – Ribéry the Muslim and Gourcuff the good French boy.' The FFF's disciplinary commission suspended four players over the World Cup fiasco: Anelka for 18 international games, Évra for five, Ribéry for three and midfielder Jérémy Toulalan, whose advisors had helped to draft the players' statement, for one. Neither Anelka nor Toulalan played for France again.

94 Ribéry admitted to having had a sexual encounter with Dehar, but said he did not know how old she was at the time and had not paid her any money. Benzema denied having ever met her.

For his first game in charge, a 2–1 friendly defeat against Norway in August 2010, Blanc decided not to select any of the 23 players who had gone to South Africa. He talked about instilling 'rigour and discipline', banned the use of mobile phones at the dinner table, forbade his players from wearing headphones when they arrived at the stadium for matches and circulated the words to 'La Marseillaise' to help them sing it before matches. After beginning their Euro 2012 qualification campaign by losing 1–0 at home to Belarus, *Les Bleus* won their next four qualifiers without conceding a goal and enjoyed prestigious friendly wins over England and Brazil. But just as the horizon appeared to be clearing, the storm clouds rolled in again.

In April 2011, the investigative website Mediapart revealed that it had obtained a secret recording of a meeting involving Blanc and other FFF coaches in which they had discussed imposing unofficial quotas on the number of players possessing dual nationality allowed to play for France's representative teams. The meeting, held in November 2010, was arranged to address the issue of players who played for France at youth level but switched allegiances to other, principally African countries at senior level. The discussion had strayed on to France's desire to emulate the kind of technical, possession-oriented football played by world and European champions Spain, which had prompted some deeply problematic remarks from Blanc. 'You get the impression that we produce the same kind of players: big, strong, powerful ones,' he said. 'And who are the big, strong, powerful ones? The blacks. That's the way it is . . . The Spanish, they say: "We don't have a problem. We have no blacks."' *L'affaire des quotas* blew a hole through the middle of the *black-blanc-beur* dream of 1998 and Blanc was publicly criticised by both Thuram and Patrick Vieira. Yet an investigation piloted by Minister of Sport Chantal Jouanno found no evidence of racism or discrimination (no quota system having actually been put in place) and Blanc, who protested that his words had been taken out of context, held on to his job. He apologised in a live TV interview, saying that the meeting had 'got out of hand'.

France qualified for Euro 2012 and reached the quarter-finals before losing to eventual champions Spain in Donetsk, but the disciplinary problems remained. Nasri and Alou Diarra had a changing-room altercation after the group-stage defeat by Sweden, Hatem Ben Arfa infuriated Blanc by answering his phone during a post-match briefing and Nasri got involved in a foul-mouthed slanging match with an Agence France-Presse journalist in the mixed zone after France's elimination by Spain. Euro 2012 effectively proved the last hurrah for three of the fabled *Génération '87* – Nasri, Ben Arfa and Jérémy Ménez – and although the fourth member, Benzema, emerged with his international status intact, he would soon have more problems to contend with.

If Blanc had started the clean-up operation after the shame of Knysna, it was left to another hero of 1998 to complete the job. Didier Deschamps had already been touted as a contender to succeed Domenech in 2010 and when Blanc stepped aside in 2012, he duly got the nod. Aged 43, the former France captain boasted an impressive managerial CV – a Champions League final appearance with Monaco in 2004, promotion from Serie B with Juventus in 2007, a first league title for Marseille in 18 years in 2010 – and he was quick to stamp his mark on *Les Bleus*. 'He insisted on discipline,' says Christophe Jallet, who made his France debut in Deschamps' first match, a 0–0 friendly draw with Uruguay in Le Havre in August 2012. 'He said: "No more behavioural problems. We have an image to uphold. We're France players and we have to be irreproachable." He said that meant on the pitch, off the pitch, on social media, all of that. At the first or second get-together, he introduced certain rules. He said: "Don't worry, be yourselves. But when you're with the France team, we're on time, we're respectful, we go and have photos taken with people, we smile. They're there for us, we're there for them. We have to restore the image of the France team. No missteps." I think he chose his squads with that in mind. He knew how to create a good overall atmosphere.'

France's diminished status denied them a place among the top seeds in the qualifying draw for the 2014 World Cup. Drawn alongside Spain, they could only finish second in their group, which pitched them into a play-off against Ukraine. A 2–0 first-leg defeat in Kyiv left Deschamps staring down the barrel of a seismic failure, but the return leg would prove the making of his team. After spending the four days between the two games energetically rallying his players, he made bold decisions for the return fixture. Nasri was dropped, never to return, with Éric Abidal, Loïc Rémy and Olivier Giroud also making way for Mamadou Sakho, Yohan Cabaye, Mathieu Valbuena and Benzema. Amid an uncharacteristically fervent Stade de France atmosphere, the crowd awash with *Tricolore* flags that had been laid out on every seat pre-game, *Les Bleus* stormed to a stirring 3–0 win, Paris Saint-Germain centre-back Sakho proving an unlikely saviour with a brace and Benzema adding the other. After the game, Giroud grabbed the stadium announcer's microphone and led the players and fans in a spontaneous chorus of 'La Marseillaise'. Évra and Ribéry, two of the villains from 2010, were both on the pitch, along with the controversy-prone Benzema, but for the first time since South Africa, everyone was singing (literally) from the same hymn sheet. 'To arrive at the stadium and see that people were really supporting us, rather than having it in for us, that was a defining moment,' says Sagna. France reached the quarter-finals in Brazil before losing 1–0 to eventual champions Germany, but a foundation stone had been laid down.

As hosts, France were not required to qualify for Euro 2016, yet the build-up to the tournament would prove more traumatic than anyone could have imagined. In early November 2015, Benzema became embroiled in another scandal when he was arrested on suspicion of attempting to blackmail his France teammate Valbuena over a sex tape. The case, known as *L'affaire de la sextape*, would rumble on for six years, with Benzema eventually found guilty – alongside four other men – and given a suspended one-year prison sentence. In consultation with FFF president Noël Le Graët, Deschamps decided not to pick the Real Madrid striker (or Valbuena) for Euro 2016. In response, Benzema accused him of having 'given in to pressure from a racist part of France'. Éric Cantona, who had dismissively labelled Deschamps a 'water-carrier' during his playing career, poured fuel on the fire when he suggested that Benzema and Ben Arfa had been overlooked due to their 'north African origins'.[95] Days later, vandals scrawled the word '*raciste*' on the wall of a house in the Brittany town of Concarneau that Deschamps shared with his wife,

---

95 Deschamps sued Cantona for defamation but the case was dismissed.

Claude. The France coach was profoundly hurt by the affair. Graver still were the events of the night of Friday 13 November, 2015, when a triple suicide bombing outside the Stade de France during a friendly game between France and Germany launched rolling attacks across Paris by Islamist terrorists that left 130 innocent people dead. France midfielder Lassana Diarra lost his cousin, Asta Diakité, in the attacks, while Antoine Griezmann's sister, Maud, escaped unhurt from the bloody siege of the Bataclan concert hall. The nation that hosted Euro 2016 was a nation in mourning.

Just as for Jacquet 20 years previously, the European Championship served Deschamps as a platform for a tilt at World Cup glory. After topping their group, France were losing 1–0 to Ireland at half-time of their last 16 match in Lyon when Deschamps made a change that instantly snapped the team's future into focus. Having started the tournament on the right flank in a 4-3-3 system, Griezmann was moved into the number 10 position in a 4-2-3-1 formation when Kingsley Coman came on for N'Golo Kanté. He responded with a two-goal salvo that sent *Les Bleus* into the quarter-finals. The pint-sized Atlético Madrid striker scored again in a 5–2 rout of Iceland and netted both goals in a heady 2–0 semi-final win over Germany in Marseille, taking his tally to a tournament-leading six. An extra-time goal by Lille striker Eder earned Portugal a 1–0 win over an uninspired France in the final, denying the hosts the moment of communal catharsis that the country had craved. But they were getting closer.

There were 10 minutes and 27 seconds on the clock at the Kazan Arena in western Russia when Kylian Mbappé confirmed his reputation as the most electrifying young player in world football. Seizing on a loose ball midway inside France's half, the 19-year-old forward burst between Nicolás Tagliafico and Éver Banega, left Javier Mascherano in his slipstream and blew past Marcos Rojo, who could only bundle him to the ground inside the Argentina box. Griezmann's penalty put France 1–0 up in the last 16 tie, but it was Mbappé's coolly taken second-half brace that ultimately proved decisive in a madcap 4–3 win that became an instant World Cup classic.

Born in Bondy in the northeastern Paris suburbs in December 1998 to a Cameroon-born father and a Franco-Algerian mother, Mbappé had exploded on to the scene with Monaco halfway through the 2016–17 season, inspiring the club to Ligue 1 title glory and a run to the Champions League semi-finals before joining PSG in a blockbuster €180 million transfer. His brace against Argentina made him the first teenager to score twice in a World Cup finals match since Pelé in the 1958 final. The Brazil great later dubbed Mbappé 'my heir'. In France, the player Mbappé brought to mind was Henry. Both hailed from the Paris suburbs, came through the ranks at Clairefontaine and started their professional careers at Monaco, both allied blistering pace with preternaturally composed finishing and both spoke to the media with disarming maturity.[96] As young as Mbappé was, the sight of him tearing the Argentinian defence to shreds came as no surprise to any of his teammates. 'I knew that he was capable of that from his first training session,' smiles former France midfielder Blaise Matuidi. 'From the very beginning, he came in and showed us that he was going to be the man for the next 10 years.'

France had toiled in their 2018 World Cup opener against Australia in Kazan, only prevailing 2–1 thanks to an 81st-minute own goal by Aziz Behich. Deschamps delivered a stinging critique of his players' effort levels in an uncompromising debrief at the squad's base in Istra, 40 miles west of Moscow, the following day. He also changed his approach, ditching the loose-limbed 4-3-3 system that he had used against Australia for a precisely calibrated 4-2-3-1 set-up in which the defensive-minded Matuidi took up a hybrid left-wing role to counterbalance the attacking raids of Mbappé on the opposite flank. Griezmann supported Giroud up front, while in the middle of the park, Deschamps took his cue from Leicester City by fielding a three-man midfield of Paul Pogba with Kanté either side. Mbappé's close-range goal secured a 1–0 win over Peru that

---

96 Mbappé has even drawn upon Henry's *spéciale* to devise a trademark finish of his own. Henry taught a generation of goalkeepers to expect that when a right-footed player drove towards goal from the left flank, they would invariably open their hips and aim a shot inside the right-hand post; Mbappé will surge towards goal and open his hips in exactly the same way, only to drill the ball inside the near post (in French he is said to *ferme son pied* or 'close his foot') at the last moment.

sent *Les Bleus* through to the knockout phase, allowing Deschamps to rest players for a dreary goalless draw with Denmark.

France produced some swashbuckling football against Argentina, not least when left-back Lucas Hernandez crossed for right-back Benjamin Pavard to make it 2–2 early in the second half with an exquisite, swerving half-volley from the edge of the area ('Back post, Pavaaaaaard!' yelped Grégoire Margotton in the TF1 commentary box). But in reality they were a team in the image of their coach, a team of grapplers and grinders, who found that they drew strength from being able to sit deep and hold their opponents at arm's length before hitting them on the break or from set-pieces. 'We tried to play, but we realised that it wasn't us,' said Samuel Umtiti, who partnered Raphaël Varane at centre-back. 'We had to play to our strengths and tell ourselves that, if we want to win, it'll be with our strengths. That's what worked: having a low block and knowing that in attack we'd have chances.'

Nobody typified that approach better than Griezmann, who ran, harried and tackled like a central midfielder and displayed all the tactical canniness that he had learned from Diego Simeone at Atlético; putting his foot on the accelerator when the game needed speeding up, adding a few extra roly-polies every time he won a free-kick when it needed slowing down. His input proved particularly crucial in the quarter-final against Uruguay, whose centre-backs Diego Godín and José Giménez both played alongside him in Madrid. Griezmann cleverly aborted and then restarted his run-up at a 40th-minute free-kick, sowing disarray in the Uruguayan defence and allowing him to pick out Varane for a glancing header that gave France the lead. After a stunning one-handed save from skipper Lloris to repel a header by Martín Cáceres, Fernando Muslera fumbled a shot from Griezmann into the net and France were in the last four.

The 1–0 semi-final win over neighbours Belgium was a rope-a-dope masterclass. Boasting the attacking talents of Kevin De Bruyne, Eden Hazard and Romelu Lukaku and having previously disposed of Brazil, Belgium dominated possession in Saint Petersburg but lost to a 51st-minute Umtiti header from a Griezmann corner. Belgian goalkeeper Thibaut Courtois accused France of playing 'anti-football', while Hazard, who came through the ranks at Lille, said: 'I prefer to lose with this Belgium than win with this France.' Their complaints were music to French ears. 'I want the [second World Cup] star and if I have the star, I don't give a shit about the football we produce,' said Griezmann. Varane described the team as 'cold-blooded killers'. Solidity in defence, opportunism in attack, lucidity in the key moments and vital goals from unlikely sources: it was like 1998 all over again. 'The match [against Belgium] could have gone on all night and we wouldn't have conceded a goal,' says Matuidi. 'We felt so strong on every level.'

France's evolution into a battle-hardened winning machine found an echo in Pogba's development over the course of the tournament. The prancing midfielder was regularly criticised for a lack of defensive discipline in his performances with Manchester United, but in Russia, motivated by football's ultimate prize, he stripped his game down to the bare essentials: fewer shots, fewer dribbles; more tackles, more interceptions. 'I want to win this World Cup and you have to make sacrifices,' he said ahead of the final. 'Defending is not my strong point – I'm not N'Golo – but I do it with pleasure.' He accepted more responsibility off the pitch as well, delivering a series of rousing pre-match team talks that took many of his teammates by surprise and fronting up to the media in a way that he had never previously done on international duty. 'I don't know how and I don't know from where, but Paul Pogba became a leader,' said centre-back Adil Rami. Pogba and his teammates got the rewards for their sacrifices in the final. Slightly fortunate to be 2–1 up at half-time, courtesy of a Mario Mandžukić own goal and a Griezmann penalty, France ran away with the game in the second half. Pogba and Mbappé both scored from outside the box and although Mandžukić embarrassed Lloris by scoring after the Tottenham goalkeeper had attempted to dribble past him, it proved immaterial. Eight years after France had stared into the void in South Africa, *Les Bleus* were back on top of the world.

After a rain-lashed trophy presentation on the Luzhniki Stadium pitch, Pogba turned master of ceremonies for the post-match celebrations, 'dabbing' in the changing room with French President Emmanuel Macron (back when it was still just about a thing) and leading the squad in hearty cries of *'Vive la France!'* and *'Vive la République!'* After the false dawn of the *black-blanc-beur* phenomenon and the soul-searching prompted by *L'affaire des quotas*, these were players who wore their multicultural heritages lightly and affirmed their allegiances proudly.

And thanks to clean-cut figureheads like the charismatic Pogba, the shy, humble Kanté and the dazzlingly articulate Mbappé, they kicked the tired old stereotype of the bad boy footballer from the *banlieues* – France's routinely demonised urban suburbs – firmly into touch.

———

France's approach at the next World Cup in Qatar underlined the extent to which romanticism had given way to pragmatism in the doctrine of the national team. The player in the number 10 shirt was a clinical striker, Mbappé, rather than a stylish playmaker in the mould of Michel Platini,[97] Zidane or even Gourcuff. The nominal playmaker, meanwhile, found himself playing further and further from the opposition goal after Deschamps elected to fully harness Griezmann's appetite for rolling up his sleeves by aligning him in central midfield. France averaged under 40 per cent of possession in their four knockout matches, registered only two shots on target in their 2–0 semi-final win over Morocco and produced a remarkably subdued performance in the final against Argentina in Doha, falling 2–0 down and failing to threaten the opposition goal until Mbappé scored with a penalty and a breath-taking volley in the 80th and 81st minutes to send the game to extra time. His second penalty, in extra time, made him only the second player to complete a hat-trick in a World Cup final after Sir Geoff Hurst for England against West Germany in 1966, cementing his place in the pantheon of France's greatest players at the age of just 23.[98] There were echoes of Seville in the final outcome – a valiant defeat on penalties after an epic 3–3 draw, a provocative opposition goalkeeper (in the form of shoot-out showman Emiliano

---

97 Platini's cultural sway has been diminished in France after FIFA's ethics committee banned him from all football-related activities for eight years – subsequently reduced to four – in December 2015 over a 'disloyal' payment of two million Swiss francs made to him by then FIFA president Sepp Blatter in 2011, forcing him to resign as UEFA president and abandon his bid for the FIFA presidency. Platini and Blatter claimed that it was backdated pay for consultancy work carried out between 1998 and 2002. Both men were cleared of fraud by a Swiss court in July 2022.
98 Mbappé turned 24 two days after the final.

Martínez), grievances about the performance of the referee[99] – but even allowing for the after-effects of a virus that had swept through the French camp prior to the game, there was bafflement as to how Deschamps' side could have contrived to play quite so badly for quite so long. Christophe Dugarry, a long-time Deschamps critic, said that the game's first 80 minutes 'were among the most catastrophic for the France team in the last 50 years'.

Matuidi gives the criticism of France's football under Deschamps short shrift. 'For me, it's not legitimate because when you play football, you play to win,' he says. 'Look at Spain, for example – it's good to make passes, to make 200, 300 passes, but if you don't win at the end, what's the point? When I get up in the morning and look at my cabinet, I see the World Cup. And why is that? Because I won. My son is not going to ask me: "Dad, how many passes did you make?" He'll ask me if I won. I think real football experts know that.'

Lauded for his achievements, but lamented for his lack of panache as both a player and a coach, Deschamps embodies the conflict that has fuelled debate around the French national team over the last 40 years. While his team's style of play may bear little resemblance to Michel Hidalgo's *football à la française* or the *jeu à la nantaise* in which he was schooled at Nantes by Jean-Claude Suaudeau, the gallant heroes of yesteryear do not hold it against him. 'With both the 2018 team and the current one, you have to look at the football that the players are capable of producing,' says Alain Giresse, silky schemer of Hidalgo's *carré magique*. 'I say: "OK, you want more elaborate football – give me the names of the players who have those qualities that stayed at home. I'm listening. Give me the names." We don't have the players that other teams have. What we have is a team that knows how to optimise its potential and win. Take the match against England [in the 2022 World Cup quarter-finals]. The English have a great team and they played well. If [Harry] Kane doesn't miss his penalty, who knows? But in the end, we're tough, we're solid and in football, you don't get marks for technical quality. It's not figure skating!'

Nothing cuts through the noise quite like victory.

---

99 Aggrieved by what they saw as Szymon Marciniak's failure to clamp down on cynical play by Argentina, *L'Équipe*'s journalists awarded him a rating of 2/10.

17

ESPAGNE

THE BALLAD OF ZZ AND KB9

'It felt like him and the ball were the same thing. It was like watching someone play football and dance at the same time.'

Álvaro Mejía, former Real Madrid defender, on Zinédine Zidane

'He always has to show what he is, what he can do. All the time. People are more indulgent with less talented players and yet with him, who is exceptional, it has to be all the time.'

Zidane on Karim Benzema

Elegantly attired in a navy-blue three-piece suit, blue polka dot tie and pale blue shirt, Zinédine Zidane removes the folded black cue card from the black envelope in his hands and opens it towards himself. After reading its contents, he flashes the audience a playful look. 'You don't want any suspense?' he says, mischievously pursing his lips. 'A bit of suspense?' There is a murmur of laughter and he continues. 'The winner of the Ballon d'Or 2022 – and I'm delighted by this reward – *c'est pour toi,* Karim Benzema.' Sitting between Sadio Mané and Kevin De Bruyne on the front row of the auditorium, a bearded, bespectacled Benzema rises from his seat to thunderous applause, buttons up his black suit jacket and slowly climbs the steps to the stage to receive the gleaming Ballon d'Or trophy from the hands of a man whose story has become intertwined with his own. '*Bravo, petit frérot,*'[100] Zidane says quietly as the pair embrace. The audience at the magnificent Théâtre du Châtelet beside the Seine in central Paris, dotted with friends, family members and key figures from Benzema's career, takes a little while to settle, but eventually the applause and the terrace-style chants of 'Karim! Karim!' subside. 'Seeing this in front of me is a source of pride,' Benzema says once he has regained his composure, gesturing towards the glinting golden sphere on the rostrum beside him. 'It was a childhood dream. I grew up with this in my head. And I had motivation because I had two models in my life: Zizou and Ronaldo.' Zidane grins; Ronaldo – the Brazilian version – looks on from the front row with a smile.

Honoured after a remarkable season in which he scored 44 goals in all competitions and inspired Real Madrid to Champions League glory almost single-handedly, Benzema became the fifth French player to win football's most cherished individual honour and the first since Zidane 24 years previously.[101] 'As a Frenchman, coming after Zizou is special, magnificent,' he told *France Football* in an interview to mark the occasion. 'He's important. He's my big brother.' The moment that Zidane and Benzema shared on stage in October 2022 provided a gilded conclusion to a collaboration that seemed to have been written in the stars. The two men's families hail from villages 12 miles apart in the hilly Petite Kabylie region of northern Algeria (Zidane's from Aguemoune, Benzema's from Tighzert). Both grew up in large families in deprived suburbs of major French cities (Zidane in La Castellane, Benzema in Bron). Both made their name with historic French clubs (Zidane with Bordeaux, Benzema with Lyon). Both overcame initial difficulties to flourish in the white jersey of Real Madrid. Although neither was particularly talkative, they spoke with the same bewitching, balletic eloquence when the ball was at their feet. And after Zidane took over as head coach at the

---

100 'Well done, little brother'.
101 The other French winners are Raymond Kopa (1958), Michel Platini (1983, 1984 and 1985) and Jean-Pierre Papin (1991).

Bernabéu in January 2016, they scaled the very highest summits in the sport side by side.

If Italy was where French players went to acquire a winning mentality and England was where they went to toughen up, Spain was where they went to perform. Beginning with Raymond Kopa at Real Madrid in the late 1950s, Spain has served as a kind of ultimate proving ground for French footballers, a place where only the very best succeed and only the very best endure. La Liga did not test your courage and your stamina like the Premier League, it did not test your mettle and your tactical cunning like Serie A, but if your football was not up to scratch, there was no hiding place.

If Johan Cruyff had had his way, Zidane's Spanish adventure might have started five years earlier than it did. Cruyff wanted Barcelona to sign him from Bordeaux in 1996, only for the midfielder to wind up at Juventus (much to the Dutchman's annoyance). Florentino Pérez dreamed of bringing Zidane to Real Madrid even before he became president at the Bernabéu, supposedly setting his heart on the Frenchman after watching his match-winning brace against Brazil in the 1998 World Cup final from the VIP seats at the Stade de France. According to the well-worn tale, Pérez put his plan into motion shortly after becoming Madrid president in 2000 during a gala dinner in Monaco on the eve of the UEFA Super Cup, passing Zidane a napkin on which he had written: 'Do you want to come and play for Madrid?' Zidane wrote his reply in English: 'Yes.' The following summer, he signed a four-year contract at Madrid in a €77.5 million deal that made him, at 29, the most expensive player in football history.

Zidane's early days in the Spanish capital were difficult. The transfer generated huge expectation and a frenzy of media interest, which marked an abrupt change from the tranquil existence he had been leading in Turin. He took time to find his feet on the pitch too, having to effectively un-learn some of the defensive discipline that had been drilled into him at Juve. 'Zidane's first three or four months at Madrid were not easy,' says former Madrid and Cameroon midfielder

Geremi, who acted as Zidane's guide following his arrival. 'He had to change the way that he played because Italian football is not the same as Spanish football. Zidane was a free midfielder. We just wanted him to get on the ball and attack. There were guys like me behind him to do the dirty work. I'd say to Zizou: "Leave it. Just stay there. Let us do our job and when we get the ball, we'll give it to you."' Zidane's initial struggles prompted jokes that Madrid's new recruit wore the number five shirt because he was only half the player that he was with France. He even found himself wondering if he had made a mistake. But eventually, inevitably, his talent told.

The first lightning bolt to spark from his boot-tips occurred in the opening minutes of a home game against Deportivo La Coruña in early January 2002. Collecting a pass from Luís Figo on the edge of the area, Zidane threw the entire Dépor defence into disarray by delicately rolling the ball to the right with the studs of his left boot and then swiftly rolling it to the left with the studs of his right boot before slamming a left-foot shot beyond José Francisco Molina in the visitors' goal. Spanish football, it transpired, was not so difficult after all. 'We knew how good he was because we saw it every day in training,' says Geremi. 'But when we saw that goal, we were like: "Wow!" Sometimes you saw Zidane do things like that and you could only laugh.'

Typically aligned on the left of midfield by Madrid coach Vicente del Bosque, Zidane said that he felt 'free' on the pitch in Spain, as if he had '50 extra centimetres to play with'. Domestically, Zidane's maiden campaign was a disappointment as Madrid finished a distant third in La Liga and lost the Copa del Rey final – at the Bernabéu, on the club's 100th anniversary – to Deportivo. But in the Champions League final against Bayer Leverkusen in Glasgow, Zidane scored the goal that he had been signed to score, the goal of his life, using his (weaker) left foot to meet Roberto Carlos' looping left-wing cross with a majestically awkward hip-high volley from just inside the box that rocketed the ball into the top-left corner. It brought Madrid a ninth European Cup and gave Zidane, after two lost finals with Juve, his first.

Zidane was the perfect footballer for the discerning spectators at the Bernabéu, with their overhead heaters and their opera house sensibilities, who came to the stadium to be entertained rather than to support. It was not just that he scored and created unforgettable goals; every Velcro-like first touch, every *roulette*, every delicately feathered pass prompted warm purrs of appreciation. Madrid legend Alfredo Di Stéfano said that he played 'as if he had silk gloves on each foot'. Even daily exposure to Zidane's gifts did not dull their impact. 'I said to my friends many times: "You have the luck to see Zidane 50 times per year during the games that we play,"' says Álvaro Mejía, a Madrid academy graduate who played alongside Zidane for three years. '"But I have the luck to see Zidane 300 days a year, every year. And there are 250 days when we are training and nobody else is watching because the cameras aren't allowed in and we have the chance to watch him. And every single day you see something different." It felt like him and the ball were the same thing. It was like watching someone play football and dance at the same time.'

Ronaldo's arrival in 2002, off the back of World Cup redemption with Brazil, took some of the spotlight off Zidane and with the pair quickly striking up an understanding, Madrid surged to La Liga glory. Then the silverware dried up, the team finally buckling beneath the unbearable weight of Pérez's *Zidanes y Pavones* project,[102] to which David Beckham was added in 2003. Zidane announced his retirement in April 2006, aged 33, saying: 'For two years I haven't been playing how I want to.' He bowed out in front of the Madrid fans with a goal in a 3–3 draw against Villarreal, delicately heading home a deep Beckham cross, before appending an unexpectedly brilliant coda to his career at the 2006 World Cup in Germany. But it would be *au revoir* to the Bernabéu rather than *adieu*.

Had the planets aligned slightly differently, Zidane and Benzema might have played together for France. The Lyon youngster received his first senior international call-up in November 2006, only four months after Zidane had traipsed off a football pitch for the final time following his infamous headbutt on Marco Materazzi in Berlin. Yet although Benzema never played with Zidane, it

----

102 Pérez's plan was to pair big-money signings like Zidane with youth-team graduates like centre-back Francisco Pavón.

was hard not to think of Zidane when you saw him play. There was the same languid ease, the same brooding expression, the same effortless manner of nudging the ball along with the outside of the foot. Pérez certainly thought so, often describing Benzema as 'a cross between Zidane and Ronaldo'. The Madrid president had resigned in February 2006, unable to deny the stark failure of the *Galácticos* era, but he would return to the role three years later with Zidane alongside him in an advisory role and new superstar signings in his sights.

There was no shortage of interest in Benzema in the summer of 2009. The 21-year-old striker had scored 54 goals for Lyon over the previous two seasons and was the subject of approaches from Manchester United, Barcelona and Internazionale. But he had always dreamed of playing for Madrid and Pérez had impressed him by visiting him at his family home on Rue Marcel-Cerdan in Bron and conversing with his family in French. The transfer fee of €35 million rising to €41 million paled in comparison beside the record-breaking amounts previously shelled out for Kaká (€67 million) and Cristiano Ronaldo (€94 million) and whereas around 55,000 people turned out for the Brazilian's unveiling and a crowd of 80,000 packed the Bernabéu for Ronaldo's first steps in a white shirt, a more modest total of 20,000 attended Benzema's presentation. His first season was similarly low-key. Principally used as back-up for Gonzalo Higuaín by Manuel Pellegrini, Benzema made only 14 league starts and scored only eight goals. Things scarcely improved under new coach José Mourinho, who continued to prefer Higuaín and upbraided Benzema for his lack of effort in training. When the Frenchman failed to find the net in a 0–0 draw at third-tier Murcia in the Copa del Rey in October 2010, *Marca*'s front page declared that he was 'dead'.

After a back injury ruled Higuaín out for several months, Mourinho provocatively flaunted his disappointment. 'If you have a dog to go hunting with, you catch more; if you have a cat, you catch less, but you can still hunt,' he told a press conference. 'We only have one attacker and that's Benzema.' Benzema, by his own admission, 'lost it' when he heard Mourinho's comments and immediately demanded a meeting with him. 'The main thing was to tell him that of course we wanted more from him,' says José Morais, who was Mourinho's assistant in Madrid. 'I think one of his questions was: "But what do you want from me?" And Mourinho told him in his very simple way: "I want you to score goals.'" Benzema had scored only one league goal since the start of the season but, freed from the competition with the sidelined Higuaín, he notched up 14 in 15 games over the run-in, finishing with a healthy tally of 26 in all competitions. At Mourinho's request, Zidane had taken up a liaison role between the coaching staff and club management in November 2010. At the end of the season, he became sporting director, notably piloting Madrid's recruitment of future France centre-back Raphaël Varane from Lens. Behind the scenes, Zidane took Benzema under his wing and became his most vocal advocate. 'The relationship between Zidane and Karim was special because Zidane thought that he was an extraordinary player with unbelievable talent,' says Morais. 'In our conversations, he was always mentioning Karim's quality.'

Benzema reported for pre-season training in 2011 seven kilogrammes lighter than he had been a year previously and began the campaign as Madrid's first-choice number nine. Spearheaded by a front four of Benzema, Ronaldo, Mesut Özil and Ángel Di María, Mourinho's team played spectacular counter-attacking football and romped to the league title in historic fashion, smashing in a record 121 goals and becoming the first side in La Liga history to amass 100 points. Benzema, who eclipsed Zidane's tally of 49 Madrid goals in mid-season, said that he felt 'full of confidence'.

Mourinho's replacement by Carlo Ancelotti in 2013 and the arrival from Tottenham Hotspur of Gareth Bale prompted changes for both Zidane and Benzema, the former becoming Ancelotti's assistant, the latter forming a new-look 'BBC' front three alongside Ronaldo and Bale. Locked into his era-defining goalscoring rivalry with Barcelona's Lionel Messi, Ronaldo was the player to whom all of Madrid's roads led, but Benzema was happy to accept a supporting role. 'The finisher was Cristiano,' he told RMC Sport in 2019. 'With him, I played in another role. More in the build-up, in movement, to create space. A number nine doesn't necessarily have to be a goalscorer. For me, Cristiano was the goalscorer. With Bale, all three of us scored goals, but Cristiano scored 30 more than the rest. And I brought him a lot.' It says much about Benzema's altruism that for all the memorable goals he scored at Madrid, perhaps his most celebrated individual moment was the remarkable byline wriggle past three Atlético Madrid players that set up a goal for Isco in the Champions League semi-finals in May 2017. A creator as well as a finisher, Benzema has always considered himself 'a number nine with the soul of a number 10'.

Ancelotti led Madrid to penalty shoot-out glory against Atlético in the 2014 Champions League final in Lisbon and when Zidane succeeded Rafael Benítez as head coach in January 2016, having spent the previous 18 months coaching the reserves, *Los Blancos* took control of the competition in a manner reminiscent of the club's 1950s heyday, winning it for three seasons running. During his storied playing career, few had considered the shy, temperamental Zidane to be manager material and he admitted himself that the idea could not have been further from his mind when he hung up his boots in 2006. But he had been quietly absorbing influences throughout his career and emerged into his first top-level role as a fully formed, Italian-style elite coach, characterised above all by his consummately calm squad management. 'It's not a method, he's just like that: he has a natural connection with the changing room,' Zidane's assistant, David Bettoni, told *L'Équipe* in July 2020. 'Sorry for those waiting for a very specific "Zidane recipe"! I'd just say that he is the modern coach par excellence. Which is to say a man who is passionate, adaptable, who works a lot and who has great control of his emotions.' Having also yielded La Liga glory in 2017 and 2020, it was an approach that turned Zidane into one of the most decorated coaches of all time.

With Benzema, he kept his advice to a minimum; encouraging him, for example, to make more aggressive runs when attacking the ball in the penalty area, rather than dropping off for cut-backs. He remained the striker's most ardent defender, repeatedly making the case for him to be recalled by France throughout his long international exile over *L'affaire de la sextape*.[103] 'He always has to show what he is, what he can do. All the time,' Zidane said in 2017. 'People are more indulgent with less talented players and yet with him, who is exceptional, it has to be all the time.' By the time Zidane returned to the Madrid dug-out in March 2019, having walked away after completing his hat-trick of Champions League victories in 2018, Benzema had entered the thrilling final

---

103 Benzema was finally recalled by France coach Didier Deschamps in May 2021 after over five years in the international wilderness. He played at Euro 2020 (staged in 2021 due to the Covid-19 pandemic) and inspired France to victory in the 2021 UEFA Nations League, but retired from international football in December 2022 after missing the World Cup through injury.

phase of his Bernabéu evolution. No longer obliged to toil in the shadows on behalf of Ronaldo, who left for Juventus in 2018, he was finally able to play as the complete, dominating centre-forward that he had always wanted to be. With extraordinary results. Having managed a meagre 12 goals in all competitions in the final season of his collaboration with Ronaldo, his goal tallies in the next five seasons went: 30, 27, 30, 44, 31. Zidane left Madrid for a third time in 2021 and the Champions League campaign that followed proved to be Benzema's crowning glory. 'KB9' bent the competition to his will with a bravura that stretched the bounds of credibility, netting tie-turning hat-tricks against Paris Saint-Germain in the last 16 and Chelsea in the quarter-finals and scoring three vital goals across two legs against Manchester City in the last four before Vinícius Júnior's goal sank Liverpool in the final to give him a fifth European crown. 'He knows how to do everything,' says his former Lyon and France teammate Sidney Govou. 'I don't think people even realise.' Ballon d'Or glory, when it finally arrived, was a formality.

By the time Benzema left, aged 35, for Saudi Arabian club Al-Ittihad in June 2023, he had scored 354 goals for Madrid – second only to Cristiano Ronaldo – in 648 appearances and won more trophies than any player in the club's history. Despite a relatively meagre international goal return of 37 from 97 caps and competition from such storied figures as Just Fontaine, Jean-Pierre Papin, Thierry Henry, Olivier Giroud and Kylian Mbappé, Benzema's partisans consider him the greatest striker that France has ever produced. 'Everyone has their favourite,' said Zidane. 'But for me, it's Karim.'

18

LE FOOT FÉMININ

LYON LIGHT THE WAY

'The boys and girls rub shoulders and for us, that sends a powerful message. From a sporting perspective, playing with the boys allows the girls to grow and to reach the highest possible level. But it also shows the boys that the girls know how to play football.'

Sonia Bompastor

After a turbulent few weeks, there is an upbeat, end-of-term feeling in the air as the players of Olympique Lyonnais Féminin walk out for training on this mild, overcast afternoon in late May 2023. Three days previously, an 88th-minute header by Danish striker Signe Bruun settled a taut title decider against arch-rivals Paris Saint-Germain at the Parc des Princes to give OL a record-extending 16th French women's championship. The club is staging an open training session at the Groupama OL Training Center in Décines-Charpieu, seven miles east of central Lyon, and around 300 fans are scattered across the white, red and blue plastic seats in the small, covered stand that overlooks the complex's main pitch, the Terrain d'honneur Gérard Houllier. The crowd is largely made up of families and young girls, some of whom wear replica jerseys with players' names on the back (MAJRI 7, CAYMAN 23, LE SOMMER D. 9). A young boy in a white OL home shirt holds up a homemade cardboard sign that reads '*16 FOIS MERCI*' ('16 TIMES THANK YOU') in red and blue bubble writing.

Sight of the players emerging from the changing room on the far side of the pitch in their light-grey training tops and shorts, the towering figure of skipper Wendie Renard immediately recognisable, is greeted by applause, the stamping of feet and a slightly timorous chant of '*Champions de France!*' After a light jog around the pitch and some plyometric drills, the players walk over for some *toro* possession exercises in front of the fans. A group of girls hanging over a steel railing at the foot of the stand scream 'Ada!' as Lyon's Norwegian superstar Ada Hegerberg approaches. The inaugural Women's Ballon d'Or winner responds with a friendly wave. The players split into three groups of seven for the *toros*: five passers and two piggies in the middle clutching blue bibs in their hands. Shouts and peals of laughter ring out as the chasers hare from player to player in pursuit of the ball. Wearing a navy-blue Adidas tracksuit, the short, blonde-haired figure of Lyon coach Sonia Bompastor walks between the groups observing, her arms loosely folded across her chest, a relaxed smile upon her face.

It is the end of an era at Olympique Lyonnais. Jean-Michel Aulas is stepping down as president after 36 years in the role and the new owner of parent company OL Groupe, John Textor, is in the process of selling the club's ultra-successful women's team to American businesswoman Michele Kang. South Korea-born Kang, who made her fortune in medical technology, has pledged to associate OL Féminin with Washington Spirit, the National Women's Soccer League (NWSL) franchise that she owns, in a new multi-club structure, all while preserving its existing identity. Aulas, who built up OL Féminin almost from scratch, had made an emotional appearance at the women's Coupe de France final between Lyon and PSG in Orléans 11 days previously, walking from the field with his eyes full of tears after greeting his players prior to kick-off.

Sitting in an office within the OL training centre shortly before the day's training session begins, Bompastor concedes that keeping a lid on her feelings has not been easy. 'It was a very difficult moment,' she says. 'I had to hide my emotions and make sure that my players stayed focused on our sporting objectives. Today, we've achieved our objectives and I can release my emotions a little. Everyone knows how important President Aulas is to his women's team. He's a man who's enabled French women's football and OL Féminin to have everything that we have today. It's hard to say to yourself that it's over, to really realise it. We have a lot of love and a lot of respect for everything that he's done. There will never be strong enough words to thank him.'

A clinical first-half brace from Hegerberg earned Lyon a 2–1 win over PSG in the Coupe de France final, completing the club's ninth league and cup Double in 12 seasons. But although OL have been the dominant force in both domestic and continental women's football over the previous 15 years, the competition are catching up. PSG, funded by their powerful Qatari owners, stunned Lyon to win the French league title in 2021, bringing an end to 14 unbroken years of OL success. Despite an unprecedented eight victories in the Women's Champions League since 2010, Lyon do not lord it over the competition as imperiously as they once did, having gone out in the quarter-finals in both 2021 (to PSG) and 2023 (to Barcelona), either side of victory over Barça in the 2022 final in Turin. The financial might of Barcelona and the major English clubs means that Lyon are no longer the only show in town in the transfer market as well. 'Just a few years ago, when you picked up the phone to call a player and say: "Do you want to come and play for Olympique Lyonnais?", the answer was yes,' says Bompastor, who spent six years playing for OL over two spells between 2006 and 2013. 'We managed to bring in all the best players. But if you look at what's been happening recently, Barcelona are a step ahead of Olympique Lyonnais and so are England with their professional league. We have to make up the ground we've lost in France to keep pace with the competition. Because it's not easy to be European champions any more. Even in France with Paris Saint-Germain, the competition has tightened up and we're seeing that again with the Coupe de France and the championship [being closer].'

Bompastor has spoken to Kang and is optimistic about what her ownership will bring ('When you look at everything she has already achieved in her career, she's not come to Olympique Lyonnais to sink the club,' the former left-back says), but as her players, their training session finished, amble over to the supporters to sign shirts and pose for selfies, the club stands poised to make a step into the unknown.

When Marilou Duringer-Erckert first started kicking a ball around in the little Alsatian village of Schwindratzheim in the mid-1960s, the notion that French women's players might one day play matches inside full stadiums, benefit from state-of-the-art training facilities and earn a living from the game would have appeared impossibly fanciful. While still in her teens, she helped to set up one of France's oldest extant women's football teams at FC Schwindratzheim (later to become FC Vendenheim after a merger with another local club). It was the beginning of a journey that would turn her into one of the most influential figures in the development of the French women's game. 'It was in 1965,' she tells me in a Zoom call from her home in Alsace, a whole lifetime of football paraphernalia (photographs, pennants, certificates) visible on the wall of her office behind her. 'We'd heard that there were women's teams in Italy and because I was always watching my friends from the village play on the boys' team, one of the directors of FC Schwindratzheim asked me if I'd be up for launching a women's team. I said: "Sure, why not?" We started training and in 1967 we played our first match against another women's team from Gerstheim in front of 1,500 spectators.' A decent crowd for a first match, I suggest. Duringer-Erckert smiles. 'Well, the men came to see the women's thighs,' she says. 'We know they didn't come to watch the football back then. Everyone told me: "Marilou, [women] playing football, it's not going to work, what are you doing, blah blah blah." For some, it wasn't a sport for women. But we persevered, we continued to exist and lots of other teams soon followed.'

Women's football had been played in France since as far back as the 1910s. The first women's match, contested by two teams from multisport club Fémina Sport, took place in Paris in September 1917. A women's championship was founded two years later and, in the spring of 1920, a French representative team toured England, playing four exhibition matches against pioneering English women's club Dick, Kerr Ladies in front of tens of thousands of spectators.[104] But the French Football Federation, established in 1919, refused to recognise women's football and after the outbreak of World War II, it was banned by the collaborationist Vichy regime in 1941. It would be another 30 years before the FFF gave the women's game its seal of approval, after a chain of events spurred

104 Dick, Kerr Ladies began life as the works team of British rail transport manufacturer Dick, Kerr & Co.

by an exhibition match that took place in Reims in August 1968. Pierre Geoffroy, a sports journalist from regional newspaper *L'Union*, was looking for a showpiece event for the paper's annual summer fair (a dwarfs' wrestling contest having taken centre stage the previous year) and decided to organise a women's football match. The women who took part, recruited via a notice in *L'Union*, enjoyed the experience so much that they persuaded Geoffroy to keep the team going. Originally known as Football Club Féminin Reims, they were absorbed by Stade de Reims in November 1969 and became the de facto French national team, taking up invitations to play exhibition matches all over Europe. Their endeavours moved the FFF to finally recognise women's football in March 1970 and a new national championship was launched four years later.

Duringer-Erckert was called up by Geoffroy for a training camp with the France team in the early 1970s, but her employer, an insurance company, refused to give her the time off. In 1985, aged 36, she became the first woman to sit on the FFF's federal council. Surrounded by disinterested grey suits, she had to fight to have her voice heard. 'They were dinosaurs,' she says. 'All so macho. It was always the last topic of the meeting, even though I had so many things to ask for and propose because nothing existed. Some of them would have their briefcases on the table, ready to leave. Others would be reading *L'Équipe*. Every time, the answer was: "We'll see about that later." I came home in tears sometimes. But I kept fighting. At the start, I'd said: "I don't need you to like women's football, I just need you not to put sticks in its spokes." And little by little, I managed to get women's football accepted.' Duringer-Erckert, who is now in her mid-70s, went on to become head of the French women's team delegation and accompanied *Les Bleues* to a string of major tournaments.

The spark for the next phase of French women's football's development came from a very unlikely source. As long-standing president of Montpellier's men's team, Louis 'Loulou' Nicollin was most widely known for his corpulence and his unapologetically coarse vocabulary, but in 2001 he agreed to a merger with local women's team Montpellier Le Crès, thereby becoming the first president of a French professional club to possess a dedicated women's section. He allowed the female players to share the men's facilities, kitted them out in brand-new kit and set out to recruit the best women's footballers around. 'When you have a president who comes to see you and tells you that he wants you, that obviously counts for a lot,' says former France playmaker Camille Abily, who joined Montpellier upon graduating from Clairefontaine in 2003.[105] 'It's true that he could be a bit vulgar and a bit sexist, but he had a real commitment and a real desire to develop his team. He really was the pioneer in France.'

Under Nicollin's stewardship, his *'gonzesses'* ('birds') won two French league titles and three Coupes de France, bringing success to Montpellier at a time when the men's team were yoyoing between Ligue 1 and Ligue 2. Nicollin was hurt when Lyon began to cherry-pick his best players, which ended Montpellier's brief reign as France's leading women's side, but Aulas at least had the grace to acknowledge his debt. 'He was my master,' Aulas said of Nicollin, who died in 2017. 'He was the one who invented professional women's football in France, not me.'

Aulas was in the process of building one dynasty at Olympique Lyonnais when a phone call in late 2003 presented him with an opportunity to construct another. FC Lyon, the city's women's team, were in dire financial straits and with Aulas beginning to enjoy success with his men's team, Lyon deputy mayor Thierry Braillard wondered if he might be able to help. Aulas duly agreed to absorb FC Lyon into Olympique Lyonnais and on 1 July, 2004, OL Féminin was born. Aulas knew as little about women's football as he had known about men's football prior to taking charge of OL in 1987, but he was guided by strong principles about gender equality that he had inherited from his mother, a mathematics teacher, who took her own life when he was 28. He saw the foundation of a women's team as an opportunity to 'set an example'.

In the early days of the team's existence, it was a case of make do and mend. 'At the start, we didn't have kit in club colours, no set changing room and we took our kitbags home with us,' said centre-back Renard, who arrived in Lyon from her native Martinique in 2006. 'We travelled by bus – the plane was

---

105 Clairefontaine began to admit female players in 1998.

reserved for the European Cup. For the French championship, we'd travel the day before and we trained when we arrived, sometimes after a seven-hour journey.' During a UEFA Women's Cup[106] quarter-final match against Arsenal in November 2007, played beneath torrential rain at Meadow Park in Borehamwood, Aulas was horrified to discover his players wringing out their shirts and socks in the changing room showers at half-time because they only had one set of kit each. At the time, French women's teams still had amateur status, obliging Aulas to find jobs for his players within the club in order to pay them salaries.

Bompastor and Abily both arrived from Montpellier in 2006, but in January 2009 they accepted offers from clubs in Women's Professional Soccer, the short-lived American championship that pre-dated the launch of the NWSL in 2013. Their departures helped Aulas to convince the FFF to introduce 'federal contracts' in March 2009, which authorised French clubs to pay their female players according to fixed salary guidelines. During her first Lyon stint, Abily had to juggle a sports science course and a coaching role in the OL academy on top of her duties as a player, but upon returning to the club in 2010, she could focus on playing full-time. 'That was the really great thing about the federal contracts,' she says. 'When I was a student and I also worked at the club, I worked from eight in the morning until nine at night, non-stop. You can't be as demanding with someone who's done a full day's work and arrives on the pitch at 6:30 p.m. as you can with a girl who does nothing else and comes to training at 10 in the morning.'

Aulas overcame resistance from within the club to give the women's players access to the same facilities as the men, which today includes the medical department, treatment rooms, a balneotherapy area and strength and conditioning equipment. 'We had everything that we needed,' says Reynald Pedros, the former Nantes winger, who coached OL Féminin between 2017 and 2019. 'You could argue that we had an even better operation than some men's teams in Ligue 1. The set-up was first-class.' The same principles hold true at academy level, where boys and girls play together from Under-7 to Under-15

---

106 Rebranded as the UEFA Women's Champions League in 2009.

level. Lyon became the first French club to set up a mixed academy in 2016, appointing Bompastor as the first director of its female section. 'The boys and girls rub shoulders and for us, that sends a powerful message,' says Bompastor. 'From a sporting perspective, playing with the boys allows the girls to grow and to reach the highest possible level. But it also shows the boys that the girls know how to play football.'

Lyon very quickly became the dominant force in the French women's game, securing the first of 14 consecutive league titles in 2006–07. Before long they were winning championships without dropping a single point.[107] Just as with the men's team, Aulas set his sights on European glory early on, announcing an ambition to conquer the continent within three years in 2006. This objective prompted a widening of Lyon's horizons in the transfer market, with Costa Rican attacking midfielder Shirley Cruz, prolific Swedish striker Lotta Schelin and Swiss midfielder Lara Dickenmann arriving in the early years, to be followed by internationally renowned players such as Hegerberg, US stars Alex Morgan, Megan Rapinoe and Lindsey Horan, England internationals Lucy Bronze and Nikita Parris, Canadian centre-back Kadeisha Buchanan and German playmaker Dzsenifer Marozsán.

Following a 7–6 defeat on penalties by German side Turbine Potsdam in the 2010 Champions League final, Lyon turned to straight-talking former Montpellier Féminines coach Patrice Lair, whose scrupulousness and sapping fitness work took OL up another gear. Lyon became European champions in 2011, scaling the one summit that had proved beyond the men's team by beating Potsdam 2–0 at Craven Cottage thanks to a first-half poacher's goal from Renard and a composed left-foot strike by substitute Dickenmann five minutes from time. 'It was magnificent, that first final, because we managed to beat one of the German giants,' says Abily, who was voted player of the match. 'They're still a great nation today, but back then, it was so hard to beat them. It was a magical moment.' Lyon successfully defended their crown the year after, beating Frankfurt 2–0 in front of 50,212 supporters at Munich's Olympiastadion, and then, after a four-year gap, emulated the legendary Real Madrid men's team of

---

107 A feat achieved in 2010–11, 2012–13 and 2014–15.

the 1950s by winning the Champions League for five seasons in a row between 2016 and 2020. Aulas had built not just the most successful club side that French football had ever seen, but one of the most dominant teams in the history of world sport.

———

In stark contrast to the men's game, club sides lead the way in French women's football and the national team lags behind. Until 2024, *Les Bleues* had never reached a major tournament final at senior level, their legacy at World Cups and European Championships a litany of what ifs, penalty shoot-out heartache and agonising near-misses. Prior to a quarter-final exit at the 2009 European Championship in Finland, the French women's team had never even made it beyond the group phase at a major competition. But two years later, at the World Cup in Germany, a run to the semi-finals put the women's game on the map.

Coached by the quirky, poetry-loving Bruno Bini, who played alongside Michel Platini at Nancy, a team featuring Bompastor, Abily, veteran skipper Sandrine Soubeyrand and quicksilver attacking midfielder Louisa Nécib eliminated England on penalties in the quarter-finals before losing 3–1 to the United States in the last four. With the men's game in disgrace after France's shameful 2010 World Cup campaign and *L'affaire des quotas*, and with OL Féminin having just conquered Europe, it put women's football in the national spotlight for the first time. 'There was a before and an after 2011,' says former France left-back Laure Boulleau. 'France had behaved very badly with the boys at the World Cup in South Africa, but we created a buzz by getting to the semi-finals. We had a great team and we were very approachable, which was the opposite of what we'd seen in 2010. When we got home, there were fans at the airport and we had a signing session at the Nike boutique on the Champs-Élysées that was crazy. There were people everywhere. That's when things started to happen with the media and sponsors, plus there was the emergence of social media. We sort of became France's favourite team.'

In response to the team's performance in Germany, newly elected FFF president Noël Le Graët increased the budget allocated to women's football and began to give *Les Bleues* the same level of logistical support as *Les Bleus*. But despite the consistent presence of a sizeable Lyon contingent well versed in the art of winning trophies, France's women have been unable to take the final step, falling in the quarter-finals at the World Cups of 2015, 2019 and 2023 and losing to Germany in the last four at Euro 2022. Milestone victories have often been within touching distance – penalties putting paid to French hopes against Denmark at Euro 2013, the great Gaëtane Thiney squandering an open goal in extra time against Germany in 2015 – but France have repeatedly come up just short. 'I think we were missing something psychologically,' says Abily, who retired in 2017 with 183 caps and 37 goals to her name. 'To find that little bit extra to put your foot in when you need to score, to counter-attack or not to concede.' Boulleau, who is now France's most high-profile female pundit, believes the team lack a 'killer edge'. 'I don't know why we lack it,' she says. 'Maybe it's a French thing, I don't know.'

In recent years, the national team's quest for glory was undermined by recurring tensions between the players and disciplinarian coach Corinne Diacre. Previously known for her breakthrough role as head coach of men's side Clermont, Diacre fell out with a succession of high-profile OL players, stripping Renard of the captaincy in 2017,[108] publicly criticising striker Eugénie Le Sommer over her positioning during the 2019 World Cup and omitting experienced midfielder Amandine Henry from her squad for Euro 2022. 'It really affected the players' morale when they returned from international duty,' says former Lyon coach Pedros. 'They weren't in a good place mentally.' Matters came to a head in February 2023 when Renard and PSG stars Marie-Antoinette Katoto and Kadidiatou Diani announced that they would no longer play for France under the team's existing management structure. Diacre was promptly dismissed by the FFF and replaced by former Zambia and Ivory Coast men's coach Hervé Renard. He would steer the team to a first ever final, in the 2023–24 UEFA Nations League, only for Seville to prove a graveyard of French ambition once again by providing the stage for a one-sided 2-0 loss to world champions Spain.

---

108 Diacre reappointed Renard as captain in 2021.

France successfully hosted the 2019 World Cup, with over 1.1 million supporters attending matches during the tournament, but in the eyes of many of those who work within the French women's game, it represented a missed opportunity. Whereas England's staging of Euro 2022 yielded a bumper new television rights deal for the Women's Super League and an enormous 172 per cent increase in domestic attendances,[109] France – which was immediately disadvantaged by the onset of the Covid-19 pandemic – experienced no such uptick after hosting the World Cup. Average attendances in the women's top flight remain stubbornly below 1,000 (compared to over 5,500 in England) and broadcasting revenues are dwarfed by those recouped on the other side of the Channel, with TV viewers often put off by matches being filmed at pitch level in poky municipal stadiums. Progress, though, may yet be at hand.

Tasked by the FFF with developing a plan for the future of the women's game in France, a special commission headed up by Aulas devised proposals to launch a fully professional league in 2024, raising hopes that an exciting new dawn might be about to break. 'When you consider everything that President Aulas has already done for women's football, his knowledge of the top level, his knowledge of women's football and his experience, I'm optimistic,' says Bompastor as she prepares to head out to lead training. 'It had to be done. But the important thing now is to get the project up and running. There's no time to lose.'

109 Announced in March 2021, the domestic broadcasting rights deal with the BBC and Sky Sports was reported to be worth around £8 million per season. Attendance figure refers to the 2022–23 Women's Super League season, taken from Ernst & Young report published in July 2023.

19

PARIS SAINT-GERMAIN

ALL THAT GLITTERS

'It took time to recover mentally from that moment. It wasn't easy for your family, for your friends, for the people who love Paris Saint-Germain. You were even ashamed to leave the house.'

Blaise Matuidi

Lionel Messi has already started drifting over towards the touchline as the last few seconds tick down in stoppage time. When the final whistle sounds, he puts his hands on his hips and gazes back towards the pitch for a moment. Then he turns and walks off, slapping hands with Marseille centre-back Duje Ćaleta-Car and a member of the OM coaching staff as they pass him, before heading straight down the tunnel without so much as a look towards the Paris Saint-Germain supporters. The jaunty strains of 'Go West' by the Village People fill the stadium and behind both goals at the Parc des Princes, pyrotechnics blaze. But the players do not linger on the pitch and the stadium quickly empties. It should be a moment for celebration: PSG have beaten arch-rivals Marseille 2–1 – effectively ending OM's faint title hopes – and closed to within touching distance of a record-equalling 10th Ligue 1 crown. It is a warm, still mid-April evening in 2022, the sky over the stadium at kick-off a soft, inky blue, and Paris have their feared 'MNM' strike-force of Messi, Neymar and Kylian Mbappé in action. Yet in this year as in so many others in the club's recent history, Paris in the spring is not a happy place.

Five weeks previously, PSG slumped to the latest in a series of seemingly endless Champions League humiliations when they were turfed out of the competition by Real Madrid in the round of 16. Leading 2–0 on aggregate with half an hour remaining in the second leg at the Bernabéu, PSG succumbed to one of the meltdowns that has become their trademark, allowing Karim Benzema to score a 17-minute hat-trick that sent Madrid into the quarter-finals. When the team returned to league action at home to Bordeaux four days later, the club's furious *ultras* jeered their own players, angrily whistling Messi and Neymar – symbols, in their eyes, of a failed project in which headline-grabbing signings had been prioritised over sporting coherence – every time they touched the ball.

The anger has diminished by the time Marseille come to the capital, giving way to an apathy that in its own way is even more problematic. The hardcore fans in the Virage Auteuil have been officially on strike since the game in Madrid, symbolised by the turning upside-down of a huge white 'VIRAGE 1991[110] AUTEUIL' banner that stretches along the bottom of the top tier at the ground's northeastern end. The stand is full, but the fans are largely silent. Although they cheer PSG's two goals – a volleyed lob from Neymar, a penalty in first-half stoppage time from Mbappé – they do not sing. The only sustained noise from the terraces comes from the Junior Club at the junction of the Virage Auteuil and the Tribune Borelli, where children respond to the steady drumbeat of a lone drummer and the chants of an official with a loudhailer by rhythmically slapping their red inflatable clappers together.

PSG lead 2–1 at half-time and the second half is a non-event, an effort from Mbappé that is ruled out for offside the hosts' sole attempt at goal. Amazon Prime Video's pitch-side pundit Thierry Henry describes the match as '*soporifique*'. When the television camera alights on Mbappé sitting on the bench after being substituted, he looks like he might be about to fall asleep. PSG coach Mauricio Pochettino, often an animated touchline presence during his five-year spell at Tottenham Hotspur, spends practically the entire match seated in the dug-out. His post-match press conference is barely more animated. Sitting beside his

---

110 In reference to the year the *ultras* first took up residence on the Virage Auteuil.

assistant and unofficial interpreter Miguel D'Agostino in a blue club tracksuit, Pochettino responds flatly in Spanish to the questions put to him by the French journalists. 'Do you think PSG deserved to win?' he is asked at one point. '*Sí*,' he replies, without elaborating. The following weekend, PSG clinch the title with a 1–1 draw at home to Lens, giving Pochettino the first championship success of his coaching career. A little over two months after that, he is gone.

As you peer down into the stadium from the press box at the back of the Tribune Borelli, the signs of the transformation that the club has undergone since its takeover by Qatar's sovereign wealth fund in 2011 are all around. The ground underwent a major €75 million renovation ahead of the 2016 European Championship and everything inside it is shiny and clean. The pitch, tended to since 2013 by award-winning Northern Irish groundsman Jonathan Calderwood, is immaculate. There are pitch-side adverts for Qatar Airways, Visit Qatar and principal shirt sponsor Accor Live Limitless, the hotel chain's loyalty programme. A Spidercam swoops and glides above the players' heads, LED screens flash and twinkle, the music booms out from a concert-worthy audio system. Messi's sensational arrival from Barcelona the previous summer, after financial difficulties prevented the Catalan giants from offering him a new contract, has had the desired effect in commercial terms. The club shifts over one million replica shirts over the course of the 2021–22 campaign, 60 per cent of which have his name and squad number (30) on the back, announces 11 new commercial partnerships and sees sponsorship revenue surpass €300 million for the first time.

From a sporting perspective, things are much less clear-cut. Tearfully torn away from the club of his life and obliged to spend his first three months in Paris living in a hotel with his wife and three sons, Messi struggles to adjust to Ligue 1's rugged football, has to overcome a bad bout of Covid and finishes the season with his lowest tally of league goals – six – in 16 years. Months later, he will experience the crowning moment of his astonishing career by captaining Argentina to World Cup glory in Qatar. But despite a second successive Ligue 1 title, the world's finest footballer will leave Paris for Inter Miami in June 2023 with the fans' jeers ringing in his ears and having made only a faint and fleeting impression upon the French game. A whirlwind of money and misery, expectation and recrimination, domestic dominance and continental calamity, it is a transfer that encapsulates the peculiar modern existence of the world's most puzzling super-club.

———

Curiously for a major European capital, Paris was traditionally something of a football backwater. Clubs from the capital shone during French football's amateur era, notably winning the first six Coupes de France in the years immediately following World War I, but a combination of factors – low municipal funding,[111] competition from slickly run provincial rivals, a high proportion of inhabitants hailing from other parts of France and therefore disinclined to support a Parisian team – meant that sides from the City of Light soon found themselves confined to the shadows. Red Star, from the working-class northern suburb of Saint-Ouen-sur-Seine, have spent almost their entire existence in the lower leagues since being relegated from the top flight in 1948, while businessman Jean-Luc Lagardère's ambitious attempt to turn Racing Club into title challengers in the 1980s fizzled out after only a few seasons.

PSG were founded in 1970 by a merger between Paris FC and Stade Saint-Germain, a club from the wealthy western suburb of Saint-Germain-en-Laye. The club's initial fortunes were encapsulated by the similarly arcing trajectories of presidents Daniel Hechter (1974–78) and Francis Borelli (1978–91). Fashion designer Hechter oversaw promotion to Division 1 in 1974 and designed PSG's famous home kit, before being brought down by a scandal in which ticketing revenue was illicitly used to top up players' salaries. Publishing executive Borelli was at the helm for the club's first league title in 1986 and installed French football's first executive boxes at the Parc des Princes, only to rack up debts of 51 million francs that would earn him a suspended eight-month prison sentence for misappropriation of funds. Eager to increase the competitiveness in a league that it had been broadcasting since 1984, Canal+ started investing in PSG in 1991

---

111 Prior to 1977, the city of Paris was managed by the French state rather than a dedicated municipal institution and did not possess an elected mayor liable to drive funding towards a local football club.

and eventually obtained full control, aiming to turn the club into a worthy rival to Bernard Tapie's Marseille. The company's backing took PSG to the next level, with star signings such as David Ginola, Raí, George Weah and Youri Djorkaeff sparking a period of success that included a second league title in 1994, Cup Winners' Cup glory in 1996 and runs to a European semi-final or better in five consecutive seasons.

The big-name transfers kept coming as the 1990s segued into the 2000s – Marco Simone, Jay-Jay Okocha, Ronaldinho, Pauleta – but the most coveted silverware did not. By the time the club was bought by a group of American and French investment firms in 2006, PSG had become a cup team, their inconsistency typified by a rollercoaster 2007–08 campaign in which they won the Coupe de la Ligue final against Lens in the 93rd minute, lost the Coupe de France final against Lyon in extra time and avoided relegation on the season's final day.

As the capital city, Paris was a place where prying journalists could be found around every corner and distractions lurked at every turn. 'There are lots of temptations,' says former PSG captain Alain Roche, who played for the club throughout the golden period of the mid-1990s. 'There'd be film stars, singers, artists, people from showbusiness at the Parc des Princes, you'd be invited to film premieres, restaurants, nightclubs. You had to keep your head on your shoulders and not be attracted by everything that was around you. The danger was there. That's what Paris is: danger.' There was danger in a very real sense at the Parc des Princes, where rival fan groups from the Kop de Boulogne and the Virage Auteuil did battle for years. When a supporter from the Boulogne end was beaten to death prior to a match against Marseille in February 2010, club president Robin Leproux declared war on the *ultras* by halting the sale of tickets in large blocks at the two ends of the stadium. It was in this febrile environment that the money men from Qatar Sports Investments (QSI) set foot when they bought the club in the summer of 2011.

The takeover was the first major play by Qatar in its bid to assert its football credentials after stunning the sporting world by securing the right to host the 2022 World Cup. Backed by the tiny Gulf state's eye-boggling wealth, accumulated from its oil and natural gas reserves, PSG became an immediate threat to European football's established order and were quickly linked to just about every superstar player on the planet. In his introductory press conference as sporting director following his arrival from Internazionale in July 2011, former Paris midfielder Leonardo sought to temper some of the giddiness, asserting that the club was 'not going to sign 10 Messis', but the Brazilian also made it clear that they were now targeting glory in both the league and the Champions League. PSG's new marketing slogan was '*Rêvons plus grand*'. Dream bigger.

Deals had already been in the pipeline for Saint-Étienne midfielder Blaise Matuidi and Lorient striker Kévin Gameiro, but the capture of willowy Argentinian playmaker Javier Pastore in a French-record €42 million deal from Palermo made the world sit up and take notice. 'It was part of the strategy, to make some noise,' admits Luis Ferrer, an Argentinian talent-spotter who spent 11 years in PSG's player recruitment department. 'We wanted to show that Paris weren't all talk, that it was real. They wanted to make a mark and it was natural to look at a player like Javier Pastore, who was the new up-and-coming star in European football.'

PSG's status as the only major football club in a metropolitan area with around 12 million inhabitants represented vast untapped potential in the eyes of the new owners. Then there was the location itself. Although PSG as a football club enjoyed only limited visibility beyond France's borders, Paris as a city was an international byword for style, culture and romance. A key plank of the Qataris' strategy was therefore to put the city of Paris at the centre of the club's branding. In February 2013, PSG unveiled a modified version of the club's circular crest (after a redesign so secretive that members of the marketing department were forbidden from communicating about it by email) in which the word 'SAINT-GERMAIN' was moved to the base of the badge to leave 'PARIS' standing alone in extra-large letters above a stylised image of the Eiffel Tower. The club stuck up posters around town showing players posing beside famous Parisian landmarks (the Eiffel Tower, the Arc de Triomphe, the Opéra Garnier), purely to entrench the association between *le club* and *la ville* in the minds of both tourists and the local population. When there was a major new signing to unveil, PSG made sure to use the Eiffel Tower as a backdrop, staging an improvised photo shoot in front of it when Zlatan Ibrahimović arrived in 2012 and arranging for it to be lit up in Neymar's honour when he joined in 2017.

PSG's new president was a trim, immaculately presented Qatari in his late 30s called Nasser Al-Khelaifi. Born into a family of pearl fishermen in Doha in November 1973, the young Al-Khelaifi excelled at tennis, representing Qatar in the Davis Cup from 1992 to 2002 and reaching a world ranking of 995. It was through tennis that he became friends with Sheikh Tamim bin Hamad Al Thani, ruler of Qatar since 2013 and a keen football fan. Al-Khelaifi effectively represents the Sheikh, who makes the key strategic decisions about PSG from the Amiri Diwan, the seat of Qatari power on the Doha waterfront. Armed with Al-Thani's patronage, an MBA from Qatar University and his own personal connections, Al-Khelaifi has acquired a dizzying number of roles. In addition to being president of PSG, he heads up QSI, the beIN Media Group, the Qatar Tennis Federation and the European Club Association (ECA), skilfully obtaining the chairmanship of the latter in April 2021 after publicly opposing the doomed European Super League project. He also sits on UEFA's Executive Committee and the board of France's Ligue de Football Professionnel and chairs the board at film company Miramax, which beIN acquired in 2016. On top of being a minister without portfolio in the Qatari government. Renowned, perhaps unsurprisingly, as a workaholic (his go-to emoji is the bicep), he is said to get by on only three hours' sleep a night. Al-Khelaifi's collaborators describe him as a man fuelled by an almost child-like ambitiousness, who squeezes in games of padel wherever his schedule will allow and who fires off WhatsApp messages and emails from three mobile phones while juggling his multiple responsibilities in Doha, Paris and Nyon.[112] For better, for worse, from the megawatt smile of the player presentation press conference to the angry scowl of the premature Champions League exit, he has been the face of PSG's Qatari era.

Seeking to turn PSG into contenders for silverware at home and abroad, the club's new hierarchy adopted an approach that had served the French game well

---

112 The headquarters of both UEFA and the ECA are located in the Swiss town of Nyon.

over the previous 30 years: they copied the Italians. Leonardo knew Serie A inside out, as a former AC Milan player and coach of both Milanese clubs, and his transalpine connections immediately opened doors in the transfer market. In addition to Pastore, goalkeeper Salvatore Sirigu, midfielder Mohamed Sissoko and winger Jérémy Ménez also arrived from Italian clubs in the summer of 2011, with the key signing of Brazil-born Italy international Thiago Motta from Internazionale following in January. Jean-Claude Blanc, a widely respected French sports marketing executive, was recruited from Juventus to work as general manager and quickly set about professionalising the club's business operations. And when former PSG centre-back Antoine Kombouaré was sacked as head coach at the end of December 2011, having led the club to the top of the table but also presided over early eliminations in the Coupe de la Ligue and the Europa League, the man who took his place was a veritable bastion of Italian coaching expertise: Carlo Ancelotti.

A two-time Champions League-winning coach with Milan, Ancelotti had been abruptly sacked by Chelsea a few months previously, having led the club to their first ever league and FA Cup Double in 2010. He quickly charmed PSG's players and staff with his natural charisma and affable manner, but it was the changes he introduced at the club's Camp des Loges training base that had the biggest impact. From one day to the next, PSG began to prepare and train like a Champions League-level side: minutely detailed training schedules, pre-training muscle activation sessions, GPS vests, enhanced statistical analysis, a new restaurant facility, personalised dietary plans and an expanded team of physiotherapists. From a place the players simply popped into for a couple of hours each morning, the Camp des Loges became a place of work. 'We had to change the mentality,' says Ferrer. 'Back then, any player who had been in Italy or Spain and then came to France had a huge culture shock. It wasn't like professional football here [in France]. The players would arrive at 09:30, training would start at 10:00, training would end, into the shower and *au revoir*! Paris Saint-Germain implemented a fixed arrival time so that everyone would have breakfast together, then a break, then do a muscle warm-up before training started. After training, showers, then usually something for the sponsors and after that a mandatory lunch. They would spend a whole part of the day at the club and that brought a professionalism, like at any big club in the Champions League, which Paris had lacked.'

With PSG adjusting to Ancelotti's methods and trademark 4-3-2-1 formation, they were beaten to the league title by an unfancied Montpellier side coached by former Bordeaux midfielder René Girard and spearheaded by Olivier Giroud. But the summer of 2012 would shift *Les Parisiens* on to a formidable new footing as, one by one, Ibrahimović, Thiago Silva, Marco Verratti and Ezequiel Lavezzi lined up to pose with the club's blue jersey. Brazil captain Silva was the world's outstanding centre-back. Argentinian forward Lavezzi brought a goal threat from wide areas and an infectious *joie de vivre* in the changing room. Verratti was 19 when he arrived from Pescara and largely unknown, but would quickly emerge as one of the most uniquely talented central midfielders in the game. And Ibrahimović shook the entire club to its foundations.

The leading scorer in Serie A with Milan the previous season, Ibrahimović's prolific finishing made him a one-man match-winner, his awesome physicality reduced opposition defences to rubble and his showman's flair raised the profile of the club – and by extension the league – all on its own. Regardless of who PSG were playing, when the swaggering Swede scored a special goal – a brilliant back-heel volley against Marseille, an outrageous taekwondo flick against Bastia, a thunderous 30-yard piledriver against Anderlecht – everyone saw it. In training, he was pitiless with teammates who failed to match his lofty standards, but although it created friction, it forced everyone to raise their game. 'He brought a stringency, a winning mindset and he pushed people to go beyond what they thought they were capable of giving,' says right-back Christophe Jallet, who was appointed captain by Ancelotti. 'It's true that it's not always easy to live with, but when it's managed correctly, it brings everyone into line.'

For all the adulation he received, Ibrahimović was not always able to conceal his apparent disdain for France, its football and even the history of his own club. He received a four-game ban for ranting about 'this shit country' while venting his frustrations with the officiating after a defeat at Bordeaux and declared shortly before he left in 2016 that PSG 'was born the day the Qataris arrived'. How did things like that go down in the changing room, I wonder? 'He wrote the history of the *new* Paris Saint-Germain, but PSG also had 40 years of history before that,' says Jallet. 'Sometimes, we'd say between ourselves that he was talking shit and you'd say to him the next day, in the dressing room: "Listen, what you said wasn't good." He'd tell you to fuck off and that what he'd said was true. But then you'd explain things and he'd say: "OK." You could discuss things with him privately – as long as you had solid arguments!' There were, at least, no qualms about Ibrahimović's football. He scored 30 Ligue 1 goals in his maiden campaign – figures not seen in France since the days of Jean-Pierre Papin – and with a 37-year-old David Beckham also on board after joining the club in January 2013 for his last hurrah, PSG won the league for the first time in 19 years.

Ancelotti left for Real Madrid shortly after, later explaining that he had been upset by what he saw as an unnecessary ultimatum from Al-Khelaifi and Leonardo that if his side did not win their final Champions League group game against Porto, he would be sacked (PSG, who had already qualified for the knockout phase, won 2–1). Ancelotti's departure dismayed the changing room and the man who replaced him, Laurent Blanc, was known to be some way down the list of the owners' preferred candidates. Yet the former France centre-back succeeded not only in turning PSG into a trophy-winning machine, but in giving the team a more effective and clearly defined playing identity than any of his immediate successors.

The blockbuster €64 million acquisition of Uruguayan centre-forward Edinson Cavani from Napoli obliged Blanc to fit two world-class strikers into his starting XI. After initially attempting to pair Ibrahimović and Cavani up front, he decided to set the team out in a 4-3-3 formation by moving the new recruit to the right flank, which had the added benefit of enabling him to assemble a three-man midfield of Motta, Verratti and Matuidi. The tall, tactically canny Motta ('a real bastard', smiles Jallet) sat in front of the back four, the tireless Matuidi powered up and down *à la* Jean Tigana in the inside-left channel and the impish Verratti kept PSG on the front foot with his audacious ability to wriggle away from danger around the edges of his own penalty area. 'We were complementary,' says Matuidi. 'I was good at getting forward, they were good at building the play up from the back. When it came to winning the ball back, it was the opposite: me and Marco would go and press high up and Thiago organised everything behind with his intelligence. Our connection was pretty incredible.'

Taking their cue from the football played by Blanc's former club Barcelona, PSG monopolised possession of the ball, wearing their opponents down with endless passing circuits before suddenly springing Ibrahimović, Cavani, Lavezzi, Pastore or Lucas Moura through on goal. No team in France could resist them. 'The number of times we'd be 2–0 or 3–0 up at half-time because our opponents had turned up knowing that there was nothing to play for,' says Jallet. 'There was a power hovering in the air even before we started playing. You'd have opponents telling you at 2–0 or 3–0: "OK, stop running, stay back, leave me alone. The match is already over!" When you hear that, you realise how hard it must be to play against you. We were a real steamroller.' PSG romped to the league title in each of Blanc's three seasons in charge – finishing nine points above Monaco in 2014, eight points above Lyon in 2015 and a staggering 31 points above Lyon in 2016 – in addition to winning two Coupes de France, three Coupes de la Ligue and three Trophées des Champions. Within five years, QSI's huge investment had, entirely logically, enabled PSG to assert total supremacy over the French game. All that was left was to conquer Europe.

'*NNNNOOOOOOOONNNNNNNNNNNNNNN!*'

In one long, anguished howl from the Camp Nou commentary box, Paul Le Guen succeeded in articulating the unthinkable sporting catastrophe that was being visited upon PSG before the incredulous eyes of the whole football world. Down in the giant stadium below him, a scene of bedlam: Sergi Roberto racing towards the corner flag with arms outstretched, Messi leaping on top of an advertising hoarding and punching the air, Luis Enrique sprinting down the touchline, Unai Emery scrunching his eyes closed in disbelief, the entire ground a mad, roiling tumult of Catalan delight. PSG had led 4–0 on aggregate at kick-off. They had led 5–3 on aggregate with two minutes of normal time to play. With 25 seconds of stoppage time left, they were still going through, and then Neymar chipped one last hopeful ball into the penalty area, Roberto darted in and stuck out his right foot and the sky came down upon their heads. '*C'est pas possible!*' yelled Le Guen's Canal+ co-commentator, Stéphane Guy. '*C'est pas possible! C'est pas possible! C'est pas possible!'* Only somehow, it was. Barcelona 6–1 Paris Saint-Germain (6–5 on aggregate), Champions League last 16 second leg, Wednesday 8 March, 2017. The greatest fightback (or the greatest collapse, depending on your perspective) in the competition's history. It became known as *La Remontada* (The Comeback) and it has haunted PSG ever since.

In the days that followed, some senior players confided to PSG staff that they never wanted to play for the club again. Cavani, scorer of PSG's goal, later revealed that it had pushed him to see a therapist for the first time in his life. A former executive told me that the club's employees felt 'traumatised'. In France, much of the anger was directed towards German referee Deniz Aytekin, who awarded Barcelona two soft penalties and failed to spot a last-man foul on Ángel Di María by Javier Mascherano that prevented the PSG winger from putting the tie to bed. But even allowing for that, it was still hard to explain the complete mental collapse to which PSG appeared to have succumbed. In the 10 minutes that elapsed between Neymar scoring the 88th-minute free-kick that made it 4–1 on the night and the final whistle, PSG completed only four passes – three of which were kick-offs. How had they lost their heads so completely?

'I think we were overcome by fear,' says Matuidi, his voice suddenly grave. 'As soon as we kick off at the start of the match, we drop back 15 metres and I think that was a mistake on our part. We spent more time looking at the clock than playing football. It was fear that did that. We should have put our foot on the ball and said to ourselves that we were going to try to play football regardless. We didn't manage to do that. We couldn't even string three or four passes together, even though that's what we knew how to do. The absence [through suspension] of a player like Thiago Motta and his experience hurt us a lot. When we got to the changing room, I told myself that I wanted to stop playing football. Because I didn't play football to experience moments like that. That's the first thought that I had when I was taking a shower. It was something that I would never have imagined. It took time to recover mentally from that moment. It wasn't easy for your family, for your friends, for the people who love Paris Saint-Germain. You were even ashamed to leave the house.'

PSG had experienced pain in the Champions League before. They had led with 20 minutes remaining away to Barcelona in the quarter-finals in 2013, only for Barça to equalise and go through on away goals. A year later, at the same stage of the competition, they were poised to eliminate Chelsea when Demba Ba smuggled in an 87th-minute equaliser at Stamford Bridge to condemn them to another away-goals exit. A toothless quarter-final defeat against Manchester City in 2016 effectively cost Blanc his job. This, though, was a different order of magnitude – and not least because they had played so impressively in the first leg. Emery, hired as Blanc's replacement after a hat-trick of Europa League triumphs with Sevilla, had struggled to impose his more vertical style of football amid changing-room resistance from players who had grown accustomed to a more patient approach. In the first leg against Barça, they had belatedly produced the kind of football that he was looking for – bold, hard-running, high-pressing – and it had worked to perfection. It made what happened at Camp Nou an even more bitter pill to swallow. And what happened at Camp Nou was only the beginning.

To compound matters, PSG also missed out on the Ligue 1 title in 2016–17, finishing second to a brilliant Monaco team featuring the talents of Radamel Falcao, Bernardo Silva, Fabinho and a teenage Mbappé. So they did what any right-thinking multi-billion-dollar sporting institution with impatient owners and practically limitless wealth would do: they went out and bought the two players who had caused them the most hurt. Their €222 million move for Neymar obliterated the world transfer record and marked a watershed moment in modern football: for the first time, a state-backed club had succeeded in wrenching a prized asset from the clutches of one of the game's traditional heavyweights. As Barcelona supporters fumed and La Liga president Javier Tebas raged, furiously calling on UEFA to investigate, the 25-year-old with the mohawk haircut was presented to his adoring new public at a sun-soaked Parc des Princes prior to PSG's opening league game against Amiens. By happy accident, PSG had already released a Brazil-style yellow change kit; the replica version bearing the name of their new number 10 flew off the rails. Mbappé arrived on transfer deadline day in a curiously structured transfer designed to keep the club within UEFA's Financial Fair Play rules: a season-long loan with a €180 million right-to-buy clause that would be automatically triggered as long as PSG avoided relegation (spoiler alert: they did). 'It was important to come home to my city,' said the 18-year-old Bondy native during a characteristically assured introductory press conference.

French football fans immediately thrilled to Neymar's virtuoso displays – the nutmegs, the stepovers, the rainbow flicks, the no-look passes – and he quickly hit it off with Mbappé. Normal service resumed on the domestic front as PSG swept all before them, although with Neymar sidelined by the first of what would prove to be a long line of cruelly timed injuries, they fell at the same round of 16 hurdle in the Champions League, this time to Cristiano Ronaldo's Real Madrid.

In marketing terms, the tandem of Neymar and Mbappé took PSG across a hallowed threshold and into the realm of the global lifestyle brand. A year after the pair's arrival and following on from Mbappé's star turn at the 2018 World Cup, the club announced an exclusive three-year partnership with Nike subsidiary Air Jordan, moving Al-Khelaifi to proclaim that PSG were now 'one of the three biggest football brands in the world'. PSG opened offices in Shanghai, Singapore and New York. A-listers like Leonardo DiCaprio, Mick Jagger, Rihanna, Kim Kardashian and Selena Gomez took in games at the Parc des Princes. Beyoncé popped up on Instagram wearing a PSG shirt embroidered with Swarovski crystals, teenagers clamoured for club-branded merchandise from Toronto to Tokyo. No French club had ever been so visible, so glamorous, so *cool*. And yet on the pitch, PSG would become a laughing stock.

In some ways, Champions League elimination by Manchester United at the Parc des Princes in 2019 was even more humiliating than what had happened at Camp Nou two years previously. Barcelona, at least, had been top of La Liga, with a full-strength squad boasting some of the world's finest footballers. United were fourth in the Premier League, missing 10 senior players through injury or suspension and finished the game with 17-year-old debutant Mason Greenwood and two 19-year-olds on the pitch. Yet after Romelu Lukaku punished errors from Thilo Kehrer and Gianluigi Buffon to put the visitors 2–1 up on the night, a stoppage-time handball by Presnel Kimpembe enabled Marcus Rashford to send United through on away goals from the penalty spot, leaving the injured Neymar mouth agape in disbelief in black cap and bomber jacket on the touchline. It was around this time that the term 'Farmers League' began to gain currency on social media as a derisive name for Ligue 1, the implication being that PSG's domestic success was irrelevant because the only opposition they faced came from plodding part-timers. PSG were the football club that had turned into a meme.

With Thomas Tuchel now in charge – another young, dynamic coach, like Emery, who favoured fast, front-foot football – PSG appeared to have exorcised their Champions League demons in the 2019–20 season by reaching their first final. After a successful second-leg fightback against Borussia Dortmund in the last 16, just as the dark curtain of Covid was falling across Europe, Tuchel's men beat Atalanta and RB Leipzig in the truncated 'Final Eight' tournament in Lisbon before narrowly losing 1–0 to Bayern Munich in the final. The game at an empty, echoing Estádio da Luz was settled by a header from Kingsley Coman, a PSG academy graduate who – like so many others – had flown the nest in search of the game time that he knew would be denied him at the Parc des Princes.[113] After tensions with Leonardo cast Tuchel into the arms of Chelsea, where he would win the Champions League within months of arriving, Pochettino could manage no better than a one-sided semi-final defeat by Manchester City in 2021 and a year later, the old fragilities dramatically resurfaced with the meltdown in Madrid. 'The secret against PSG is to press them,' said Benzema, who exploited blunders from goalkeeper Gianluigi Donnarumma and captain Marquinhos to net his decisive Bernabéu hat-trick. 'And then, when we scored, they told themselves that they'd lost the match, even though it was only 1–1 [on the night and 2–1 to PSG on aggregate] . . . That often happens to them. They let go mentally.'

PSG's modern existence has become a kind of football *Groundhog Day*. Their dominance of Ligue 1 has turned them into the most successful club in French top-flight history, the Parc des Princes is always full and they are now part of the European football establishment, yet almost every spring, they fall to pieces in the Champions League. Senior players freeze. Cohesion evaporates. The team stares into the abyss of elimination and finds itself powerless to avoid toppling in.

113 See also: Christopher Nkunku, Moussa Diaby, Alphonse Areola, Mike Maignan.

The years pass, the coaches change, but there has been little sense of unity, little sense of players identifying with the club, little sense, even, of the megastars actually wanting to be there in the first place: learning French, embracing life in Paris, building meaningful connections with the club and the city that endure beyond the final payslip. 'It hasn't felt like a strong club,' says Alain Roche. 'You haven't felt that the players know the club's history, that they've become imbued with it. You have to feel that when things aren't going well, the directors and the president will impose themselves. You haven't felt that pressure, that the club is stronger.'

That may, however, be changing. After an 11th league title and a fifth last 16 exit in seven seasons in the Champions League under Christophe Galtier in 2023, PSG turned to Luis Enrique, architect of *La Remontada*. The talk was of discipline and humility, of a younger, hungrier, more French squad, of no more kowtowing to big egos. Shortly before leaving Paris, Messi was suspended and fined over an unauthorised trip to Saudi Arabia. Suspecting Mbappé, now the club's all-time record scorer, of having agreed to join long-standing suitors Real Madrid upon the scheduled expiry of his contract in 2024, PSG axed him from their squad for a pre-season tour of Japan and South Korea (before eventually striking the latest in a long line of uneasy truces with the forward). Neymar and Verratti were both allowed to leave. In came a posse of French players – Lucas Hernandez, Ousmane Dembélé, Randal Kolo Muani, Bradley Barcola – to give the club a new, homegrown core.

So have this newly tough and uncompromising PSG finally got things right? Or – and with Mbappé, the last remaining superstar, now poised to leave as well – squandered the best chance of winning the Champions League that the club will ever have?

20

ALLEMAGNE

LA NOUVELLE VAGUE

'All of them are dreaming of the Premier League, but making the step
from Ligue 1 at the age of 18 or 19 to the Premier League is quite
difficult . . . So the Bundesliga is the perfect step in between.'

Bayern Munich chief scout Markus Pilawa

Mathys Tel has attacked his fledgling career as a professional footballer with such
impatience that it should probably come as no surprise when he arrives 15 minutes
early for our interview. Tall and broad-shouldered, wearing a grey Nike hoodie,
matching tracksuit bottoms and white trainers, the 18-year-old striker politely
shakes my hand and introduces himself before settling into a chair in the first-floor
meeting room that has been set aside for us at Bayern Munich's Säbener Straße
headquarters. It is a grey afternoon in mid-May 2023 and the rain is hammering
down outside the window, spattering on to the broad green leaves of the tall
Norway maple trees that line the street. Bayern are one point clear of Borussia
Dortmund with three games remaining in one of the most exciting Bundesliga title
run-ins in recent memory, but Tel has noticed no dramatic increase in tension as
the finishing line looms into view. 'No, it's just like normal,' he says. 'There isn't
really any fuss.' Two days after our encounter, he scores the fifth goal in a 6–0 rout
of Schalke. Despite a 3–1 home defeat by RB Leipzig in their next game, Bayern
finish the season as champions for the 11th year running after Dortmund are
unable to beat mid-table Mainz on the final day. Even after a deeply underwhelming
season, even after presenting their nearest rivals with an open goal, Bayern get their
hands on the trophy. It is just what they do around here.

Tel had joined Bayern from Rennes on a five-year contract the previous summer in a deal worth €20 million plus €8.5 million in potential bonuses. Even before the transfer was officially announced, Bayern head coach Julian Nagelsmann told reporters that Tel had the potential to become a 40-goal-a-season striker. He had rolled off the same Rennes production line as Sylvain Wiltord, Yoann Gourcuff, Ousmane Dembélé and Eduardo Camavinga, making his first-team debut against Brest in August 2021 at the age of just 16 years and 110 days, which broke Camavinga's club record. Quick, versatile and possessing exceptional dexterity with the ball at his feet, Tel played only 79 minutes of first-team football for Rennes over the course of the 2021–22 campaign, stretched across 10 matches, but Bayern's recruiters were simultaneously following his progress with France's Under-17s and Under-18s and they liked what they saw. He became Bayern's youngest ever goalscorer when he netted on his full debut at Viktoria Cologne in the DFB-Pokal aged 17 years and 126 days, then became the club's youngest Bundesliga scorer by converting a cut-back from Alphonso Davies in a 2–2 draw with Stuttgart at the Allianz Arena. 'I remember the stadium announcer saying "Mathys!" and all the fans shouting "Tel!"' the teenager says, his eyes widening at the memory. 'I was getting back into position, but my heart was all over the place.'

The Bundesliga has become the springboard of choice for young French footballers looking to reach the highest level, with Dembélé, Kingsley Coman, Christopher Nkunku, Marcus Thuram, Moussa Diaby and Randal Kolo Muani among the players to have lit up the German top flight in recent years. German clubs do not hesitate to give playing time to promising youngsters from France and it was by showing Tel a clear pathway to first-team football that Bayern succeeded in convincing him to join them. 'It's about playing,' says the striker, who made 28 first-team appearances in his maiden season in Bavaria, scoring six goals. 'German clubs really trust [young] players. If they take you, it's not to have you sitting around, but to play you. Young players who aren't playing for French clubs are saying to themselves: "If I go to Germany, I'll play." Bayern said that they had a really great project for me, that they were going to play me and that they wanted to build me up to become a very big player. That's exactly what I want.'

Tel, who grew up in Villiers-le-Bel in the northern Paris suburbs, is taking one-on-one German classes for an hour before training every morning. If a brief mid-interview exchange with the Bayern press officer is anything to go by, they are going very well. His parents are both living with him in a house near the training ground that the club helped him to find. His elder sister visits from France from time to time. The family are Christians and they have found a church in the city centre that they like. Despite playing for one of the world's biggest clubs, Tel can go about his business in Munich without being hassled. 'People leave me in peace,' he says. 'There's a great deal of respect with regard to that. I can walk around without my hood up or a hat on. It's great to be able to live like a normal person.'

His adaptation at Bayern has been facilitated by the fact that he is surrounded by compatriots. Bayern have a long-standing association with French players and their squad in Tel's first season includes France internationals Coman, Benjamin Pavard, Lucas Hernandez and Dayot Upamecano, as well as France-born Senegal international Bouna Sarr. A mid-season change of coach brings a French-speaker into the dug-out in the shape of Thomas Tuchel, who picked up the language during his time at Paris Saint-Germain, and there are several Francophones on the staff.

Although he admits to having felt nervous on his first day of training ('I didn't know where to put myself!'), Tel soon found his feet and has been attentively watching his teammates for things that he can add to his game. 'Joshua Kimmich, for example, before receiving the ball, he looks around three or four times to see if he is unmarked,' he says. 'I didn't even use to look once, so I've tried to take that from him.' The famous Bayern winning mentality, meanwhile, manifests itself as a constant, steady drumbeat within the squad. 'I felt it without them even talking,' says Tel. 'I felt it in their attitudes, how they say hello, how they behave in training. That mentality of always wanting to win, always being at your best in everything you do. There's not a single little thing that they don't do to the max.'

With a smile and a handshake, he departs for a driving lesson in the rush-hour rain, the latest French youngster preparing to take German football by storm.

Germany has not always been such a happy hunting ground for French footballers. In 1976, 23-year-old France international Marc Berdoll joined FC Saarbrücken from Angers with a reputation as one of the most prolific young strikers in Europe, having racked up 71 league goals over the previous three seasons, only to return home a year later with his tail between his legs after scoring one goal in 17 Bundesliga appearances. Jean-Pierre Papin's spell at Bayern was overshadowed by a serious knee ligament injury that he sustained in his first competitive match. Although he won the UEFA Cup in 1996, he departed having scored only three league goals in two years. Youri Djorkaeff fell out with head coach Andreas Brehme at Kaiserslautern and was so desperate to leave that he forced through a mid-season move to Bolton Wanderers in January 2002. 'The club made me sick of Germany,' Djorkaeff wrote in his 2006 autobiography, *Snake*. 'Even today, when I hear conversations in that language in a restaurant, my stomach tightens. Then I put down my fork. Meal finished.' Ouch. Other French players found that German football suited them perfectly well. Gilbert Gress' flowing locks and mazy dribbles turned him into a pin-up at Stuttgart in the late 1960s, while fellow winger Didier Six made a similarly strong impression at the same club in the early 1980s.

Bayern's love affair with French footballers truly began in the summer of 1997 when Bixente Lizarazu arrived after an injury-plagued one-season stint at Athletic Bilbao. The boxy Basque was initially taken aback by the intensity of the training sessions, but he gave as good as he got, famously cuffing club legend Lothar Matthäus around the head during a training-ground contretemps in August 1999. 'At the big clubs, you have to mark your territory,' he later explained. Whereas most of the leading French players who ventured overseas in the 1990s and early 2000s were shaped by experiences in either England or Italy, Lizarazu reported for international duty during that period with a different set of influences in his luggage. 'The Germans have a determination and a self-confidence melded with relaxation,' he said. 'That state of mind enables German players to win even with less talent than their opponents. The challenge sublimates them; it generally tends to inhibit the French and those from the Latin countries. I "Germanised" myself from that point of view.' Over the course of nine seasons in Bavaria, only interrupted by an unhappy six-month spell at Marseille in 2004,

Lizarazu confirmed his status as one of the world's outstanding left-backs, winning six Bundesliga titles and five DFB-Pokals and playing a starring role in Bayern's conquest of the Champions League in 2001. His surging runs up the left flank earned him the nickname *Kraftpaket* or 'Power Pack'. Willy Sagnol, who amassed a comparable silverware collection while playing on the other side of the Bayern defence between 2000 and 2009, was known as *Flankengott* ('Crossing God'). But in the Bayern nickname stakes, there was no competing with *Kaiser Franck*.

Franck Ribéry had lived an extremely peripatetic footballing existence prior to joining Bayern in 2007: four seasons at amateur level with hometown club Boulogne-sur-Mer, Alès and Brest, six-month stints with Metz and Galatasaray and then a two-year spell at Marseille, during which his explosive dribbling and spectacular long-range shooting won him a place in France's squad for the 2006 World Cup. Bayern paid a club-record fee of €25 million to bring him to Bavaria and he repaid them multiple times over during a record-breaking 12-year stay in which he made 425 appearances and scored 124 goals, winning nine Bundesliga titles, six DFB-Pokals and the 2013 Champions League.

Ribéry, in the words of former Bayern president Franz Beckenbauer, was 'the salt in the soup'. On the pitch, he formed a devastating duo with right winger Arjen Robben, the pair ceaselessly cutting in from their respective flanks to sow mayhem in opposition defences. Off the pitch, he was an inveterate practical joker, be it smearing toothpaste on the door handle of Lukas Podolski's hotel bathroom, tipping a bucket of water over Oliver Kahn from the Säbener Strasse roof or crashing the team bus during a winter training camp in Dubai. His performances and his pranks, coupled with his command of German and his whole-hearted embrace of Bavarian life in all its Lederhosen-clad kookiness, took him into Bayern fans' hearts. And when his reputation plummeted in his homeland in the wake of *L'affaire Zahia* and his prominent role in France's meltdown at the 2010 World Cup, Munich became his refuge. 'I'll never be loved as much as I am here,' he said in 2013. Ribéry had long had a strained relationship with the country of his birth. As a child, he was taunted over the facial scars he sustained in a car crash at the age of two. As an adult, he was mocked for his thick northern accent and inarticulate speech and fustigated for his disciplinary problems. But in the leafy Munich suburb of Grünwald, beside the calm waters of the River Isar, he found peace. His experiences in Munich echoed Éric Cantona's in Manchester 15 years earlier: scorned at home, loved abroad, each finding acceptance in a red number seven shirt as a king in a foreign land.

The one major disappointment of Ribéry's Bayern years was his failure to win the 2013 Ballon d'Or. He had been Bayern's stand-out player in a season that culminated in a historic Treble, notably creating Robben's 89th-minute winner against Dortmund in the Champions League final at Wembley with a characteristically inventive back-heel. But after FIFA extended the voting period because too many voters failed to meet the initial deadline, Cristiano Ronaldo tipped the balance in his own favour by scoring a decisive hat-trick for Portugal in a World Cup qualifier against Sweden. Ronaldo took the award, with Ribéry finishing third behind Lionel Messi.[114] 'I still haven't digested it,' he told *L'Équipe* in 2019. 'I had nothing to envy Cristiano Ronaldo or Lionel Messi for that year.' He had, nevertheless, opened the door for a generation of French footballers to follow in his footsteps.

———

Having spent 11 years working as a scout at Dortmund, where he helped to recruit players such as Dembélé, Jadon Sancho, Erling Haaland and Jude Bellingham, Markus Pilawa knows a promising young footballer when he sees one. In the summer of 2022, to the dismay of Dortmund's fans, he travelled the well-trodden path to Munich to take over as chief scout at Bayern. Moving in the opposite direction was Laurent Busser, the Frenchman who had previously headed up Bayern's scouting department and who had been responsible for the recruitment of French players like Pavard, Hernandez, Upamecano and Tel. Although Busser has taken his in-depth knowledge of the French market with

114 FIFA and *France Football* jointly presented the Ballon d'Or between 2010 and 2015, during which time it was voted for by a combination of journalists and national team coaches and captains (as opposed to journalists only when organised by *France Football*). Muddying the waters yet further, several national team coaches claimed that their votes in the 2013 ballot were incorrectly logged.

him to Dortmund, Pilawa is adamant that it will have no impact on Bayern's ability to sign players from France. While Bayern do not have any scouts permanently stationed across the border, they closely monitor French youth-level football using video scouting platforms such as Matchfeed and Eyeball and possess a tried and trusted network of agents and intermediaries. 'We're not lacking information,' Pilawa says. When you are only interested in signing the very best, you can be confident that the talent will not escape your attention.

So what is it about young French footballers that makes them so attractive to German clubs? In Pilawa's view, the thriving street football culture that exists in the diverse suburbs of France's major cities has equipped French players with skillsets that their German counterparts simply do not possess. 'The development of football is about speed, dynamism, intensity, transitions and physical condition and the French players are all about that,' he tells me. 'I think it's also because of their history and their colonial period. You have a big diversity of profiles – African profiles, North African profiles – which are maybe more focused on individual technical skills. They have a big range of profiles – not like in Germany. A lot of the players are from poorer backgrounds, so they're still hungry. Then with academies like Rennes, Lyon, Paris Saint-Germain, Lens, even Marseille, there is obviously very, very good education on the players' technical side. Plus they're more self-confident and they have more individuality. There have been big discussions here in Germany for two or three years because we realise that we put all the young guys into a structure where they can only play in patterns and there is no space for individuality. The French players are given space to show their individuality on the pitch, whereas in Germany they'd get substituted because all 11 players have to do the same things in the same patterns. In France it's not like that and the personality of their players takes them to a higher level than the German players.'

Whereas the French players who came to Germany in the 1990s and 2000s invariably saw it as the country where they would spend their peak years as footballers, their modern equivalents recognise that the Bundesliga can serve a more strategic role. Germany is a place where the football is fast and frenetic, where the stadiums are always full and where the leading clubs are capable of competing for the highest honours in the European game, but as French players such as Dembélé (Dortmund to Barcelona), Nkunku (RB Leipzig to Chelsea), Diaby (Bayer Leverkusen to Aston Villa) and Ibrahima Konaté (Leipzig to Liverpool) have shown, it can also serve as a stepping stone to one of the two Spanish giants or the hallowed ground of the Premier League. 'All of them are dreaming of the Premier League, but making the step from Ligue 1 at the age of 18 or 19 to the Premier League is quite difficult,' says Pilawa. 'There are some guys who are ready for that, but not a lot. So the Bundesliga is the perfect step in between. The Italians only buy in the Italian market, Spanish football is not a good fit for French players, the Netherlands and Belgium are too small, so it's only England and Germany where French players really fit. But in England the squads are too big, they have too much money, they can sign whoever they want. So we are the perfect league for the French players.'

For some mid-ranking German clubs, buying players cheaply from the French market and selling them at profit to the Premier League has proved an invaluable source of income in recent years. Mainz alone made sizeable profits on the sales of Jean-Philippe Gbamin (Everton), Jean-Philippe Mateta (Crystal Palace) and Moussa Niakhaté (Nottingham Forest), all of whom were bought from French clubs, while Hoffenheim spent a reported €500,000 to sign Georginio Rutter from Rennes in 2021 and sold him to Leeds United two years later for a fee rising to €40 million.[115] With such huge windfalls to be had, it pays to keep an eye on the talent coming out of France.

During the 2012–13 season, Ribéry was one of only three French players playing in the Bundesliga.[116] At the start of the 2023–24 campaign, there were 31. On both sides of the Rhine, they know that they are on to a good thing.

---

115 Gbamin came through the youth system at Lens, but was born in Ivory Coast and plays for Ivory Coast at international level. Niakhaté was born in France and plays for Senegal.
116 The others were Matthieu Delpierre (Hoffenheim) and Jonathan Schmid (Freiburg).

EPILOGUE

HOW NOT TOULOUSE

'French football is springboard football. We produce
players for other people.'

Alain Roche

It was at a sushi restaurant in Mayfair one January evening in 2020 that the
star-spangled banner first began its ascent of the flagpole at Toulouse FC.
Damien Comolli had just left his role as sporting director at Fenerbahçe and
was invited to a meeting with representatives from American private equity
firm RedBird Capital Partners, who were looking for a European football club
to buy. An experienced football executive whose previous clubs included
Arsenal, Tottenham Hotspur, Liverpool and Saint-Étienne, Comolli had been
in touch with people at RedBird for years, but it was only now that the stars
had aligned for a collaboration. Over the sashimi and the soy sauce, they talked
tactics and arranged to meet again in Miami the following month, where
Comolli was due to watch the San Francisco 49ers – the NFL team he had
fallen for during a year living in the Bay Area as a teenager – play the Kansas
City Chiefs in the Super Bowl.

In Miami, he was shown the fruits of RedBird's research. Over the previous
few years, the firm's analysts had studied over 70 different European clubs,
visiting 50 of them, and drawn up granularly detailed descriptions of each one's
operations from shareholder structure down to academy facilities. 'We defined
four criteria that would summarise which type of club RedBird would want to
purchase and that I would want to run for them or with them,' Comolli says. 'It
came down to: a great city, easy to access from New York or from the US; very
dynamic, both economically and demographically; it had to have a very good

academy and youth development programme; and it had to have very good facilities and a very good partner on the ground. And when we looked at all of these, I said: "Look, if Toulouse is up for sale, Toulouse ticks all the boxes." And they said: "OK, let's go for Toulouse."' RedBird acquired an 85 per cent stake in the club at a reported cost of around €11 million in July 2020 and appointed Comolli as president.

Toulouse had just been relegated at the time, but when I visit the club two years later, they are celebrating promotion back to the top flight. It is the first day of pre-season and there is a sunniness in every smile, an extra bounce in every *bonjour*. The players arrive early in the morning, breezily strolling into the Stadium de Toulouse in T-shirts and shorts beneath a blue sky streaked with low stratus clouds. The Ligue 2 trophy, a golden oblong secured with a 2–1 home win over Nîmes two months previously, stands, still unengraved, on the third-floor reception desk. High up on the white cupboards behind the desk, someone has stuck a piece of paper upon which 'REDBIRD WAS HERE' has been scrawled in black felt-tip pen. Toulouse, a student city in southwest France with a population of around 500,000 people, has long been associated with rugby union thanks to the exploits of five-time European champions Stade Toulousain, but *Le Téfécé* are determined to grab a share of the limelight for themselves. 'When we bought the club, we were very clear,' Comolli, who hails from nearby Béziers, tells me in his office. 'We said: "We are the fourth biggest city in France. We have to be top six in Ligue 1." I don't know if it's three years or four years or five. But the first thing about next season is: no limitations.'

Challenging the stereotype of the committed but clueless American owner, RedBird, which was founded in 2014 by Philadelphian financier Gerry Cardinale, came equipped with its own football expertise courtesy of its investment in sports data company Zelus Analytics. Co-founded by Luke Bornn, a Canadian former Harvard statistics professor who previously worked as head of analytics at Roma, Zelus employs a team of largely US-based analysts who provide Toulouse with the data upon which all of the club's decision-making is based. When it comes to recruitment, Zelus possesses a vast database of player profiles that allows the club to pursue targets that will correspond exactly to the team's needs on the pitch. 'It's moving to an approach where, rather than having scouts watch one or two or even four or five games, let's use data to look at the player's last 40 games and let's understand really what this player does, what they do well from a data perspective and is it repeatable,' Bornn tells me in a Zoom call from his home in Sacramento. 'The starting point is: how do we make our information better? How do we make sure that we're getting players who aren't just good because some person watched a game or two and said: "I really like this guy, he's got great technique"? We're looking over a longer sample size to say: "Is this player actually contributing positively to his team's success?"'

Toulouse's approach was resoundingly vindicated by their successful Ligue 2 promotion campaign. English striker Rhys Healey, recruited from League One side MK Dons for around €500,000, topped the Ligue 2 scoring charts with 20 goals, while midfielder Branco van den Boomen, who arrived from Dutch second-tier outfit De Graafschap in a €350,000 deal, finished the campaign with a league-leading 20 assists. 'When we brought Healey in, the consensus from traditional football people on the ground was: "You can't – this guy's not good enough to play in Ligue 2,"' says Bornn. 'And he's basically been one of the best players in the league for the last two years. You can tell the exact same story with Van den Boomen. "We can't play this guy, he's from a lower-tier league." And of course once he comes in, he lights out. I think he had 20 assists this year, which is like an insane number, MVP, the whole lot. The good thing with data is that it allows you to be totally unbiased and objective.'

Comolli has long been an advocate of data analysis, having first used it to recruit players while director of football at Tottenham in 2006, and his faith in it is total. When I put it to him that Toulouse are effectively engaged in a giant data experiment, he disagrees: 'For me, it's not an experiment because it works.' Following relegation in 2020, the club's analysis of successful Ligue 2 promotion campaigns found that teams that attacked well stood a better chance of going up than teams that defended well. Former Nottingham Forest manager Philippe Montanier was recruited as coach on the basis of his attacking philosophy and led Toulouse to promotion with a record tally of 82 goals. They intend to play the same kind of football in Ligue 1.

———

Down the corridor from Comolli's office I find general manager Olivier Jaubert, who runs the business side of the club. The pair have a bi-weekly business call and a weekly football call with representatives from RedBird, but Comolli estimates that when it comes to day-to-day operations, they make '95 per cent of the decisions on our own'. A former Nike executive who speaks faultless English, Jaubert knows the terrain of American investment in French football better than anyone. He previously spent two years working as chief revenue officer at France's Ligue de Football Professionnel (LFP), where his role involved staging roadshows in New York designed to encourage US investors to put money into Ligue 1 clubs. The pitch, he says, was a simple one. 'When you look at football right now, where is the best place to invest?' he asks. 'It's simple. The UK is so expensive it's almost impossible to buy – even in the Championship! In Germany, you cannot own the clubs.[117] In Italy, there are a few possibilities, but there's not a lot of efficient player development programmes. There are already some investors in Spain, but La Liga is strong so it's complicated. And I think that France had the best potential: strong academy programmes, good facilities – mainly because of the '98 World Cup, Euro 2016 and the [2023] Rugby World Cup – and the clubs are not that expensive.'

American investors have to stomach the fact that almost all French clubs rent their stadiums from local authorities rather than owning them outright, which diminishes their match-day earning power. On the flipside, the regulation guaranteed by financial regulator the Direction Nationale du Contrôle de Gestion (DNCG) provides reassurance of financial stability. At the start of the 2023–24 season, nine French clubs were under full or partial American ownership: Marseille, Lyon, Strasbourg, Lorient, Le Havre and Toulouse in Ligue 1, Caen in Ligue 2 and Nancy and Red Star in the third-tier National. It has not been plain sailing for all. Red Star's traditionally left-wing fanbase mounted angry protests against the Parisian club's acquisition by US investment firm 777 Partners in May 2022, while financial mismanagement at Bordeaux by

---

117 Germany's '50+1' rule guarantees 51 per cent of voting rights to a club's fans, preventing investors from owning more than 49 per cent of a club.

General American Capital Partners contributed to *Les Girondins* dropping out of the top flight for the first time since the dog-end of the Claude Bez era.

French club ownership is an increasingly international affair. In addition to the Americans, there are the Qataris at Paris Saint-Germain, British billionaire Sir Jim Ratcliffe at Nice, Russian oligarch Dmitry Rybolovlev at Monaco and Chinese entrepreneur James Zhou at Auxerre, while Troyes are part of the Abu Dhabi-owned City Football Group. But for all the advantages that buying a French club offers – low entry prices, modern stadiums, access to France's world-leading player development programmes, a highly competitive league (PSG aside) – recent years have brought unprecedented challenges.

The Covid pandemic hit Ligue 1 particularly hard. A characteristically bureaucratic decision to curtail rather than suspend the 2019–20 season (contrary to what happened in England, Germany, Italy and Spain) contributed to a 16 per cent fall in revenues across the league and matters were compounded by the collapse of what had been perceived as a game-changing €3.25 billion domestic television rights deal with Chinese-backed Spanish broadcasting company Mediapro. State-guaranteed loans and wage reduction schemes helped Ligue 1 clubs to withstand the initial blow of the pandemic, staving off DNCG warnings of potential bankruptcies, and Amazon swooped in to pick up the pieces from the Mediapro fiasco (sidelining historic football broadcaster Canal+ in the process). Although Ligue 1 clubs reported cumulative losses of €581.9 million for the 2021–22 season, the robustness of the market for French player sales meant that that figure was expected to fall to around €300 million in 2022–23.[118] In addition, the €1.5 billion sale of a 13 per cent stake in Ligue 1's media rights to Luxembourg-based private equity fund CVC Capital Partners in April 2022 (echoing a similar deal between CVC and La Liga) has enabled French clubs to look to the future with more certainty. With Ligue 1 having been reduced from 20 clubs to 18 at the start of the 2023–24 season, bringing it in line with the Bundesliga, the French elite's shared revenues are now being more tightly pooled as well.

---

118 Figures taken from DNCG Annual Report 2021–22 (published in April 2023) and interview with DNCG president Jean-Marc Mickeler in *L'Équipe* on 29 July, 2023.

Not that French football needed a once-a-century worldwide health crisis to create problems for itself, of course. Fan disorder has surged since Covid protocols were eased in 2021, with supporters attacking players, fighting with each other and mounting violent pitch invasions. Two Marseille matches had to be abandoned during the 2021–22 season – one against Nice, one against Lyon – after Dimitri Payet was twice struck on the head by water bottles thrown from the stands. Ephemeral Lyon coach Fabio Grosso nearly lost an eye after Marseille fans hurled missiles at the OL team bus prior to an October 2023 league game at the Vélodrome and a month later, a Nantes supporter was fatally stabbed before a match against Nice. The chaotic scenes that preceded the 2022 Champions League final at the Stade de France, meanwhile, shone an unforgiving spotlight upon France's treatment of match-going fans. After thousands of Liverpool supporters were dangerously kettled, arbitrarily denied access to the stadium and callously tear-gassed by police, a UEFA-commissioned report deemed it 'remarkable' that there had been no loss of life.

On top of the violence, French football continues to demonstrate an unparalleled propensity for scandal. From accusations that former PSG midfielder Aminata Diallo hired a group of thugs to assault her clubmate and positional rival Kheira Hamraoui to the forced resignation of Noël Le Graët as French Football Federation president over allegations of sexual harassment, the French game has shown that for all the 'Farmers League' jibes on social media, when it comes to generating improbable headlines it has few peers.

Happily, France also remains a world-beater in a more prized – and valuable – domain: churning out brilliant footballers. In its annual study of the world's leading exporters of football talent, the CIES[119] Football Observatory in Switzerland placed France second behind only Brazil as of May 2023, with 1,033 France-trained players playing in 135 national leagues around the world. For players aged 23 or under, France came out on top, placing 202 players across the globe to Brazil's 174. In addition to transforming

119 International Centre for Sports Studies.

Les Bleus into one of the world's foremost national teams, it has turned Ligue 1 into a global reference for what tends to be referred to in France as *le trading*: namely, recruiting and developing young footballers, blooding them in the professional game and then selling them for huge fees to other, richer clubs in other, richer leagues.

In an ideal world, French football would prefer its most gifted offspring to hang around at home for a little longer, but in an economic climate of restrictively high social charges and revenues that lag well behind those in England, Germany, Spain and Italy, the talent production line is what keeps Ligue 1 afloat. The LFP subtly acknowledged Ligue 1's status as a supplier of rival championships by rebranding it as *La Ligue des Talents* in January 2019. Be it Eduardo Camavinga (Rennes) and Aurélien Tchouaméni (Bordeaux) at Real Madrid, Christopher Nkunku (PSG) at Chelsea or Dayot Upamecano (Valenciennes) at Bayern Munich, yesterday's up-and-coming *talents* now dot the pitches of Europe's grandest clubs. With exciting teenagers popping up in Ligue 1 on an almost weekly basis – Warren Zaïre-Emery at PSG, Eliesse Ben Seghir at Monaco, Désiré Doué at Rennes, Leny Yoro at Lille – the shelves are never empty. 'French football is springboard football,' says Alain Roche, former sporting director at PSG and Bordeaux. 'We produce players for other people. And we need to keep doing it.'

Ligue 1 has long been a distant fifth among Europe's 'Big Five' leagues. After narrowly clinging on to fifth place in UEFA's coefficient standings during the 2022–23 season (an outcome that hinged on West Ham United's semi-final victory over Dutch side AZ Alkmaar in the UEFA Conference League), France is assured of sending four automatic qualifiers into the revamped Champions League when it launches in 2024. But the challenge, from the Netherlands, Portugal, Belgium and others, will not go away.

———

It is now 40 years since Michel Platini's goals and Michel Hidalgo's *football à la française* swept France to glory at the 1984 European Championship. In keeping with Hidalgo's romantic outlook, and in a reflection of the footballing structures of the age, France's first European champions were brought together on the fly. In the 1984 version of the *carré magique* (Platini, Alain Giresse, Jean Tigana, Luis Fernandez), Tigana and Fernandez were both late starters in the professional game and the sum total of the quartet's international experience at youth level was a handful of Under-21 caps. The success that *Les Bleus* have enjoyed since the 1998 World Cup has been built upon more systematised foundations, reflecting the work carried out in the 1970s by Georges Boulogne to equip both the amateur and professional game with formalised coach education programmes and structured youth development pathways. From Zinédine Zidane and Patrick Vieira in the academy at Cannes to Blaise Matuidi and Kylian Mbappé at Clairefontaine, France's modern greats are walking, talking, trophy-hoarding advertisements for *la formation à la française*. Yet if France has plenty to teach the world about how to produce footballers, it has much less to say for itself about how to play the game.

Since the end of the Platini era, and for all the success that the national team have enjoyed, French football has had no real signature style, no prevailing, instantly recognisable overall philosophy. Whereas rival European national teams have been able to pluck groups of players schooled in a certain style of football from dominant club sides, such as Spain have done with Barcelona or Germany with Bayern, the difficulty that French clubs have in holding on to their best young footballers makes that impossible in France. 'Didier Deschamps picks up players who play in teams whose styles are completely different, with coaches whose ideas are completely different,' says respected former Nantes coach Raynald Denoueix. 'What's France's style today? For Didier Deschamps, it's the result.'

PSG's playing identity in the Qatar Sports Investments era has depended on the varying individual philosophies of the men who have succeeded each other in the Parc des Princes dug-out, with efforts to impose any semblance of tactical coherence stymied in recent years by the obligation to squeeze superstar players such as Mbappé, Neymar and Lionel Messi into the starting XI. At Marseille, coaches such as Marcelo Bielsa and Igor Tudor have enjoyed relative success in recent times by harnessing the volatility of the Stade Vélodrome crowd with hard-running football and anachronistic man-to-man marking. At Monaco,

Mancunian former sporting director Paul Mitchell drew on his experiences within the Red Bull network to instil a German-style approach founded upon counter-pressing and quick transitions. But there is no French *tiki-taka*, no French *gegenpressing*, no uniquely French vision that crystallises France's perception of the game.

'What is the real French playing philosophy?' former France skipper Hugo Lloris asked during a 2018 interview with *L'Équipe*. 'I've been watching France's matches for 20 years, or I've played in them, and I don't know what the precise idea of French football is. Athletic teams with above-average talents, yes, but beyond that?' Frank Lebœuf describes France as 'the bastards of Europe'. 'We've taken a bit of everything,' he said during a 2017 debate on SFR Sport. 'It's our strength, but also our weakness. We were world champions without having an identity. We won the matches. Stop asking for a style of play – we never had one.' Hubert Fournier, the current Directeur Technique National, believes that at youth level, French football has turned that adaptability into a virtue. 'Our model doesn't rely upon a very clear identity, like the Spanish for example, but rather upon the idea of giving our youngsters a methodology so that they can adapt,' the former Lyon coach told *L'Équipe* in 2022. 'Football evolves and they'll have a multitude of coaches during their careers, they'll play pretty much all over Europe. We try to give them a toolbox.' Rather than turning out youngsters who can only play a certain way, France produces players still in their factory settings: expertly engineered smartphone footballers, cleanly built and neatly boxed, ready to be shipped around the world and slotted into whichever playing system they might encounter.

The absence of a universally recognised 'French school' has contributed to the increasing sparsity of French coaches on the international scene. Where Arsène Wenger, Gérard Houllier, Denoueix[120] and Zidane once flew the *Tricolore* on foreign touchlines, the only French head coach working in one of Europe's top four leagues at the start of the 2023–24 season was Rudi Garcia at Napoli. And he had been sacked by the middle of November. The feeling in France is that the absence of a globally lauded French football blueprint has made homegrown

120 Denoueix led Real Sociedad to a second-place finish in La Liga in 2002–03.

coaches less attractive. Coupled with poor language skills (a traditional French failing) and competition from countries such as Portugal, whose coaches benefit from well-established professional networks and the support of influential agents like Jorge Mendes, it has contributed to French coaches falling out of fashion. They are even becoming scarce in France. With squads increasingly cosmopolitan in their make-up and overseas owners often keen to appoint their own coaches, foreigners outnumbered Frenchmen (10–8) in Ligue 1 dug-outs for the first time ever as the 2023–24 campaign got under way.[121] The native coaches are not giving up without a fight, however. In Bruno Génésio (Lyon, Rennes), Julien Stéphan (Rennes, Strasbourg) and, in particular, Franck Haise, whose swashbuckling 3-4-2-1 system led Lens to a superb second-place finish behind PSG in 2023, some French coaches have succeeded in demonstrating that there might be life yet in *football à la française*.

For a promoted side, Toulouse's return to top-flight football could scarcely have gone much better. *Les Violets* finished 13th in Ligue 1 in 2022–23, a comfortable 13 points clear of a relegation battle that was rendered even more fraught than usual due to the fact that four teams went down rather than the usual 2+1 (the side finishing third-bottom traditionally facing a play-off against the winners of the Ligue 2 play-offs) to facilitate the shift to an 18-team league. Even better, they crushed holders Nantes 5–1 in the Coupe de France final at the Stade de France, after racing 4–0 up inside the first 31 minutes, to bring the trophy back to the *La Ville Rose* for the first time since 1957.[122] 'Even in my dreams, I couldn't have imagined a final like that,' said a delighted Montanier. Stadium de Toulouse enjoyed its highest attendances in 18 years, with the season average up nearly 10,000 compared to the 2019–20 relegation campaign. The club also pressed

121 This counts Montpellier coach Michel Der Zakarian, who grew up in France but played for Armenia – his country of birth – at international level, as a foreign coach.
122 Toulouse FC won the Coupe de France in 1957 but folded 10 years later after a curious merger with Parisian side Red Star. The modern Toulouse FC, founded in 1970, considers itself a continuation of the club's previous iteration, but strictly speaking it is a different club.

ahead with plans to build a new, 3,500m² training facility beside the stadium, which is expected to open in 2025. An article in *L'Équipe* published on the morning of the Coupe de France final described Toulouse's collaboration with RedBird as '*trois ans d'idylle*' ('a three-year romance'). But then things got a bit untidy.

Two weeks on from the Coupe de France final, Toulouse were plunged into a homophobia scandal after three players – Moussa Diarra, Zakaria Aboukhlal and Saïd Hamulić – were left out for a league game against Nantes because they refused to wear jerseys with rainbow-coloured squad numbers in support of the International Day against Homophobia, Transphobia and Biphobia. Morocco international Aboukhlal was then suspended by the club over allegations that he directed a misogynistic insult at a local official during a celebratory reception at Toulouse city hall. Reports emerged that Danish centre-back Rasmus Nicolaisen had borrowed €100,000 from his teammates to pay off gambling debts. Supporters said sad goodbyes to five popular players – Healey, Van den Boomen, captain Brecht Dejaegere, goalkeeper Maxime Dupé and Dutch midfielder Stijn Spierings – who left after their contracts expired. Montanier was sacked (Comolli having declared that Toulouse's bottom-half finish was an underachievement according to the club's metrics) and replaced by his Catalan assistant, Carles Martínez Novell. Jaubert left too. Because RedBird also owned AC Milan, several of the firm's directors – including founder Cardinale – had to resign from the Toulouse board before UEFA would allow both clubs to compete in European competition in the 2023–24 campaign (*Le Téfécé* having qualified for the Europa League by winning the Coupe de France). Amid reports that RedBird were poised to walk away from the club altogether, Toulouse enjoyed a famous European win over Liverpool but were sucked into a relegation battle in Ligue 1 and dispossessed of their Coupe de France crown following a penalty shoot-out defeat by third-tier FC Rouen.

Two steps forward, one step back. Glory one day, gloom the next. Such is the messy, stubbornly shapeless modern history of French football, where talent abounds, triumph and disaster go hand in hand and you can never be entirely sure, as the ball speeds its way towards goal, whether or not the goalposts will be on your side.

ACKNOWLEDGEMENTS

A huge thank you, first and foremost, to all the players, coaches and officials – past and present – who gave up their time to be interviewed for this book: Jean-Michel Larqué, Patrick Revelli, Maxime Bossis, Alain Giresse, René Girard, Luis Fernandez, Henri Émile, Alain Roche, Éric Di Meco, Jean-Pierre Papin, Mark Hateley, Tony Cascarino, Eric Black, Reynald Pedros, Raynald Denoueix, Nicolas Ouédec, Massimo Bonini, Olivier Dacourt, Guy Roux, Allan Saint-Maximin, Gary Pallister, Lee Sharpe, Gilles Grimandi, Robert Pirès, Emmanuel Petit, Jamie Carragher, Rémi Garde, Damien Comolli, Bacary Sagna, Claude Dusseau, Grégory Coupet, Sidney Govou, Armand Garrido, Christophe Jallet, Blaise Matuidi, Geremi, Álvaro Mejía, José Morais, Sonia Bompastor, Marilou Duringer-Erckert, Camille Abily, Laure Boulleau, Luis Ferrer, Mathys Tel, Markus Pilawa, Luke Bornn and Olivier Jaubert. Thanks also to Philippe Tournon, Olivier Rouyer, Julien Bée, Jean-François Pérès, Phil Dickinson, Arsène Wenger, Corinne Bernegger, Laurent Amat, Patrick Mignon, Michel Mimran and David Sugden for help with background detail.

Thanks to Bill Campbell, Richard Campbell, Richard McBrearty, Peter McKinney, Pat Lynch, Paul Bayliss, Martin Westcott, Chris Oldnall and Neville Farmer for helping me to fill in the blanks in the remarkable story of the *poteaux carrés*. At Saint-Étienne, thanks to Philippe Gastal, Laurent Chastellière, Jean-Christophe Venville, Alex Mahinc and Yves Verrière for taking the time to show me around Stade Geoffroy-Guichard and its wonderful museum (which is well worth a visit). For help setting up interviews and sourcing contacts, thanks to Henri Galipon, Karen Govou, Antoine Atta, Darren Tulett, Florence Papin, Emery Taisne, Youness Bengelloun, Stanislas Touchot, Mickaël Landreau, Alexandra Dubois, Guillaume Kuentz, Will Unwin, Guillaume Lainé, Yohanes Zewdu, Katie Bingle, Robert Pirès, Grégory Sertic, Dan Levy, Olivier Cailler, Jean-Claude Laffont, Kurtys Saint-Maximin, Assia Le Gall, Leris Mayala, Lee Marshall, Francisco Barros, Gadiri Camara, Damien Riso, Holger Quest,

Florent Deligia, Jeanne Sigismeau, Laure Boulleau, Vincent Duluc, Valentin Pauluzzi and Njie Enow Ebai. For general advice, assistance and feedback, thanks to Michael Cox, Uli Hesse, Álvaro Romeo, Serafino Ingardia, Philippe Auclair, Jérôme Latta, Dermot Corrigan, Jack Lang, Duncan Alexander, Dom Kullander, Sid Lambert, Martin Cloake, Mike Collett, Hugo Steckelmacher, Marcus Alves, Alexandre Aflalo, Matt Dickinson, Amy Lawrence and Matt Slater. Thanks in particular to Patrick Kendrick for breaking off from his wedding preparations to help me set up an interview with Massimo Bonini and to James Eastham for kindly reading over the manuscript (and weeding out a couple of glaring errors). A full bibliography follows, but I was particularly indebted during my research to Geoff Hare's 2003 book *Football in France: A Cultural History*.

At Canal+, a big *merci* for various forms of assistance to David Barouh, Hervé Mathoux, Patrice Pilven, David Rivet, Zahir Ouassadi, Katy Eutrope-Sylvère, Raphaël Domenach and Marielle Begoc. Special thanks to Dorian Faucherand for selflessly trawling through the Canal+ archives in search of relevant match footage. Thanks to Allan Kelly and Dave James, my old bosses at Agence France-Presse, whose tolerance of my keenness for all things French football back in 2009 unknowingly paved the way for this book to come into existence. Lee Walker and, in particular, Seán Fay laid the foundations for some of the writing that appears in these pages with their commissions for Bleacher Report. Thanks in a similar vein to Clive Petty and James Restall at *The Times* and to Alex Kay-Jelski, Tom Burrows and Ben Burrows at The Athletic.

Thank you to my literary agent, Melanie Michael-Greer, for helping me to find the right approach to this book after several years of kicking the idea around. At Bloomsbury, thanks to Matt Lowing and Caroline Guillet for their guidance, patience and encouragement. Thanks to Chris Stone for his careful copyediting. Thanks to Laura Bennett and Jae Marple for their tireless work translating and transcribing interviews and to Anne-Isabelle Perou for answering an endless succession of linguistic queries. For putting a roof over my head on occasional stays in Paris, thanks to Dom and Lynsey O'Shea (not forgetting Elodie O'Shea and Adeline O'Shea), Andy Scott and Liz Manning. Thanks to the British weather for serving up one of the most miserable summers in recent memory while I was cooped up indoors battling a looming deadline (even if a compelling Tour de France and a thrilling Ashes series provided distractions of their own). Thanks, as always, to my family for their love and support – special mention for my sister, Ffion Williams, for coming to my rescue after I set off to Paris to conduct an interview one day, having left the notepad containing all my questions at home in Finsbury Park.

BIBLIOGRAPHY

BOOKS

Adams, Tony with Ridley, Ian, *Sober: Football, My Story, My Life* (Simon & Schuster, 2018)

Allen, Clive with Olley, James, *Up Front: My Autobiography* (deCoubertin Books, 2019)

Ancelotti, Carlo with Brady, Chris and Forde, Mike, *Quiet Leadership: Winning Hearts, Minds and Matches* (Portfolio Penguin, 2017)

Auclair, Philippe, *Cantona: The Rebel Who Would Be King* (Pan Books, 2010)

Auclair, Philippe, *Thierry Henry: Lonely at the Top: A Biography* (Pan Books, 2013)

Aulas, Jean-Michel with Blanc, Olivier, *Chaque jour se réinventer* (Éditions Stock, 2023)

Barbier, Joachim, *Ce pays qui n'aime pas le foot* (Hugo & Cie, 2012)

Basse, Pierre-Louis, *Séville 82: France-Allemagne: le match du siècle* (Éditions Privé, 2005)

Béoutis, Didier, *Le Duel : Anquetil – Poulidor, dix ans de confrontation (1960–1969)* (Mareuil Éditions, 2018)

Bernès, Jean-Pierre with Pascuito, Bernard, *Je dis tout : les secrets de l'OM sous Tapie* (Albin Michel, 1995)

Boli, Basile with Askolovitch, Claude, *Black Boli* (Éditions Grasset et Fasquelle, 1994)

Boli, Basile with Lanoë, Jean-Marie, *Mémoires d'hOMme : Marseille, Tapie, les grands soirs* (Éditions First, 2022)

Bouchard, Jean-Philippe, *Dans la tête de Didier Deschamps : Tous ses secrets d'entraîneur* (Éditions Solar, 2018)

Caioli, Luca and Collot, Cyril, *Benzema : Buteur sans limites* (Marabout, 2022)

Carlin, John, *White Angels* (Bloomsbury, 2005)

Carragher, Jamie with Bascombe, Chris, *Carra: My Autobiography* (Corgi Books, 2009)

Cascarino, Tony with Kimmage, Paul, *Full Time: The Secret Life of Tony Cascarino* (Simon & Schuster, 2000)

Chaumier, Denis, *La légende du FC Nantes* (Hugo Sport, 2020)

Coupet, Grégory with Danet, Benjamin, *Arrêt de jeu* (Éditions du Rocher, 2011)

Cox, Michael, *The Mixer: The Story of Premier League Tactics, from Route One to False Nines* (HarperCollins, 2017)

Cox, Michael, *Zonal Marking: The Making of Modern European Football* (HarperCollins, 2019)

Cross, John, *Arsene Wenger: The Inside Story of Arsenal Under Wenger* (Simon & Schuster, 2018)

Dauncey, Hugh and Hare, Geoff (eds), *France and the 1998 World Cup: The National Impact of a World Sporting Event* (Frank Cass Publishers, 1999)

Degorre, Damien and Raymond, Raphaël, *Histoire d'un scoop* (Éditions L'Équipe, 2010)

Desailly, Marcel with Broussard, Philippe, *Capitaine* (Éditions Stock, 2002)

Djorkaeff, Youri with Ramsay, Arnaud, *Snake* (Éditions Grasset & Fasquelle, 2006)

Domenech, Raymond, *Tout seul* (Flammarion, 2012)

Dubois, Laurent, *Soccer Empire: The World Cup and the Future of France* (University of California Press, 2010)

Dugarry, Christophe with Riolo, Daniel, *Le foot vu par Christophe Dugarry* (Éditions Hugo & Cie, 2009)

Duluc, Vincent, *La grande histoire de l'OL* (Éditions Prolongations, 2007)

Duluc, Vincent, *Le livre noir des Bleus : Chronique d'un désastre annoncé* (Éditions Robert Laffont, 2010)

Evra, Patrice with Mitten, Andy, *I Love This Game: The Autobiography* (Simon & Schuster, 2021)

Eydelie, Jean-Jacques with Biet, Michel, *Je ne joue plus !* (Éditions de l'Archipel, 2006)

Ferguson, Alex with McIlvanney, Hugh, *Managing My Life: My Autobiography* (Hodder & Stoughton, 2021)

Ferguson, Alex with Moritz, Michael, *Leading* (Hodder & Stoughton, 2015)

Fernandez, Luis with Chaumier, Denis, *Luis* (Hugo et Compagnie, 2016)

Fievée, Alexandre, *Dans le vestiaire de l'OM : les années Tapie* (Hugo Sport, 2019)

Fort, Patrick and Philippe, Jean, *Zidane : de Yazid à Zizou* (L'Archipel, 2006)

Franck, Dan with Zidane, Zinédine, *Zidane : le roman d'une victoire* (Éditions Robert Laffont-Plon, 1999)

Fratani, Marc with Hamel, Ian, *Le mystificateur : 25 ans dans l'ombre de Bernard Tapie* (L'Archipel, 2019)

Gaillard, Claire, *La grande histoire des Bleues : Dans les coulisses de l'équipe de France féminine* (Hachette Livre, 2018)

Garcia, Vincent and Hermant, Arnaud, *La deuxième étoile* (Éditions de l'Archipel, 2018)

Gerrard, Steven with McRae, Donald, *My Story* (Penguin Random House, 2015)

Giesbert, Franz-Olivier, *Bernard Tapie : Leçons de vie, de mort et d'amour* (Presses de la Cité, 2021)

Gildea, Robert, *France Since 1945* (Oxford University Press, 2002)

Ginola, David with Silver, Neil, *Le Magnifique: The Autobiography* (CollinsWillow, 2000)

Giresse, Alain with Sévérac, Dominique, *Né pour jouer* (Robert Laffont, 2021)

Giroud, Olivier with Rouch, Dominique, *Always Believe* (Pitch Publishing, 2021)

Glassmann, Jacques, *Foot et moi la paix* (Calmann-Lévy, 2003)

Goethals, Raymond with Henry, Philippe and Trimpont, Serge, *Le douzième homme* (Éditions Robert Laffont, 1994)

Goldblatt, David, *The Ball is Round: A Global History of Football* (Penguin Books, 2007)

Govou, Sidney with Jay, Edward, *Je ne pensais pas aller si loin* (Éditions Jacob-Duvernet, 2011)

Griezmann, Antoine with Ramsay, Arnaud, *Derrière le sourire* (Éditions Robert Laffont, 2017)

Grimault, Dominique, *Les Bleus : Le livre officiel de l'équipe de France (1904–2001)* (Solar, 2001)

Hardy, Martin, *Touching Distance: Kevin Keegan, The Entertainers and Newcastle's Impossible Dream* (deCoubertin Books, 2016)

Hare, Geoff, *Football in France: A Cultural History* (Berg, 2003)

Hateley, Mark with Aird, Alistair, *Hitting the Mark: My Story* (Reach Sport, 2021)

Hermant, Arnaud, *Mbappé : Le phénomène* (Éditions de l'Archipel, 2019)

Hermel, Frédéric, *Zidane* (Flammarion, 2019)

Hesse, Uli, *Bayern: Creating a Global Superclub* (Yellow Jersey Press, 2016)

Hidalgo, Michel, *Les buts de ma vie* (Éditions Robert Laffont, 1986)

Hidalgo, Michel with Olive, Karl, *Les carnets secrets de Michel Hidalgo* (Hugo et Compagnie, 2012)

Hoddle, Glenn with Steinberg, Jacob, *Playmaker: The Autobiography* (HarperCollins, 2021)

Houllier, Gérard with Chaumier, Denis, *Je ne marcherai jamais seul* (Hugo Sport, 2020)

Ibrahimović, Zlatan with Garlando, Luigi, *Adrenaline: My Untold Stories* (Penguin Books, 2022)

Jacquet, Aimé with Tournon, Philippe, *Ma vie pour une étoile* (Éditions Robert Laffont-Plon, 2018)

Keane, Roy with Dunphy, Eamon, *Keane: The Autobiography* (Penguin Books, 2002)

Kuper, Simon, *Barça: The Inside Story of the World's Greatest Football Club* (Short Books, 2021)

Kuper, Simon and Szymanski, Stefan, *Why England Lose and Other Curious Football Phenomena Explained* (HarperCollins, 2009)

Lacombe, Bernard with Genard, Romain, *L'instinct du foot* (Éditions Solar, 2021)

Lahouri, Besma, *Zidane : une vie secrète* (Flammarion, 2008)

Larqué, Jean-Michel, *Nos années en vert* (L'Artilleur, 2016)

Lawrence, Amy, *Invincible: Inside Arsenal's Unbeaten 2003–04 Season* (Penguin Books, 2015)

Lebœuf, Frank, *Destin, quand je te tiens . . .* (Flammarion, 2002)

Le Calvez, Jean-Michel and Jouison, Cyril, *La saga des Girondins de Bordeaux* (M6 Editions, 2009)

Lemoine, Patrick, *Le carré magique: Quand le jeu était à nous* (Éditions Talent Sport, 2016)

Leplat, Thibaud, *Football à la française* (Éditions Solar, 2016)

Lewis, Roger and Delattre, Mathieu, *100 exploits du foot français* (Éditions Solar, 2020)

Lizarazu, Bixente with Ramsay, Arnaud and Bungert, Jacques, *Bixente* (Éditions Grasset & Fasquelle, 2007)

Lizarazu, Bixente, *Mes prolongations* (Éditions du Seuil, 2018)

Lowe, Sid, *Fear and Loathing in La Liga: Barcelona vs Real Madrid* (Yellow Jersey Press, 2013)

Makélélé, Claude, with Hayes, Alex, *Tout simplement* (Éditions Prolongations, 2009)

Matuidi, Blaise with Pinton, Ludovic, *Au bout de mes rêves* (Éditions Solar, 2016)

Menuge, Alexis, *Franck Ribéry : L'incompris* (Talent Sport, 2014)

Neville, Gary, *Red: My Autobiography* (Corgi, 2012)

Ollivier, Daniel, *L'alchimie du jeu à la nantaise : D'Arribas à Denoueix, le pouvoir du collectif* (Éditions Solar, 2022)

Papin, Jean-Pierre with Heuzé, Denis, *Franc jeu* (Éditions Ramsay, 1998)

Pérès, Jean-François with Christopher, *L'histoire illustrée de l'Olympique de Marseille* (Hugo BD, 2018)

Petit, Emmanuel with Le Fauconnier, Jérôme, *À fleur de peau* (Éditions Prolongations, 2008)

Pirès, Robert with Rivoire, Xavier, *Footballeur: An Autobiography* (Yellow Jersey Press, 2003)

Pitoiset, Anne and Wéry, Claudine with Karembeu, Christian, *Christian Karembeu, Kanak* (Don Quichotte éditions, 2011)

Platini, Michel with Mahé, Patrick, *Ma vie comme un match* (Robert Laffont, 1987)

Platini, Michel with Ernaut, Gérard, *Parlons football* (Hugo & Cie, 2014)

Platini, Michel with Jessel, Jérôme, *Entre nous* (Éditions de l'Observatoire, 2019)

Ramsay, Arnaud, *Laurent Blanc : la face cachée du Président* (Éditions Fetjaine, 2012)

Rees, Jasper, *Wenger: The Legend* (Short Books, 2014)

Renard, Wendie with Dalmat, Syanie and Hautbois, Yohann, *Mon étoile* (Talent Sport, 2019)

Rethacker, Jean-Philippe and Thibert, Jacques, *La fabuleuse histoire du football* (Éditions de la Martinière, 2012)

Robinson, Joshua and Clegg, Jonathan, *Messi vs Ronaldo: One Rivalry, Two GOATs and The Era That Remade the World's Game* (Mariner Books, 2022)

Rocheteau, Dominique with Quillien, Christophe, *On m'appelait l'ange vert* (le midi libre, 2005)

Rouch, Dominique, *Didier Deschamps : vainqueur dans l'âme* (Édition°1, 2001)

Roux, Guy with Alain, Alexandre, *Confidences* (Talent Sport, 2021)

Rühn, Christov (ed), *Le Foot: The Legends of French Football* (Abacus, 2000)

Saha, Louis, *Thinking Inside the Box: Reflections on Life as a Premier League Footballer* (Vision Sports Publishing, 2012)

Sedan, Alexandre, *Les Bleus à l'Euro* (De Boeck Supérieur, 2016)

Spiro, Matthew, *Sacré Bleu: From Zidane to Mbappé – A Football Journey* (Biteback Publishing, 2020)

Stein, Mel, *Chris Waddle: The Authorised Biography* (Simon & Schuster, 1997)

Thuram, Lilian with Burnet, James, *8 juillet 1998* (Éditions Anne Carrière, 2004)

Torres, Diego, *The Special One: The Secret World of José Mourinho* (HarperSport, 2014)

Tournon, Philippe, *La vie en bleu* (Éditions Albin Michel, 2021)
Trésor, Marius with Granjou, Denis, *Au-delà de mes rêves* (City Editions, 2021)
Trezeguet, David with Torchut, Florent, *Bleu ciel* (Hugo & Companie, 2016)
Vella, Christian, *Roger Lemerre : Les Bleus au cœur* (Éditions du Félin, 2002)
Vieira, Patrick with Beckerman, Debbie, *Vieira: The Autobiography* (Orion Books, 2006)
Wenger, Arsène, *My Life in Red and White: My Autobiography* (Weidenfeld & Nicolson, 2020)
Williams, Richard, *The Perfect 10: Football's Dreamers, Schemers, Playmakers and Playboys* (Faber and Faber, 2006)
Wilson, Jonathan, *Inverting the Pyramid: The History of Football Tactics* (Orion Books, 2014)
Wilson, Jonathan, *The Barcelona Legacy: Guardiola, Mourinho and the Fight for Football's Soul* (Blink Publishing, 2018)
Wright, Ian with Bradley, Lloyd, *A Life in Football: My Autobiography* (Constable, 2017)

NEWSPAPERS, JOURNALS, MAGAZINES, WEBSITES AND PODCASTS

11Freunde; 11v11; 20 Minutes; BBC Sport; *Daily Mail*; Dailymotion; Europe 1; Football Scotland; Foot O Féminin; *FourFourTwo*; France Bleu; *France Football*; Get French Football News; Institut national de l'audiovisuel; *La Dépêche*; *La Provence*; *Le Figaro*; *L'Histoire*; *Le Monde*; *Le Parisien*; *Le Progrès*; *L'Équipe*; *Les Cahiers du Football*; *Les Échos*; Les Poteaux Carrés; Les Violets; *Le Télégramme*; *Le Temps*; *L'Express*; *Libération*; Lyon Mag; Mediapart; OM4ever; *Ouest-France*; Panenka; Playing Pasts; RMC Sport; Sky Sports; *So Foot*; Sport Business; *Sud Ouest*; The Athletic; The Big Interview with Graham Hunter; *The Guardian*; *The Herald*; *The Independent*; *The New York Times*; *The Scotsman*; The Set Pieces; *The Times*; *The Worcester News*; Transfermarkt; Twitter/X; Web Girondins; Who Scored; Wikipedia; YouTube

DOCUMENTARIES

C'est l'histoire d'un but (Basile Boli Évènements, 2011)
Claude Bez, grandeur et décadence (L'Équipe Enquête, 2016)
Claude Bez : le 13e homme (France Télévisions/Mara Films/Les Films du Mahana, 2016)
FC Nantes, record inégalé (L'atelier Transmédia, 2022)
Glenn Hoddle: Extra Time (BT Sport Films, 2021)
La légende de Séville : RFA – France (INA/FIFA, 1982)
Le K Benzema (Wild Side/Canal+, 2017)
Les Bleus 2018 : Au cœur de l'épopée russe (TF1, 2018)
Les joueuses : #paslàpourdanser (Rouge Distribution, 2020)
Les yeux dans les Bleus (Canal+, 1998)
Saint-Étienne : L'épopée 1976 (Canal+/INA/AS Saint-Étienne, 2016)
Thierry Henry: Legend (ITV, 2008)
Un peu + près des étoiles (OL Média, 2022)
Zinédine Zidane, comme dans un rêve (Canal+, 2002)
Zinédine Zidane, son nom est Yazid (L'Équipe Enquête, 2022)

INDEX